D0780862

TOURO COLLEGE LIBRARY
Midtown

WITHDRAWN

Autism

Education at SAGE

SAGE is a leading international publisher of journals, books, and electronic media for academic, educational, and professional markets.

Our education publishing includes:

- accessible and comprehensive texts for aspiring education professionals and practitioners looking to further their careers through continuing professional development
- inspirational advice and guidance for the classroom
- authoritative state of the art reference from the leading authors in the field

Find out more at: **www.sagepub.co.uk/education**

Autism

Educational and Therapeutic Approaches

Efrosini Kalyva

WITHDRAWN

TOURO COLLEGE LIBRARY
Midtown

Los Angeles | London | New Delhi
Singapore | Washington DC

Greek edition first published 2005 by Papazisí Publications
© Efrosini Kalyva
English language edition first published 2011 by SAGE
Publications Ltd © Efrosini Kalyva
Illustrations © Panagiotis Tsakiris

First published 2011

Apart from any fair dealing for the purposes of research or
private study, or criticism or review, as permitted under the
Copyright, Designs and Patents Act, 1988, this publication
may be reproduced, stored or transmitted in any form, or by
any means, only with the prior permission in writing of the
publishers, or in the case of reprographic reproduction, in
accordance with the terms of licences issued by the Copyright
Licensing Agency. Enquiries concerning reproduction outside
those terms should be sent to the publishers.

SAGE Publications Ltd
1 Oliver's Yard
55 City Road
London EC1Y 1SP

SAGE Publications Inc.
2455 Teller Road
Thousand Oaks, California 91320

SAGE Publications India Pvt Ltd
B 1/I 1 Mohan Cooperative Industrial Area
Mathura Road
New Delhi 110 044

SAGE Publications Asia-Pacific Pte Ltd
33 Pekin Street #02–01
Far East Square
Singapore 048763

Library of Congress Control Number: 2010937015

British Library Cataloguing in Publication data
A catalogue record for this book is available from the British
Library

ISBN 978-0-85702-488-6
ISBN 978-0-85702-489-3 (pbk)

Typeset by Dorwyn, Wells, Somerset
Printed in Great Britain by CPI Antony Rowe, Chippenham, Wiltshire
Printed on paper from sustainable resources

11/1/11

Contents

About the Author

Efrosini Kalyva is a psychologist, practitioner, writer and academic specialising in education and treatment of individuals with special educational needs. She holds two Masters degrees and two PhDs and she is a trainer of professionals working with children with special educational needs in a variety of settings. She is currently based in Thessaloniki (Greece), where she is Senior Lecturer in Psychology at City College, an International Faculty of the University of Sheffield. She is also a guest lecturer in public universities and delivers speeches and seminars on the education and treatment of individuals with special educational needs. Moreover, she is the co-author of another book, in Greek, on research methods in special needs education and she has published her work in international scientific journals.

Efrosini is co-owner, together with her husband, of a private rehabilitation centre for children with special educational needs. She very much enjoys her therapeutic work with these children and tries to work together with their families and their teachers in order to provide them with the best possible services. She has always believed that no reward can match the joy that derives from helping children with special educational needs, and their families, reach their full potential.

Preface

I would like to dedicate this book to all the children with ASD that I have worked with and their families who inspired me and taught me important lessons about what really matters in life, as well as to my husband (Vlastaris Tsakiris) and my family who provided me with the love and support to do what I chose in life – work with children with special educational needs.

I decided to write this book in 2004 because I wanted to give parents and professionals living and working with children with ASD information regarding the effectiveness of available treatments of ASD. It was published in Greek in 2005 and I was happy to see that it was very well received by the target audience and it was cited by official websites relating to the education of children with ASD in Greece. The second reason for writing this book was that I wanted to use it as a textbook for a university course on teaching and educating children with ASD. The students found it very helpful and a lot of them also used it as a resource when working with children with ASD. This version of the book is based on the Greek original and is enriched with all the latest studies. I hope that you will find it as interesting and as helpful as the Greek audience, and I would be delighted to answer any queries at: kalyva@city.academic.gr

Finally, I would like to thank: Amy Jarrold and Alex Molineux from Sage Publications and especially Jude Bowen for believing in my vision and helping me realise it; the anonymous reviewers of the book proposal and the sample chapters for their constructive and helpful comments; the reviewer of the whole book for taking the time to make very useful and critical suggestions; Panagiotis Tsakiris for his drawings; Vaya Papageorgiou who wrote the preface of the Greek edition of the book and some friends and colleagues for their help and advice at various stages of my career (in alphabetical order) – Ioannis Agaliotis, Vaios Dafoulis, Angeliki Gena, Maria Georgiadi, Anastasia Kasiara, and Vlastaris Tsakiris.

Efrosini Kalyva, BSc, MSc, MmedSci, PhD, PhD

Introduction

Autism is a pervasive developmental disorder with severe difficulties in communication skills, together with difficulties in regulating attention, cognitive, sensory, motor, and affective process (APA, 2001). Autism is no longer considered a rare disorder, since it is more common than Down syndrome, cystic fibrosis and diverse forms of childhood cancer (Fombonne, 1998; Gillberg, 1996). This is one of the reasons why many scientists explored facets of autism spectrum disorders (ASD), with 3,700 published articles between 1990 and 2004 (Volkmar et al., 2004).

Infants with ASD do not exhibit the anticipated attachment behaviour towards significant others, such as their parents. However, the most characteristic behaviour, which is observed by parents and leads experts to the diagnosis of autism, is the absence of interest in other people (Rapin, 1997). Many children with ASD experience delays in communication (for example, they do not understand the meaning and the importance of the communicative process) and in social skills (for example, they fail to create and sustain relationships with other people). Moreover, it is estimated that 75 per cent of children with classical autism are low functioning (Waterhouse et al., 1996).

Autism is often diagnosed in infancy and causes understandable distress to the child's parents and the broader family, while Asperger syndrome and atypical autism, which are usually not diagnosed until middle or even later childhood, are equally distressing. Many parents report that they feel relief at first because they can finally give a name to the inexplicable behaviour of their child; however, later on they are often left to their own devices with minimum guidance and support. Of course, this is not the case everywhere, but in many countries there is no support for parents after the diagnosis. So, parents are faced with a plethora of treatments that guarantee spectacular outcomes and they are usually willing to try any 'promising' therapy in order to help their child overcome ASD. Parents see a child who looks perfectly 'normal' and believe that a 'typical' child is 'hiding' somewhere waiting to 'come out'. Therefore, parents look for what many treatments promise – a cure for ASD. However, most professionals working with children with ASD know that there is no cure; the therapies that promise a cure either lack scientific background or exaggerate some effectiveness that they have in dealing with some characteristics of ASD (Herbert and Sharp, 2001).

Most scientists agree that the criteria and the limits that are set to distinguish pure science from pseudoscience are not always clear-cut and practical, since the differences are more qualitative than quantitative (Bunge, 1994; Herbert et al., 2000; Lilienfield, 1998). The therapies that are based on pseudoscience are promoted often by individuals or organisations that have a direct and substantial financial benefit from their commercial success. These therapies are based on anecdotal evidence from parents, who may not be able to objectively assess what is happening. Moreover, it is possible that some parents exaggerate the positive effects that a certain therapy had on their child because even the slightest improvement is essential to them. Some therapists choose very carefully the data that they reveal and the way they are presented, while automatically rejecting any counter-evidence or criticism. So, they are spread either by word of mouth or through web pages in the Internet or through books and printed material that is largely uncontrolled and should be viewed with great caution (Green, 1996a, 2001; Herbert and Sharp, 2001; Smith, 1996). Some ineffective therapies are based on unsubstantiated theories on the aetiology of ASD – for example, infection by mucus candida (Adams and Conn, 1997; Siegel, 1996), random incidents that coincide with the appearance of ASD – for example, childhood vaccinations (Dales et al., 2001; Kaye et al., 2001; Manning, 1999) or outdated theories – for example, unloving mothers (Bettelheim, 1967; Mahler, 1968; Tustin, 1981).

It is encouraging, on the other side, that many promising programmes have been developed for addressing the characteristic behaviours of ASD and have added an optimistic flavour. These approaches have been assessed using scientifically acceptable research methods, despite some methodological limitations, and have been proven effective when properly implemented. However, no single approach can successfully address all the characteristic behaviours of ASD and it is therefore advisable to combine the most effective treatments and to adjust them to the needs of every individual with ASD in order to achieve the desired outcome. This is the suggestion of the Committee of Science and Practice of the American Psychological Association (Gresham et al., 1999; Rogers, 1998).

All the contemporary and scientifically proven information regarding the effectiveness of the methods that are used to treat ASD are either presented at scientific conferences or published in scientific journals. Therefore, it is likely that many parents and professionals who work with children with ASD and their families do not have access to these sources of valid information. Moreover, each individual with ASD may exhibit such diverse symptoms that it is extremely challenging to identify the most appropriate treatment method. For example, there is such great variability in reactions to medical treatment, that a psychotropic medicine may exacerbate the symptoms of one individual and decrease those of another. Children mature as they grow older and it is difficult to disentangle the effects of maturation from the effects of a treatment. So, many parents, educators or, even, mental health professionals wonder where the harm is in trying a therapy that is not scientifically tested. I suggest to parents and professionals that they should be fully aware of the advantages and disadvantages of any intervention that they choose to adopt (Dempsey and Foreman, 2001). Each therapy has its cost; apart from the financial and psychological cost, children may waste valuable time with ineffective therapies (Fenske et al., 1985). Finally, you should consider the possibility of serious physical harm, as has happened many times in the past, caused by medicines that were ultimately found to have severe side-effects (Gorman, 1999).

In this context, I start with the approaches that deal most effectively with ASD, according to valid published scientific data, such as applied behavioural analysis, TEACCH and cognitive-behavioural therapy. Then I refer to therapies that are used to deal with the difficulties that children with ASD face in some developmental areas, namely, social interaction, communication and play. Then, I discuss supplementary therapies with limited scientifically proven effectiveness: sensorimotor, pharmacological and other approaches.

My aim is not to just describe these therapies, but to promote the concept of healthy scepticism in parents, educators, therapists and mental health professionals working with individuals with ASD. This book is not a recipe book with a sample of treatments, but a basis for critical thinking regarding the effectiveness of the most prominent treatments of ASD. They should be adjusted to individual needs, the level of functioning, the receptive and expressive language of every individual with ASD, as well as the diverse educational, political, cultural and financial contexts. I have chosen to review the specific approaches, since they are widely used in several countries and there is published scientific data to either support or question their effectiveness. Moreover, they are included in the treatments presented by most international organisations related to individuals with ASD, their families and mental health professionals working with them. Finally, there are the therapies that are included in most units covering autism and reviewed by students in papers and dissertations.

I would also like to stress that even the most effective intervention may not bring about the desired outcomes if it is not implemented properly. Therefore, you should bear in mind when reading this book that it is the people who implement the intervention that could make the difference, but their influence cannot easily be scientifically documented and studied. Moreover, I strongly believe that the focus of any intervention should not just be to change and improve the behaviour of the child with ASD, but also to help you realise that the environment needs to change and to adapt to the specific child. I learned from working with children with ASD that the only way to be effective is to accept them as they are and to find a way to evolve together, to find joint ways of communication, expression, affection, respect, freedom and development.

When I refer to an individual with ASD from now on, I will use the pronouns he/his/him, since most individuals with ASD are males. When I refer to parents, adults, therapists from now on, I will use the pronouns she/hers/her, to make the distinction from the individual with ASD. I use the term 'therapist' because the person who designs and implements the approach should be a trained professional, but this does not mean that all individuals with ASD receive professional treatment. The therapist could be a parent, a teacher, a peer or anyone working and living with the individual with ASD. I would also like to stress that the terms 'therapy' and 'therapist' do not imply that ASD can be cured, but that the individual's level of functioning could improve.

1

Cognitive-Behavioural Approaches

Chapter overview

I begin this chapter with a critical review of the approaches that have proven most effective for the treatment of ASD according to relevant published studies. I refer in particular to applied behaviour analysis (ABA) and TEACCH, which have been used successfully with individuals with ASD for many years in a variety of countries and cultural contexts. Applied behaviour analysis targets primarily young children with ASD, recognising the vital importance of early intervention that can bring about noticeable changes in the symptoms, while TEACCH provides a 'cradle to grave' service. Both methods that I will present and analyse in more detail have advantages and disadvantages that should be taken into consideration when assessing their effectiveness. You should also bear in mind that there is no individual therapeutic or educational approach that has been proven to address all the characteristic behaviours of all children with ASD.

At the end of this chapter, I refer to some approaches that are based mainly on behaviour modification techniques and have been applied to a lesser extent. Cognitive-behavioural therapy (CBT) is designed mainly for high-functioning children with ASD who can communicate adequately. The Denver Health Sciences Programme, the DIR/Floortime method, the LEAP programme and the Miller method are behaviourally oriented programmes that were designed to help children with ASD and their families. Despite the fact that these methods differ in the way that they are implemented, a common underlying feature is the instruction of learned behaviours that leads to mastering a specific skill.

Applied behaviour analysis

Applied behaviour analysis is a behavioural approach that has been used for more than 40 years with satisfactory success rates (Foxx, 2008; Heflin and Alberto, 2001). It is based on fundamental principals of operant conditioning (the relation that exists between the stimulus and the response), as well as other principles of behavioural instruction that aim at changing a problematic or unwanted behaviour (Cooper et al., 1989), which should be improved or stopped by the end of the intervention (Baer et al., 1968; Sulzer-Azaroff and Mayer, 1991). Target behaviours for children with ASD include social skills, communication, academic performance and adaptation skills, such as gross and fine motor skills, preparation and consumption of food, use of toilet, getting dressed, personal hygiene, the ability to find their way around in the house and the community, skills that are needed to find a job and understand concepts such as time and money (Maurice et al., 1996).

Applied behaviour analysis is based on the observation that ASD is a syndrome of behavioural deficits and excessive reactions that have a neurological basis, but can be significantly improved within controlled frameworks (Lovaas et al., 1989). More specifically, ABA focuses on the systematic instruction of small and measurable behavioural units. It is essentially an objective science that is based on the reliable measurement and the objective evaluation of a behaviour that you observe and you wish to modify. In order to reliably measure the change in behaviour, you must first understand and define it accurately (Powers, 1992). Certain behaviours, such as eye contact, can be easily defined because they are discernible, they have measurable duration and they can be easily perceived. However, there are many vague, multidimensional and complex behaviours, such as anger, depression and aggression, that you may wish to modify or extinguish. In order to record directly the frequency, the duration and other measurable variables of a behaviour, you must first define it using observable and quantifiable terms (Sulzer-Azaroff and Mayer, 1991). For example, aggressive behaviour could be defined as: 'attempts, episodes, or instances of biting, scratching, pinching or hair pulling'. The 'initiation of social interaction with peers' could be defined as: 'eye contact with the peer and use of an appropriate greeting gesture'. Once you succeed in defining these behaviours in an objectively acceptable way, you can then observe them and conclude whether they improved after the implementation of a behavioural intervention, and present convincing evidence to support your claims (Baer et al., 1987). The behaviours that you wish to alter are usually assessed in the contexts where they are observed – usually the house, the school and the wider community. A thorough evaluation of the effectiveness of the intervention is accomplished by (Sulzer-Azaroff and Mayer, 1991):

- choosing a behaviour that you wish to improve (for example, lack of eye contact);

- identifying and defining the desirable targets (for example, to increase the frequency and duration of eye contact);

- defining a way to measure the behaviours that you study (for example, record how often the child looks at people in his environment and time the duration of this eye contact);

- evaluating the current level of performance (for example, to have a reference point; if you want to be able to conclude whether the intervention was effective, you must know the duration and the frequency of eye contact before the beginning of the intervention);

- designing and implementing the appropriate intervention to change the problematic behaviour by teaching new alternative skills (for example, to reward the child every time that he looks in your eyes by giving him something he wants);

- assessing the target behaviours continuously in order to determine the intervention's effectiveness (for example, to collect measurements, at regular intervals, of the frequency and the duration of eye contact in order to estimate whether the desirable changes have taken place);

- evaluating constantly the effectiveness of the intervention and the appropriate modifications to maintain and/or to increase the effectiveness and the efficacy of the intervention (for example, if you have not succeeded in increasing the frequency and the duration of eye contact, then you must attempt to identify the mistakes that you made and correct them). When you meet your targets, you must then make sure that the change is permanent and can be generalised to other settings and to other individuals. To return to the example of eye contact, you must be certain that it remains increased after a period of 3 to 5 months or that it has been incorporated into the repertoire of the child's behaviours. You should also examine whether the child can maintain eye contact with different people in different contexts, that is, to generalise the skill that he has mastered (Green, 1996b). If the child has not achieved this, then the intervention is not complete and you need to work further on the concept of generalisation.

You can use ABA to address a wide range of skills and behaviours that impede and inhibit the progress of children with ASD, such as aggressive behaviours, which are characterised by lack of understanding of the child's own agency and the effects on others (Sigafoos and Saggers, 1995), self-help skills (Matson et al., 1990), self-stimulation (Epstein et al., 1985; Lovaas et al., 1987), play skills (Thorp et al., 1995), communication skills (Bryen and Joyce, 1985; Koegel et al., 1988) and academic skills (Kamps et al., 1994). It is worth emphasising that ABA aims not just to reduce or stop undesirable behaviour, but also to encourage the development of appropriate and desirable behaviour.

Before presenting ABA, I refer to discrete trial learning that constitutes one of its fundamental teaching methodologies and aims at controlling the wealth of information and the interaction opportunities that are usually presented to children with ASD. Since a child with ASD might have difficulty reacting to many stimuli simultaneously, he must learn to handle effectively a small amount of stimuli every time (Koegel et al., 1982a). This method helps children with ASD to control the learning process, so that they can more easily master the skills that they need to function effectively. They initially achieve the first step and then they move to the next, until they reach the final target.

Every teaching unit includes five basic stages that remain stable regardless of the skill that constitutes the final target:

1. The teacher or the therapist presents a short and concise instruction or question (stimulus) (for example, sit on the chair).

2. The instruction is followed by a prompt to promote the correct response (for example, the chair is there, go and sit on the chair).

3. The child reacts correctly or incorrectly (response) (for example, the child does not move, or sits on the floor or sits on the chair).

4. The teacher or the therapist responds appropriately to the child's behaviour. She reinforces and rewards the correct responses with something that the child likes – something edible, a toy, a hug or praise – while she ignores or corrects inappropriate responses (for example, gives some chocolate to the child who sits on the chair or physically guides the child who does not respond to sit on the chair).

5. The teacher or the therapist records the behaviours that she observes in order to create a profile of the child's abilities. This profile will help her decide the skills that she will teach the child and organise them according to the level of difficulty (for example, a child with problems in fine motor skills must first learn to hold the pencil appropriately and then manage to write or draw).

 Question for discussion

Think of a behaviour that you would like to teach to a child with ASD. How would you use these stages to accomplish your goal? What would you use as reinforcers/rewards? What problems could you encounter and how would you handle them?

Newsom and Rincover (1989) explained that discrete trial learning can be used to teach basic skills – such as focusing and maintaining attention – and many more elaborate verbal and social skills that are important for independent function. The therapy starts with two primary aims: (a) the instruction of learning readiness skills, such as the ability to sit on a chair and pay attention to what is going on in the environment, and (b) the decrease of behaviours that inhibit learning, such as lack of compliance, temper tantrums and aggression. Discrete trial learning is also the basis for practising and achieving social interaction skills.

As soon as the child learns to sit quietly and pay attention, he can be taught more complex skills, such as social behaviours and communication. Social skills training starts with eye contact (which should be meaningful) and continues with imitation, learning through observation, the expression of affection, and social play. You usually teach social skills by helping the child initially to understand the procedure of naming objects (for example, to realise that the round thing that bounces off the floor is called ball), to name objects on his own (for example, to show the ball and say 'ball') or to use complete sentences (for example, 'this is a red ball'), and, finally, to look for spontaneous communication (for example, to approach his mother and say, 'Mum, can you give me the ball?', but without asking him previously if he wants to play with the ball). If the child is non-verbal, then he can use alternative forms of communication to enhance these social skills, as will be discussed in Chapter 3. As soon as the child masters these social skills, he learns to express himself in order to get what he wants, that is, to be rewarded for exhibiting the appropriate behaviour. Then the child has to generalise the ability to communicate with other people apart from his mother and in other settings apart from the house (McGee et al., 1985). Since children with ASD do not usually learn spontaneously from the environment, you must teach them almost everything that they need to do (Green, 1996b), even if you believe that it is self-evident.

Discrete trial training in combination with other principles and methods that make up ABA have been shown to be extremely valuable in designing instruction in the classroom; in defining the motives that you must provide to children with ASD in the classroom; in choosing classroom behaviour management strategies; and in devising assessment procedures and techniques for the child (Martens et al., 1999). In order to achieve the best possible outcome, you have to be particularly sensitive to the individual differences of children with ASD. You can deal successfully with each child's individual needs by observing him and collecting data about his behaviour in an attempt to locate the factors that you must take into account in order to design an effective intervention. The targets that you set within the context of ABA programmes are the following (Dunlap et al., 2001):

1. You locate the objects or the situations that could motivate a child with ASD to express and to maintain a positive behaviour by acting as rewards or reinforcers (for example, listening to music, walking to the playground). To do this, you have to observe the child and collect supplementary information from his parents or teachers, and initially use primary and direct rewards, which are more powerful (for example, food or toys), while later you move on to secondary and indirect rewards, which delay gratification and are more socially oriented (for example, verbal praise). The ultimate goal is to start withdrawing the rewards gradually, so that the child can experience pleasure from exhibiting the desired behaviour and not from receiving a reward. At the same time you could identify and remove any objects or situations that cause stress or fear to the child and prevent him from functioning normally or that make him feel insecure.

2. You define the child's weaknesses and deficits and try to create the appropriate tasks that will help him to fill any cognitive gaps and keep up with his peers. If you want to get a full picture of the child's range of abilities you have to test him thoroughly using all the appropriate standardised tests, and bear in mind that he might perform adequately in some tasks and face problems in others.

3. You teach the child to generalise the skills and abilities that he has mastered to other settings in order to overcome his limitations (for example, to be able to read a text both at school and at home or to cooperate both with his parents and with his teacher).

4. You show the child the techniques and strategies that he needs in order to control his behaviour without needing the intervention of an adult to bring him back to order (for example, when he feels that he misses the meaning of the text that he reads, then he can start underlining the central ideas; when he gets angry at the child who sits next to him, he should tell the child to be quiet and not hit him). If he manages to gain self-control, he will be able to function more effectively in the classroom, since he will exhibit less disruptive behaviour and will facilitate the teacher's role. It is important to understand that in order to include a child with ASD in a mainstream setting, he has to develop not only academic but also social skills.

Therapists who practise ABA have, over time, reviewed some of the basic principles that they have adopted and that have proven to be either dysfunctional or ineffective. So, they have reached a point where they have introduced new practices to ABA that include positive behavioural support, functional assessment and training in functional communication.

Positive behavioural support aims to enable children to acquire behaviours that will help them adjust and become socially acceptable. In order to achieve this, they have to overcome the behaviours that are destructive, dysfunctional and stigmatising (Koegel et al., 1996). A primary aim of positive behavioural support is the teaching of functional and desirable behaviours that will ultimately replace problematic and undesirable behaviours. Therapists modify the existing environment to show the child that a problematic behaviour is irrelevant, ineffective and inadequate (Horner et al., 1993, 1996). O'Neill et al. (1997) reported that in order to create a plan to support the child's positive behaviour you must pursue the following actions (while remembering that it is just as important to assess the environment to see what needs to be changed there):

1. Assess the child and identify undesirable behaviours.

2. Implement the procedure that I described above in an effort to replace undesirable behaviours with more acceptable and effective behaviours.

3. Suggest an intervention that does not come into conflict with the values and the beliefs of the child and his family. If you choose a programme that parents and teachers cannot implement because they lack the necessary training or because it is too expensive or demanding, then it will fail.

4. Evaluate consistently the child's behaviour so that the intervention can bring about the desired outcome.

The second technique that was introduced in the context of ABA is functional analysis, namely, the process of gathering information that can be used to maximise the effectiveness of interventions that support positive behaviours (O'Neill et al., 1997). Functional behaviour analysis can be achieved when you:

• Provide an accurate description of the problematic behaviours: you need to know if the child is aggressive. You need to be aware of all the aggressive behaviours that he exhibits, so that you can deal with them more effectively. An important distinction, for example, is whether the child is aggressive towards others or whether he hurts himself. The more accurate the description the more effective the intervention you can plan.

• Identify and determine the events and the conditions that precede the undesirable behaviour: you may observe that the child reads with difficulty when the teacher asks him to stand up, whereas he does not have any problem when he reads sitting down. If you are familiar with those patterns, then you can protect the child from exposure to situations and facts that might disturb him and impede his progress. It is also likely that the problematic behaviour is more intense in a specific time frame. For example, the child is going to concentrate more in the morning than in the afternoon. If you have realised this, then you must try to teach him some of the most challenging skills in the morning.

- Observe and determine the consequences of a behaviour that you either reinforce or extinguish: if the child wants to eat and starts throwing objects on the floor, your reaction will determine whether he adopts this behaviour or not. If you give him something to eat, then the child will connect the demand for food with throwing objects on the floor and will act this way every time he is hungry. If you ignore his behaviour and do not give him something to eat, then he will stop acting this way and will find another way to express his need. This is when you can step in and show him the proper way to ask for food (for example, to say the word 'food' or, if he cannot speak, to point to the food or to a card with something edible printed on it).

Functional analysis constitutes a strict method of evaluating the child's responses and behaviours that is built on experiential observation. Many studies have shown that interventions which are based on the findings of careful and thorough functional evaluations are more likely to be effective in comparison with the traditional interventions that are not based on empirical data from observations of the target child (Durand et al., 1989; O'Neill et al., 1997; Repp et al., 1988). Functional analysis is not used exclusively with individuals with developmental disabilities, but with a range of other disorders. Moreover, it often includes a combination of assessment procedures. Berg et al. (1995), Cooper and Harding (1993), Dunlap et al. (1991), Mace and Lalli (1991) and Sasso et al. (1992) describe methods that combine procedures of direct, descriptive and functional analyses. Functional analysis is not limited to the analysis of problematic behaviours. Daly et al. (1997) describe a model of functional analysis for the evaluation of academic performance.

The third technique is the training in functional communication, which teaches the child the way in which he can use the appropriate means of communication to get an object that he desires. Hagopian et al. (1998) believe that this is a method to replace the undesirable behaviour with another behaviour that is more effective and socially acceptable.

Applied behaviour analysis is the study of human behaviour. In the past 30 years, thousands of published studies have demonstrated its effectiveness in a range of:

1. Populations (children and adolescents with mental disorders, developmental disabilities and learning disabilities).

2. People who implement the interventions (parents, teachers, and mental health professionals).

3. Contexts (school, home, institutions, hospitals, and enterprises).

4. Behaviours (speech, social, academic, recreational and functional skills, aggressiveness, self-injuries and stereotypic behaviours).

This does not mean, of course, that ABA does not have limitations, such as the underexplored sustainability of long-term effects and the difficulty in fostering understanding and generalisation skills.

Imitating actions with objects in a safe environment

ABA and autism

Simpson (2001) claims that ASD is the only disorder that is manifested in so many ways and therefore numerous attempts have been made to address it (Olley and Gutentag, 1999). Applied behaviour analysis is based on the accurate interpretation of the relationship that exists between certain events or situations (stimulus) and the consequences that they have on the child with ASD (response). This relationship is analysed and the collected information is used to design a systematic programme that aims at changing the child's behaviour and teaching him new, useful skills (Alberto and Troutman, 1999). This approach has fanatic followers and opponents. Some people believe that the techniques of ABA are the only 'salvation' for the child with ASD and his family, whereas others consider them to be rigid and dogmatic. I believe that this approach is effective when it is implemented properly and it is adjusted to the needs and the specific characteristics of every child with ASD – but at the same time recognising its flaws. However, ABA does not constitute a total therapeutic approach to ASD, since it cannot deal effectively with all ASD's characteristic behaviours.

The most popular ABA programme was initiated by Ivar Lovaas in 1970 and it aimed at improving the functioning of young children with ASD through an intensive and extremely structured behavioural programme implemented by a highly and properly trained person. At the end of 1960 and 1970, Lovaas (1977) worked with institutionalised children with ASD. He tried to improve their verbal communication through ABA techniques. At the time he was criticised by many of his colleagues who argued in favour of the psychodynamic and other approaches, since most of these children lost the verbal skills that they acquired when the programme stopped and they returned to their life at the institution. He observed, however, that the children who returned to their families improved much more, because their families were interested in implementing the programme at home to help their children. So, he realised the vital importance of parental contribution to the educational process.

Later, Lovaas started working with younger children aged 2–4 years old at their homes and with the active participation of their parents to ensure the maintenance of newly acquired skills. The first step of the intervention programme is to develop attention, motor and verbal imitation, followed by basic language and self-help skills, and then moving on progressively to the instruction of non-verbal and verbal imitation skills and occupation with toys. As soon as the child conquers these basic skills, he progresses to the second stage, where he learns to express himself (either verbally or through cards and pictures, according to his level) and to play interactively with his peers. The first sessions always take place in the same setting, because children with ASD have a problem with generalisation – but as time goes by they can be taught both at home and at school.

Behaviour modification is based on the assumption that reward increases the chances that a positive behaviour will reoccur, whereas deprivation of privileges decreases the chances that a negative or undesirable behaviour will reoccur. In the 1960s and 1970s behaviour analysts used aversive techniques in an effort to deter the child from doing things that were potentially harmful either for him or for others (for example, they painted the child's nails with a bitter nail polish so that he would not bite them). Behaviour modification has been criticised extensively because it was considered a serious violation of the child's human rights and dignity. Lovaas initially defended the use of aversive techniques in cases where the child engaged in self-injurious or self-stimulatory behaviours and claimed that these techniques made up just 1 per cent of the typical interactions of his programme and are no longer used after the first few weeks. Lovaas's model (1993) no longer uses aversive techniques and it places greater emphasis on processes for positive reinforcement of behaviours. However, there are still some therapists who resort to aversive techniques, which they use as 'punishers' of inappropriate or unwanted behaviours.

Lovaas and his colleagues argue that even though some children with ASD never reach typical functioning, they usually manage to decrease inappropriate behaviours and to accelerate the acquisition of basic language. As you will see later, some of these claims are exaggerated and based on ambiguous data. The interest in Lovaas's method was rekindled after the publication of the book *Let Me Hear Your Voice* by Catherine Maurice (1993), where she talks about using the Lovaas approach with her two children (Buckman, 1995). This book became a best-seller for parents who read it and tried to implement the tasks and the advice that it contained with their children, without the expected outcome in many cases. The programme is meant to run for many hours when the child is awake (something that can be physically, psychologically and financially unbearable) and family involvement is crucial. The therapy is implemented initially at the child's house and then it extends to the community and the school setting. However, although the directions for the implementation of the programme are quite clear, there is inadequate advice on inclusion practices in the school and in the wider community.

Lovaas published his first study in 1987 where he presented the results of therapeutic intervention for 40 or more hours per week for at least two years with 19 young children with autism. This research involved two control groups – one group of 19 children who received 10 or fewer hours of therapy per week and one group of 21 children who did not attend any intervention. In order to measure the participants' progress, the researchers decided to use two variables: the child's intelligence quotient (IQ), which they measured before and after the intervention, and school attendance (if the child attended a mainstream or a special school). However, Schopler et al. (1989) observed that the measures that were used to evaluate the gains may not reflect substantial and generic changes in the level of functioning. For example, an increase in IQ could reflect increased compliance and familiarisation with the evaluation process and not real changes in the cognitive level. Moreover, the change in the school setting may result from parental efforts or changes in legislation and not from improved academic performance. Moreover, the children who were chosen to participate in the experimental group were quite high functioning and had a good prognosis, and were not representative of the wider population of children with ASD. They also mentioned that the design of the study was not truly experimental, since the assignment of children to the experimental and control groups was not random. So, Schopler et al. (1989) concluded that it is impossible to determine the effects of the particular intervention based on Lovaas's study.

Despite the serious methodological problems that I mentioned, Lovaas reported that the observed results were spectacular. He also suggested that after two years of intervention almost half of the children in the experimental group had normal IQ and functioned effectively at mainstream school without any additional support. However, these children had normal IQ even before the beginning of the intervention and their satisfactory performance at school could be explained by their potential. Moreover, it is difficult to identify and to isolate the effects of maturation, especially since the control children did not share the same characteristics with the experimental children. Lovaas (1987) actually claimed that children in the experimental group 'recovered' from autism, while only one child from the control groups exhibited similar gains. Since autism can be treated but not cured, this statement is exaggerated.

Lovaas attempted to respond to the criticism of his work and to prove that the findings of his 1987 study were real by conducting a supplementary study in 1993 together with his associates McEachin and Smith (McEachin et al., 1993). They re-examined the same participants after seven years and concluded that the differences in IQ persisted. Eight out of the nine children with the best performance were still in mainstream classes. But this is expected, since the children who had a normal IQ and attended mainstream schools drew knowledge from their environment and so kept up with their peers. This does not prove, however, that these behaviours are necessarily attributed to ABA.

Gresham and MacMillan (1998) adopted the limitations and the criticisms that were expressed by Schopler and his colleagues and noted that the studies by Lovaas (1987) and by McEachin et al. (1993) should be interpreted with caution. Mesibov (1993) reported that Lovaas did not assess some behaviours and skills that are linked directly to ASD, such as social interactions and perceptive skills. Furthermore, Mundy (1993) said that many high-functioning children with ASD have normal IQ – even with minimal therapeutic intervention – and the increase that is occasionally reported in IQ by scientists such as Birnbauer and Leach (1993), Sheinkopf and Siegel (1998), Anderson et al. (1987), Fenske et al. (1985) and Harris et al. (1991) is due to the child's ability to interact more effectively with his environment. So, it could be argued that the specific approach is promising and effective, because it teaches the child with ASD the proper way to interact with his environment and not because it suddenly increases the IQ and eliminates autism.

The methodological limitations that were mentioned so far impede the generalisation of the findings to the general population of children with ASD. Schreibman (2000) argued that researchers must not ignore the limitations of their studies, but acknowledge them and try to improve them. She also noted that when children with ASD are young and start attending an early behavioural intervention, they then have a greater chance of improving substantially in many developmental areas and increasing their level of functioning. The improvement can be explained by the fact that they receive an intervention on an almost daily basis and there is an adult who spends time with them exclusively. Applied behaviour analysis is based on well-grounded learning theories that were articulated at the beginning of the twentieth century, and stresses the value of scientific methods in assessing its effectiveness (Smith, 1993).

Matson et al. (1996) completed a comprehensive review of the behavioural studies that were applied to children with ASD in the areas of inappropriate behaviours, social skills, speech and language, self-help skills and academic skills. They concluded that ABA has contributed to the development of practical techniques for the treatment of autism-related problems. Hall (1997) also published one more review of behavioural research on ASD and claimed that 'three decades of research have shown that applied behaviour analysis has offered a range of strategies that have been proven effective for individuals with autism because they decrease stereotypic behaviours and they increase language and skills of initiations of social interactions' (p. 150). It cannot be established, however, to what extent the maturation of the children who participated in these studies has contributed to the improvements of some of their behaviours.

Green (1996a) produced a review of behavioural interventions that were applied to children with ASD up to the age of 5, in their houses, at school or in an educational setting. She concluded that early intervention based on ABA can bring about important, comprehensive, long-term and notable improvement in significant developmental domains for many children with ASD. She also reported that behavioural intervention is more effective for those children than the lack of intervention or other interventions, and that the outcomes are better for children who started the programme before the age of 2 or 3. However, it is expected that a child who follows an intervention has more changes in his behaviour than a child who does not. It is equally reasonable to assume that a child who starts any therapy before the age of 2 has a better prognosis than a child who starts the same therapy at the age of 7. Moreover, it is not clear how long the therapy should last and when it should cease. ABA methods are used to support individuals with ASD in at least six ways, by:

- increasing the desirable behaviours (for example, rewards increase desirable behaviours in social interactions);

- teaching new skills (for example, procedures of systematic instruction and rewarding teaching new life and communication skills, as well as social skills);

- maintaining the mastered behaviours (for example, self-control can help maintain and generalise work skills);

- generalising or transferring a behaviour from one situation or condition to another (for example, studying at home and studying at school);

- limiting and, if possible, eliminating the conditions and the circumstances where disruptive behaviours are expressed (for example, modification of the learning environment);

- decreasing disruptive behaviours (for example, self-injury or stereotypic behaviours).

Hingtgen and Bryson (1972) reviewed more than 400 research papers about people with ASD that were published between 1964 and 1970 and reached the conclusion that the interventions based on behaviourism had the most consistent effects. They do not clarify, however, which were the other interventions and where they base their assumption that behavioural approaches are superior to others. Similar findings were reported by DeMyer et al. (1981) who analysed 1,100 more studies that were conducted in the 1970s. Baglio et al. (1996) reviewed 251 studies from 1980 to 1995 and commented on the effectiveness of ABA in treating ASD. They said that behavioural interventions lead to positive outcomes. They studied the areas of deviant behaviours, language, daily life skills, survival in the community, academic performance and social skills. Despite the fact that the number of studies conducted and reviewed was impressive, you should bear in mind that not all of them were properly designed (Lynch, 1998; Perry et al., 1995).

Herbert and Brandsma (2002) noted that ABA tends to be applied exclusively to children with ASD at the end of the twentieth century (Hayes, 2001). The New York State Department of Health (1999, available at http://www.nyhealth.gov/community/infants_children/early_intervention/disorders/autism/ch4_pt2.htm) published some directives for the clinical treatment of ASD, in which it is mentioned that ABA is recommended for treating childhood autism. It is important to make a distinction between the implementation of a complete behavioural programme and other interventions that are used for the treatment of certain problems that are linked to ASD and other developmental disorders, such as self-injury (Rogers, 1998). Even if the original study by Lovaas (1987) did not have methodological limitations, it would not suffice to support the argument that ABA can treat ASD. It should also be stressed again that children who receive ABA face a basic difficulty in generalising their skills, abilities and knowledge (Gamby, 2002).

Having presented numerous studies that deal with the effectiveness of ABA, I now summarise the elements that a comprehensive treatment should include in order to produce the desirable outcomes (Simeonnson et al., 1987):

1. You have to place emphasis on the development of the desirable behaviour. This can be achieved with the reinforcement of appropriate behaviours with the appropriate rewards, as I have mentioned before (Koegel et al., 1996).

2. The family should participate actively in treatment. Without family participation, the gains that are observed in professional settings such as special educational programmes, clinics and hospitals rarely lead to improved functioning at home because of the inability to generalise (Bartak, 1978; Lovaas et al., 1973). Indeed, Hastings (2003) reports that ABA can also be used to facilitate the functioning of children with ASD.

3. The child–therapist ratio is one-to-one. For the first six months of the therapy, teaching must be at individual and not group level, because children at the initial stage respond better to an individual approach (Koegel et al., 1982a). Therapy can be done not only by professionals, but also by students or family members who have received the appropriate training (Lovaas and Smith, 1988).

4. The child with ASD must be incorporated into society. When a child is capable of becoming part of a group, the composition of the group must be as balanced as possible. Children with ASD function much better when they are placed in an environment with other typically developing children than with other children with developmental disabilities (Strain, 1983). However, it does not suffice that children with ASD simply coexist with typically developing children; the former need formal instruction from trained facilitators to interact effectively with their peers (Strain, 1983), as you will see later.

5. The child with ASD must understand communication: because the child exhibits a few appropriate behaviours, new behaviours must be taught one by one. This happens because teaching a behaviour rarely leads to the appearance of other relevant behaviours that have not been taught. For

example, teaching language skills does not lead directly to the emergence of other language skills or the motive for communication.

6. You have to determine the therapy's duration and intensity. Successful implementation demands 40 hours per week; 10 or 20 hours do not suffice (Anderson et al., 1987). The greatest part of the 40 hours for the first six months should be dedicated to speech and language rehabilitation. When the child cannot communicate verbally he must learn to communicate alternatively. Later, the sessions will be divided between integration with peers and improvement of cognitive and communicative deficits. More recent data indicate, however, that 40 hours per week was a completely arbitrary number and 15 hours per week is sufficient (Green, 1996b).

So far I have presented numerous studies that have demonstrated that ABA can deal effectively with some of the symptoms of children with ASD when used in combination with other effective approaches (Schreck and Mazur, 2008). However, this does not mean that you have to disregard their weaknesses, as identified by researchers (for example, Tews, 2007). If you manage to acknowledge and overcome them, then you will manage to improve the intervention. More specifically, there are questions that supporters of ABA have to work on resolving:

1. Which are the most appropriate and effective forms of ABA? More studies are needed to compare ABA with other interventions in order to examine its effectiveness (Hilton and Seal, 2007). Until more research is conducted, it is recommended to avoid claiming that the benefits of ABA are unique and cannot be achieved by other interventions.

2. What are the reasonable expectations for the progress of children who receive ABA? The prerequisite for realistic expectations is the identification and realisation of the advantages and disadvantages of the method, as well as the questioning of its 'curative' properties.

3. Is ABA more effective when implemented in isolation or in combination with other effective strategies? There is no single intervention that can resolve all the problems and difficulties of children with ASD. The most effective programmes are those that apply a variety of practices and evaluate systematically and constantly all the interventions and the methods that they use.

4. Which staff are required for the effective implementation of ABA? The professionals who train children with ASD must have the necessary knowledge and skills to design, implement and evaluate ABA programmes. Since the role of the therapists is very demanding, it is important to provide them with appropriate support to increase their self-efficacy and to reduce the likelihood of high work demands causing

burnout (Gibson et al., 2009). There is a controversy regarding the use of teachers for coordinating such programmes. It has been established that the desirable child–therapist ratio is one-to-one, but this presupposes the proper training of the expert; otherwise, the results may be destructive for the child. Moreover, it is difficult to maintain this ratio in the school setting where there are usually one or two teachers for a whole class. Even in inclusion classes, one teacher is asked to teach many children often who have diverse special educational needs.

Studies regarding the effectiveness of ABA are extensive and have contributed significantly to the development of many educational techniques that have been used with children with ASD either at home or at school. The most important contribution of this approach is the realisation that the sooner the child starts an intervention, the more chances he has to cover some developmental gaps and to become integrated into the family, school and social contexts. An issue that many therapists and families have to deal with is how much time needs to be given to children with ASD in order to gain the maximum possible benefit. In many studies the hours of therapy vary from 15 to 40 or more per week. The only study that compared the effectiveness of different durations of the intervention was that of Lovaas (1987), who reached the unjustified conclusion that 40 hours weekly are essential for the successful treatment of children with ASD.

However, the recommended hours of therapy are not always feasible given that such an intervention can be financially unbearable for many families who do not receive any funding and have to pay for it from their own resources. Moreover, some children might not have the ability to attend a structured programme for such a long period of time. You may wonder also whether it is realistic and acceptable for young children to spend all their time in a structured indoors setting when they should be outside playing and discovering the world. The problem is, however, that many do nothing or engage in undesirable behaviours when they are left alone.

One more parameter that you need to take into serious consideration is that if the children spend all their time with a therapist, then they do not learn to interact effectively with their family members – unless this is something that the therapist and the family work on. So you observe occasionally that parents whose children attend behavioural interventions might feel insecure about their parenting skills. They think that they cannot handle their child's behaviour without the help of an expert and so sometimes schedule therapeutic sessions even during the weekend in order to limit the time that they have to 'face' their children alone.

This is an essential factor that you need to take into account when you decide if parents should be actively involved in their child's treatment. Parents should realise that therapists must not replace them, but teach them how to interact effectively and meaningfully with their child. So, some argue that parents should also be trained as therapists for their children in order to feel more able to communicate with them or to manage their undesirable, or even risky, behaviours. There are, however, some parents who do not have the strength or the ability to work with their children and to set the limits that they need to teach them new skills. In this case it is better that parents are not asked to introduce new tasks, but focus on the maintenance and generalisation of the skills that their children have mastered. So, a challenge for the therapists is to plan some activities in which the whole family can participate in order to improve the relationship between them and to empower the parents. Such a task may ameliorate the social life of many families if it is significantly restricted because they are afraid or ashamed to leave their house.

Many parents were excited with the spectacular results that Lovaas and his colleagues promised, and adopted ABA, but then did not see the progress that they expected. This could be explained by the different characteristics of the children who participated in the studies; the duration and the frequency of the therapy; the age of onset; the level of family participation; or the accuracy of its implementation. Since there is not enough evidence to justify why some children have remarkable progress and others do not, you must be very careful not to make overgeneralisations. Moroever, you should keep in mind that more children did poorly in the Young Autism project than did well (Green, 1996a). It is also worth mentioning that some results – even if they are positive, such as the decrease of unwanted behaviours – do not last for long and are not generalised if there is no relevant provision. So the aim of the intervention is to change not only the behaviour of the child, but also the surroundings.

Some other points of the programme that warrant further attention are that ABA may be applied very rigidly and fail to meet the individual needs of each child. Children with ASD may become extremely dependent on rewards and reinforcers and not gain any pleasure from the activity itself but only from its positive consequences. Emphasis is placed on the cognitive development that is linked to school inclusion, while more attention should be devoted to social skills and play, as well as emotional and psychological problems which remain largely unexplored (Ross, 2007). However, despite the shortcomings that were mentioned, ABA interventions that were properly designed and implemented were proven instrumental in improving the behaviour and the skills of children with ASD, worldwide.

TEACCH programme

The second therapeutic approach is based on the philosophy of the Treatment and Education of Autistic and Communication related handicapped CHildren (TEACCH) programme (Schopler and Reichler, 1971) and has been used in many countries all over the world (Schopler and Mesibov, 2000; Tsang et al., 2007). TEACCH is a comprehensive programme that deals with the diagnosis, the treatment, the professional training and the lives of individuals with ASD. When I use the term 'TEACCH' in this book I refer to the part of the programme that addresses exclusively children's education. The cornerstone of TEACCH is structured instruction that is used systematically to make the environment predictable, to help the child understand the environment and to function feeling safe, to make use of his skills and to practise them. Although, as mentioned in the introduction, ASD is linked to biological and neurological factors, the environmental conditions promote the child's ability to improve his level of functioning.

TEACCH has incorporated some behavioural principles for treating children with ASD, but it differs from ABA in some fundamental respects. The most prominent differentiation is that it focuses on maximising the children's skills using their abilities instead of offering 'recovery' from ASD. The programme has been designed to offer structured settings where children with ASD will be able to develop their skills. Teachers organise individual working spaces, where every child can perform different activities. They offer visual cues to balance the deficit of children with ASD in processing auditory information. TEACCH values the cooperation between parents and teaching staff, while the parents are encouraged to establish routines at home similar to those at school (Gresham et al., 1999).

The teacher has to structure the classroom in such a way that she will be able to more effectively teach children with ASD. Even the arrangement of the furniture within the classroom can reinforce or impede the child's independent functioning, as well as his ability to recognise and comply with the rules. Many children do not know where they have to go and how to get there faster. The structured environment offers a sense of safety, together with the visual cues that help the child understand the room's functioning. If the teacher is allowed to choose the classroom, she should take into account some issues, such as its size, the neighbouring classes, the number and the degree of accessibility to electricity sockets, the distance from the nearest toilet, the lighting, as well as if there is some furniture that cannot be moved easily. For example, it is good to choose a quiet classroom.

Since some children need limits to manage to function more effectively, the teacher can artificially create them using rugs, shelves, partitions, tape on the floor, or desks. The aim is not to limit the child's mobility or autonomy, but to enable him to quickly locate the area where he needs to go in order to complete an activity. Another variable that the teacher should take into account when organising the classroom is the special needs of every individual child and to create an individual daily schedule and a group daily schedule. The daily schedule consists of verbal instructions, photographs, pictures or objects (according to the child's level of understanding) that are placed one under the other to provide a sense of order and sequence. The child is trained to understand the function of the daily programme and to learn to follow the order in which the activities are presented. Structured teaching involves arranging activities with new and less preferred tasks preceding more favoured ones, which then serve as 'reinforcers' for the earlier tasks. For example, an individual daily schedule can include the following photographs: good morning, drawing, chocolate, reading, music, maths and break. The reward must be compatible with the child's interests and preferences, it should vary and it should consist mainly of secondary reinforcers (for example, verbal praise or a smile). The activities that are incorporated into the individual daily schedule vary according to the child's level of functioning and understanding and it should be checked and modified when the situations or the needs of the child change. I would like to remind you that the child who sees the individual daily schedule for the first time does not know automatically what to do, but he is systematically trained until he understands and applies it.

Given that the main feature of TEACCH is an individualised instruction programme, every child and every classroom need different levels of structure. Low-functioning students will need more structure and more limits and directions or prompts in comparison to high-functioning students. A classroom that caters for young students should include, apart from the academic areas, some special educational areas for playing, for eating and for the development of self-help skills. There is also an area for group activities (aimed at developing interaction and socialisation between children). A classroom for older students should include, separately from areas for individual instruction, an area for recreation and an area that is like a laboratory (where the child can learn to work, for example, with clay), an area for practising domestic skills and, finally, an area for self-help skills and for grooming. All the classrooms must have some space where the students can place and keep their personal belongings (for example, lockers, drawers or special boxes). The teacher's desk should also be clearly defined.

The layout of the classroom is dictated by the skills and the abilities of the students who attend it. As soon as the students enter the classroom, they look at the group daily schedule that presents the daily events and is placed in a visible spot so that all the students can see it at any time. Then the student goes to his working area where he can see his individual daily schedule that usually contains his photograph or his name. In the working area there is a desk, a chair, the materials that the child needs in order to perform his activities and a box where he places his assignment in order to show that he has finished. If the student does not know where to find the materials, how to start or how to complete an activity, or what to do when he finishes, then it is difficult to complete an activity and to follow his individual daily schedule. The desks are placed so that the students look at the wall and the individual daily schedule and not at other students or at the windows. This helps them concentrate. Students with severe attention deficit see only a white wall, so that there are no distractions. The teacher should sit in a place that allows her to supervise all the areas – especially if she does not have any assistant in the classroom and needs to control which part of the daily schedule the student is at. Another practical point that I would like to raise regarding the layout of the classroom is that it is good to make sure that recreational areas are not located near the exits so that the students cannot go out if the teacher's attention is distracted. Of course, this layout is not feasible in a mainstream classroom, but is feasible in special or inclusion classes that are used to instruct children with severe developmental disabilities.

TEACCH has been designed, as its name reveals, to teach and educate children with ASD and other disorders and its basic principles can be summarised as follows:

1. It aims to improve the child's adjustment to his social surroundings. This is accomplished through the implementation of two strategies that could improve the child's skills (more specifically, training and modification of the environment), but also through the instruction of new skills that can compensate the deficits that he has both in the cognitive and in the social areas.

2. It establishes a cooperative relationship between professionals or teachers and parents. Parents are trained to work as co-therapists of their children, so that they can continue the implementation of the techniques at home.

3. It evaluates thoroughly the child's skills in an attempt to create an individualised teaching schedule that will address his unique academic and social needs.

4. It promotes the concept of structured teaching. Children with ASD benefit more from a structured educational setting, because they need the

predictability that creates a sense of safety.

5. It aspires to improve the child's skills. The evaluation identifies the child's skills in order to improve them and render them more functional and socially acceptable. The same rationale is applied to the education of parents and staff; that is, their skills are assessed and improved through training to make them better and more effective trainers.

6. It is used as the basis of cognitive-behavioural therapy. The educational processes are guided by the theories of cognition and behaviour, which suggest that difficult behaviour may result from subjective problems in perception and processing. When these problems are overcome, then the child can replace the problematic behaviours with more acceptable and functional behaviours.

7. It trains professionals to cope with a range of behaviours. They are trained to understand all aspects of the child's behaviours and they do not specialise as psychologists, speech therapists, and so on.

 Question for discussion

How easy do you believe it is to create a highly structured environment for the child with ASD? Are all parents able to acts as co-therapists of their child?

TEACCH has drawn a clear distinction between diagnosis for bureaucratic reasons and evaluation for individualised instruction and management of the child's behaviour and problems (Mesibov and Howley, 2003; Schopler and Olley, 1980). For younger children with ASD, the programmes are implemented at school and for adolescents or young adults at professional settings, such as competitive industries or protected laboratories (Van Bourgondien and Schopler, 1996). The basic philosophy of TEACCH is that ASD is a developmental disorder that could be treated better with a psycho-educational approach that places emphasis mainly on the detailed evaluation of all the aspects of the individual and his environment. It also supports the individual with ASD throughout all the phases of his development – from infancy to adulthood.

Williams (1995) states that in the framework of TEACCH it is essential for the child to understand the reason (the cause) and the means of communication. Some activities to motivate the child with ASD to communicate are:

1. The adult can initiate a fun and pleasant activity for the child that will be repeated several times. Then she will stop performing it and wait for

the child to initiate it. Since the child will want to enjoy his favourite activity, he will attempt to find a way to motivate the adult to do what he wants. So a basic prerequisite for communication is created, namely, desire.

2. The adult does not allow the child to approach the objects that he desires or to carry out a desired activity. As the child tries to do what he wants, he will try to communicate his desire.

3. The adult creates artificial problems/situations that need to be resolved. For example, she may place in a high spot the object that the child wants to play with. So, he will have to find a way to reach it by asking for the adult's help.

4. The adult observes the situations that upset the child and teaches him to express his emotion by asking her to stop performing the unpleasant activity. The adult must avoid at any cost causing extreme stress or fear to the child, which could lead to more disruptive behaviour. Since you cannot teach emotions effectively in artificial ways merely using cards or photographs, you have to work through them as you experience them in the context of everyday interactions and label them, so that the child can identify them.

5. The adult has to make sure that all his favourite objects are in plain view – whenever possible – throughout the day. So, if the child wants to take something, he is likely to ask for the adult's help or permission to get it. If you cannot have all his favourite objects in visible places, then you can put them in boxes or drawers, where you stick photos of their contents.

TEACCH recognises the necessity to prepare children with ASD to integrate and to function successfully in society, given that they all have the same right to education. Children who are placed in a specific setting should be able to benefit from it and to function properly. The offered activities must be based on the individual evaluation of the child's skills and abilities, and supported by trained professionals who want to offer assistance and can objectively judge the suitability of an activity. Children with ASD who have the potential should be fully included, otherwise partial inclusion could be the second option. Special classes and special schools should be offered only to children with ASD who cannot benefit from attending a mainstream setting.

Children with high-functioning ASD often fail to meet the emotional demands of the classroom. The teachers must be alert in order to identify any changes in behaviour that could be signs of depression, high levels of disorganisation, isolation, chronic fatigue or even talks about suicidal tendencies. The children who face many emotional problems should be placed in a highly structured educational environment, where they can receive individualised instruction, so that they can start experiencing success and productivity. Moreno and O'Neal (2004) give the following advice to parents of high-functioning children with ASD:

1. Individuals with ASD have deficits in their organisational skills, regardless of their intelligence or age. Even a top student who has a photographic memory can find it impossible to remember to bring a pen to the class or to recall the deadline for an assignment. The help that is provided to him should not be intrusive (for example, you could glue the photograph of a pen on the cover of his book or create a list with all the deadlines for all the assignments that he has to hand in). You should not lecture him about it, because this would only make matters worse. These students have either the most organised or most messy desks in the whole school. In the case of the latter, they must learn to organise their things following specific little steps.

2. Individuals with ASD may have impaired abstract thought, which could be supported by visual cues, such as drawings or written information. You should, however, avoid rhetoric, abstract or open-ended questions, which must be taught explicitly in relevant sessions and through incidental teaching.

3. The increase of unusual or challenging behaviours could lead to an increase in the child's anxiety levels that are created by a sense of loss of control. The anxiety is decreased when the student is kept away from stressful events or situations. In that case, organising a programme to help the student get reinstated and deal with the stressful situation is recommended. A 'safe' place or person could prove to be extremely useful. It would be even more desirable to train the child to express that he is feeling stressed, so that you can advise him or help him overcome it.

4. You should not take the undesirable behaviour personally, since it usually stems from the child's attempt to overcome experiences that cause confusion, disorientation or terror, and they have trouble understanding other people's reactions.

5. Individuals with ASD use and interpret speech literally, so you should try to avoid using metaphors, ambiguous expressions, sarcasms, nicknames and pseudonyms. This does not mean, however, that you should not provide him with explicit training in these topics.

6. When the student has trouble learning a new task, you should divide it into smaller parts or present it in different ways.

7. You should use clear and short sentences when you realise that the student does not understand something.

8. You should prepare a written or pictorial individual daily schedule that will help the student face everyday challenges.

9. Behaviour management is effective, but if it is not applied properly it can encourage mechanical behaviour, offer a short-term behavioural change or lead to some form of aggression.

10. When the high-functioning student with ASD uses repetitive verbal arguments, statements, or questions, you should interrupt him before this behaviour turns into a ritual. You could achieve this by asking him, for example, to note down his questions or his opinions and to show them to the teachers at the end of class. Since the student is not usually genuinely interested in the content of the question, you should ask him to write it down and then answer him in writing. This may help the student relax and then stop the stereotypical behaviour. If this does not prove to be effective, then ask him to try to write a reasonable answer to his question in order to distract him and to make him express his disappointment or frustration in a more productive way.

11. Since some students may not note a significant piece of information and forget to pass it on to their parents, you should train them systematically in the context of the intervention (Schopler and Mesibov, 1984).

12. When you evaluate the students' skills, do not assume that they possess exactly the same skills in every developmental area. For example, a child with ASD may be extremely good at algebra, but lack the ability to calculate the change that he gets when he goes shopping. Uneven skills are a trademark of ASD and should be addressed systematically.

In order to give a more comprehensive description of TEACCH, I provide an example of its application for teaching physical activities to children with ASD, by analysing the logic and the steps that Schultheis et al. (2000) followed. They implemented a successful programme of physical activities for children with ASD that focuses on two areas: stamina and motor skills. The structured recreational programme of TEACCH includes the following elements: physical layout, individual daily schedules and individual organisational systems. Each element is modified to be incorporated into the environment of physical education and to include the unique features and preferences of children with ASD.

When discussing the education of children with ASD, it is essential to remember that physical education is included in the definition of special needs education. However, there are very few physical activity programmes designed especially for children with ASD, since their unique behaviours can pose serious challenges for physical education teachers (Weber and Thorpe, 1992). One of the main principles of TEACCH is modifying or redesigning a programme in order to incorporate the unique characteristics of ASD.

TEACCH emphasises that the use of physical limits can help many children with ASD develop their independence. As noted by Schopler and Mesibov (1984), children with ASD are more able to organise and complete their assignments when there are clear visual limits that specify the place that is designated for specific activities. This happens because they have at their disposal the essential aids to organise their space and their actions. When children are familiar with the surroundings, they become more independent and they associate specific activities with specific areas. So, they can follow successfully the teachers' instructions with fewer verbal prompts. Limits seem to increase children's sense of safety. Some suggestions that might be helpful for the layout of the room are:

• remove the obstacles that might distract attention;

• provide four to five activity areas;

• use 'waiting' chairs so that the child does not wander aimlessly;

• close the curtains or cover the windows with paper to isolate external visual distractors;

• avoid taking breaks during class that could disrupt the course of instruction.

The individual daily schedules present the activities that have been assigned to every student and the order in which they should be carried out during class, so that he does not feel lost. These schedules have been designed especially to incorporate and to address the difficulties that each student faces and to help him conceptualise the terms 'what', 'where', and 'when'. Schopler and Mesibov (1995) presented arguments for the existence and use of individual daily schedules:

• They minimise problems caused by deficits in maintaining attention.

• They decrease the time needed to complete an activity and deal with organisational problems.

• They address problems of language comprehension.

• They make the student more independent.

• They increase the student's motivation for learning.

Sherrill (1998) suggested that when children with ASD perform a physical activity, they should be encouraged to think what to do in different situations through the use of pictures or words. Coucouvanis (1997) wrote that the functional system can use visual aids, such as objects, photographs, diaries, labels or lists to decrease disruptive behaviour. If the child stops wandering aimlessly or loitering, then he can be trained to spend his time doing the homework that he was assigned and so accelerate the completion of his physical education programme. The lists of activities to be completed are put up on a big noticeboard using a series of activity cards glued with self-adhesive tape. The individual daily schedule of every child has been designed to cover his needs and includes his photograph or name. When he gets to the gym, he learns to go to the noticeboard to check his individualised programme. He is trained to look at the activity card, to understand what he has to do and to carry out the physical exercise. Then he returns to the daily schedule and follows the same procedure as described before. The teacher is next to the child to make sure that he carries out the appropriate behaviours and to guarantee the effectiveness of the programme by:

- Using a big noticeboard that is placed next to the entrance so that the child sees it before wandering off.

- Teaching the child to read his daily schedule following the proper sequence of activities.

- Making sure that the child's photo or name is on the schedule.

- Using words, pictures, colours or symbols for each specialised activity area.

- Making a pocket where the child can place the cards after finishing with them.

- Using symbols that match the child's developmental level.

- Organising the tasks to enable the child to understand and perform them according to the schedule. This organisation involves the use of objects, photographs, colours, numbers and/or words (Schopler and Mesibov, 1995).

- Presenting the schedule to the child in advance until he becomes familiar with the concept.

- Using a timer to help the child understand when he has completed an activity, unless he is sensitive to noise, in which case, the teacher can use a clock and move the hands manually.

- Placing the necessary equipment in the room before the child arrives, so that he can find everything and avoid confusion. If the child is more skilled, then the teacher can train him to take out the equipment himself and return it when he completes the activity, in an effort to become more independent and responsible.

- Showing to the child only the equipment that is necessary for each task so as not to distract his attention and cause him to forget what he should use in each case.

- Providing the exact amount of equipment for the completion of the activity.

- Making individual seats (circles with the child's photograph and/or name) at the beginning and the end of class.

- Providing verbal and visual representations for every activity that will remind the child once again what he has to do.

- Using coloured drawn footprints that are glued on the floor and show the direction that the child has to go in order to complete an activity or to reach his next target. This could also help the child develop and practise his balance.

Although these are important as first steps, later the child needs to learn to select what is necessary for himself.

 Question for discussion

Now that you have looked carefully at the steps needed to ensure the success of a structured activity, think of something that you would like to teach a child with ASD. How would you go about planning the activity? Which steps would you take? How would you try to deal with unexpected occurrences?

As you can understand by observing the application of the TEACCH method, the basic element of success is the constant reminder that every child is unique and so the programme should adapt to his individual needs. The main aim of instruction during physical education is to offer opportunities to develop the skills that are essential for the child to play games and to participate in activities with his peers. The ultimate goal of the programme should be to free the child from prompts and enable him to perform the appropriate activities without needing to consult the schedule all the time, as well as to generalise the desirable outcome in other settings to achieve independence.

Furthermore, Mesibov and Schopler (1983) mention that sexual education of children with ASD constitutes another basic need that TEACCH covers. Individuals with ASD at different levels of functioning have different sexual education needs. For low-functioning individuals, the focus of the training is on sexual behaviour in public places. They need to learn to use the toilet properly and privately, to dress themselves and to masturbate privately. Individuals who can communicate and understand more should become more aware of their bodies and the changes that take place. Individuals with high-functioning ASD should be informed about the whole range of heterosexual issues. In a relevant study that I conducted with teachers, they identified the same issues as basic concepts and practices to be addressed (Kalyva, 2010). TEACCH professionals help parents realise on time that individuals with ASD have sexual needs; they also help parents deal with their feelings and values once these needs are expressed. However, they do not impose their opinion on parents. Since a proportion of individuals with ASD are likely to be homosexual, they need to understand all sexuality, according to their ability and emotional stage.

Presenting activities in a structured order

TEACCH has developed a training programme for typically developing children regarding diversity and empathy for children with ASD. It has been designed for primary school and junior school, whereas adjustments are made for higher grades. It introduces basic concepts and issues about inclusion, but there is no particular reference to the specific characteristics of a child or a group of children. The introductory programme is followed by briefing about special or inclusion classes and the children who attend them. There is also an extensive discussion on the target child with ASD, in his absence. The teacher must get consent and permission from the parents of the child with ASD and the child himself, if he can provide it, to go ahead with the implementation of the specific programme (Panerai et al., 1997).

Panerai et al. (2002) report that many studies have demonstrated the effectiveness of TEACCH for children with ASD and severe handicaps in reducing self-injurious behaviours (Norgate, 1998), for high-functioning children with ASD (Kunce and Mesibov, 1998) and for individuals who enter the workforce through supportive programmes (Keel et al., 1997). Panerai et al. (2002) compared the effectiveness of TEACCH and the intervention that some children with ASD were receiving at school. They concluded that children who participated in TEACCH improved significantly in fine motor skills and eye–hand coordination. No change was observed in their maladaptive behaviour, but the researchers did not provide adequate information for the other intervention that was implemented at school in order to draw more valid conclusions. Adolescents and adults with ASD who had never received any kind of intervention or training attended TEACCH and there was a significant decrease in their challenging behaviours (Siaperas et al., 2007) and increases in their social abilities and their functional communication skills (Siaperas and Beadle-Brown, 2006).

Schopler et al. (1982) collected information from 348 families who participated in a programme through the use of questionnaires. Individuals with ASD who participated in the study were between the ages of 2–26 and their IQ varied significantly. Most parents reported that the programme was particularly helpful. Only 7 per cent of the individuals who practised TEACCH ended up in an institution, in comparison with between 39 and 75 per cent of the general population of individuals with ASD. However, the particular study has quite a few methodological weaknesses: the sample was quite heterogeneous; there was no structured control condition; there were no standardised and independent assessment measures; and data about institutionalisation were misleading, since some governments over time have changed their policy regarding institutionalisation and this led to the reported decrease (Smith, 1996). Moreover, the conclusions are based mainly on parental beliefs that may have been influenced by numerous subjective factors and were expressed almost 30 years ago.

Ozonoff and Cathcart (1998) tested the effectiveness of educating children with ASD at home using the TEACCH method. The parents were taught interventions for preschool children with ASD that focused on the areas of cognitive and academic skills that were linked to school success. The intervention group consisted of 11 preschoolers who followed TEACCH for four months at home and were assessed with PEP-R (Psychoeducation Profile – Revised; Schopler et al., 1990). The control group did not follow TEACCH and was assessed with the same measure. Children in the intervention group improved in the areas of imitation, fine and gross motor skills and perceptive skills.

Although this study presents evidence that supports the effectiveness of TEACCH, there are again some methodological considerations (lack of random control condition and lack of evaluation of the reliability of the measures). It is obvious, though, that parents who learn to apply TEACCH properly can handle their children's behaviour more effectively and this is instrumental both for their self-confidence and for family functioning.

Persson (2000) examined whether seven men with low-functioning ASD – aged between 20 and 50 years – who had never used TEACCH would become more independent and improve some skills and their overall quality of life after attending it. When the intervention was completed, the behavioural problems that they exhibited were limited. In this case it is natural not to expect spectacular results given that the participants are quite old and the importance of early intervention has been established. Van Bourgondien et al. (2003) noted that the application of TEACCH is linked to the gradual reduction of behavioural problems, while no difference was observed in acquiring new skills. However, they do not provide adequate information on how they reached this conclusion.

Schopler (1991) mentions that he conducted more than 250 studies on TEACCH or in relation to TEACCH between 1964 and 1990 regarding the nature of autism, structured teaching, cooperation with families, evaluation, speech and communication, independence, professional skills, social and recreational skills, as well as behavioural management. The most spectacular results were observed among young children who had not developed language before the intervention (Lord and Schopler, 1989). However, extensive research includes a few studies that were conducted with researchers who did not practise or were not trained to use the TEACCH method. Dr Gary Mesibov (1997) also confirmed the difficulty of objectively verifying the effectiveness of TEACCH, which is a big and complex programme. The problem is complicated by the organic basis of ASD and the focus of TEACCH on lifelong adaptation that does not leave room for superficial therapies. Research conducted by TEACCH and some reports about TEACCH offer promising results, but its effectiveness has not been extensively documented by independent researchers.

There are six basic principles that guide TEACCH's clinical and research practice (Campbell et al., 1996):

1. The ultimate goal of the intervention is to promote adaptation improving the child's skills and developing environmental adaptations to autism-related deficits.

2. There are official and unofficial evaluations for the development of an

individualised educational plan using the Childhood Autism Rating Scale (CARS; Schopler et al., 1988) and the Revised Version of Psychoeducation Profile that extends to adolescents and adults (PER-R; Mesibov et al., 1988).

3. Priority is given to cognitive and behavioural therapy that is considered to constitute a successful intervention strategy.

4. Improvement is observed in the skills and abilities of children with ASD.

5. The use of visual prompts or cues is introduced to ensure optimal training for compliance and treatment of auditory processing deficits by enabling visual processing.

6. A holistic approach is implemented that promotes multidimensional training and the use of symbols.

Some critics (for example, Sallows, 2000) suggest that TEACCH does not promote the individual's inclusion into society, but isolates him cognitively from his environment and, thus, reduces his social acceptance. It focuses excessively on prompts and individual daily schedules and so the children who follow it are stigmatised by their peers. However, TEACCH programmes do target the inclusion of children with ASD in the school setting – a fact that constitutes an important step towards full social inclusion (Ferraro, 2001). More specifically, TEACCH's attitude towards the inclusion of children with ASD is reflected in the following principles (Marcus, 2004):

- All the individuals with ASD must be taught to function effectively with as few restrictions as possible.

- No child with ASD should be denied the opportunity to attend the proper educational environment (Panerai et al., 2009).

- The activities that are offered should be based on the individual evaluation of the children's skills and abilities to function and participate in the particular setting.

- Full inclusion is desirable for the students who can meet its demands, while other students are destined for partial inclusion. Special schools should be an option only for students who cannot benefit from mainstream education.

Trehin (1998) suggests that TEACCH is not a simple approach or method, but a state programme that attempts to address the needs of individuals with ASD using the most available approaches or methods. The aim of TEACCH is not to 'cure' autism, but to help children maximise their autonomy through the enhancement of communication skills, social awareness and independent decision-making skills. Lord and Schopler (1994) reported that TEACCH aims primarily to design protected settings that help children use the skills that they already possess instead of helping them enter more 'normal' or 'typical' frameworks of development. The next step is to encourage and foster the independence of children with ASD so that they can function effectively in the social setting.

Applied behaviour analysis and TEACCH

Dawson and Osterling (1997) noticed that there are quite a few similarities between ABA and TEACCH and stressed the importance of training in five basic skill domains: selective attention to some objects in the environment (for example, facial expressions, gestures); verbal and motor imitation; receptive and expressive language; appropriate play with objects; and social interaction skills. The emphasis that is placed on each skill varies according to the programme, but is included everywhere.

The specific programmes are characterised by predictability and routine. They are extremely structured and contain sets of routine actions on a daily basis. They are based on the functional approach of problematic behaviours. They employ techniques such as the selection and use of the child's favourite activities. If the above techniques are not effective, then the therapists implement a functional evaluation and analysis of the behaviour that focuses on its functions or 'causes', such as social attention, access to reinforcers and automatic or sensory reinforcement (Carr, 1994; Hall et al., 1995).

They pay a lot of attention to transition from preschool to primary school and they teach the necessary skills, such as following the teacher's instructions, asking for access in certain activities, working in conditions of delayed reinforcement, and so on (Hall et al., 1995). The participation of the family in the therapeutic process is instrumental. For example, parents are often used as co-therapists and play an important role in the education of their children. In some programmes the training takes place at home, at school, or at both settings.

Both approaches that seem to be effective in addressing the symptoms of ASD have advantages and disadvantages, as well as points of convergence and divergence. This is why I have adopted the concept of a 'selective approach' – that is, I have collected the strengths of these approaches and have concluded that an effective intervention should include the following characteristics:

1. Emphasise not only cognitive skills, but also communication and social skills of children with ASD.

2. Provide and teach acceptable alternative behavioural models that children with ASD can follow.

3. Use visual aids that seem to be more effective than verbal aids in guiding or training children with ASD.

4. Ensure that the teaching process is predictable in order to create a sense of safety and security for children with ASD.

5. Emphasise and remember the importance of play in the development of cognitive, emotional and social skills in children with ASD.

6. Ensure that the skills that children with ASD have achieved in different areas of development can be maintained and generalised to other people and settings.

7. Encourage parents to participate actively in the therapeutic or educational treatment of their children's symptoms in order to fulfil their role more comprehensively and effectively.

8. Promote the concept and application of both individualised instruction and group instruction in school units for children with ASD.

 Question for discussion

After having read all the information so far on ABA and TEACCH, could you try to compare and contrast them?

At this point, and having stressed the need for individualised educational plans (IEPs) for children with ASD, I present briefly the logic and the content of IEPs that are implemented in the school settings. An IEP is an official document that presents in an analytic way the education and training of a child with ASD. As the name implies, the educational plan should be adjusted to the needs and the characteristics of each student to provide the maximum educational benefit (Kohler et al., 1997; Meyen, 1978). The keyword is 'individualised'. A plan that works with one child with ASD may not be suitable for another (Schreck, 2000). The IEPs determine the educational goals for the academic year, the services that the child needs to meet these goals and an evaluation method of the student's progress.

It is not just a theoretical plan, but forms the basis for the training that the child will follow. The people who are usually called upon to decide on an IEP are: one or both parents; the educator who teaches or will teach the child; a representative of a public service who is equipped to provide, supervise and evaluate the special services that the child receives; the child himself – if he is able to attend the meeting; and other people invited by the parents or the experts (for example, a doctor, a lawyer or another family member). However, I would like to stress that not all countries have the required infrastructure to engage all these parties in the formation of an IEP.

The parents should be included in every group that makes decisions about the educational course of their child with ASD (Fish, 2006). These meetings should take place at least once a year – more often if deemed essential. Although teachers and teaching staff may come to those meetings with some suggestions for educational goals and plans, the meetings end only after extensive discussions have taken place and all the involved parties have agreed to sign the document. Parents have the right to participate in these meetings as equal partners with suggestions and opinions about their children's education. The meeting should be arranged at a time and place that is convenient for both teaching staff and parents. In order for the collaboration to be successful, all involved parties should express openly the information and the knowledge that they have at their disposal. Parents could make suggestions and proposals in the following areas (Simpson and Fiedler, 1989):

1. What is the vision for their child – both long-term and for the coming academic year?

2. What are their child's strengths, needs and interests – especially when he is not able to express himself?

3. What are their basic concerns regarding their child's education?

4. Has the training that their child has received so far been proven effective or not, and why (if they have this information)?

5. Is the experts' assessment of their child's skills compatible with their impression about their child?

6. Which technique that has been used at home has helped their child?

The IEP should address all the areas where the child needs help and could be either academic or non-academic, such as functional skills (for example, getting dressed, crossing the street safely), social skills, and other relevant services (for example, speech therapy, occupational therapy and physiotherapy). The IEP should include a list of the contexts where each service is provided, as well as a list of the professionals who provide these services. This is the content of IEPs:

- A report of the child's current level of educational performance.

- A statement of the annual goals that the child can reasonably achieve within the next 12 months – together with a series of measurable and direct steps for the attainment of long-term goals. This will help parents and teachers learn if the child progresses and benefits from his education. The development of specific and clearly determined goals is vital for the provision of proper training for the child.

- Appropriate objective criteria, assessment procedures and time schedules that determine whether the child has met the goals set by IEPs.

- A description of all the special needs services and the relevant supportive services that the child needs, as well as the exact time that he will devote to each activity or context.

- If the child is 16 years or older, IEPs should include a description of available services for the transition from school to extra-curricular activities.

The child with ASD should receive any relevant services that maximise treatment benefits, are determined on an individual basis and do not depend exclusively on the disability or the disorder. Examples of such services are counselling, medical care, speech therapy, occupational therapy and music therapy. Although the goals of IEPs should be child centred, the document must contain information that is useful for training inexperienced teachers, who may be asked to study some training material or to attend a seminar. The goals that are set could be either broad (for example, John will increase his language comprehension and communication) or more specific (for example, John will learn to interact more effectively with his peers in non-academic settings, such as break or lunch time). They describe the process that the child needs to follow in order to reach his goal, and the teachers and parents need to check the child's progress (Simpson, 1995).

For example, if the ultimate goal is for John to increase his verbal responses to questions during the academic year and the short-term goal is that he should attend speech therapy at least four times per week for half an hour with an expert at school, then John should answer verbally with 85 per cent accuracy. The speech therapist will send weekly reports both to parents and teachers. Therapy will start on 1 September and end on 30 June, with intermediate breaks during the school holidays. This goal states:

- the service to be provided (speech therapy);

- the professional who delivers the service (professional speech therapists);

- the context of the provided service (inclusion class);

- the frequency of the service provision (four times per week);

- the duration of the provided service (30 minutes per session from 1 September to 30 June).

To evaluate whether John has reached his goal, the speech therapist should determine if John meets the goal of 85 per cent accuracy and send weekly reports to parents and teachers. Other methods of evaluation are participation in a test, videotaping, peer reports, daily diaries and worksheets. If parents do not agree with the IEP, then they have the right to negotiate the document with the other parties until they reach an agreement. When negotiating, it is important to bear in mind that the IEP aims at addressing their child's needs and not their own.

When the IEP is complete, the constant communication between parents and teachers should remain to promote the child's success. The IEP is a work in progress that must be flexible and modified to meet the developing needs and skills of children with ASD. Adding goals or steps at any point in time, in agreement with parents and teachers, is also likely. As you can see, the IEP incorporates the basic principles of ABA and TEACCH, but it does not preclude the parallel provision of complementary therapies that could help the child with ASD in a specific area, as you will see later with approaches such as music therapy.

 Questions for discussion

Think of a measurable goal that you can set for a child with ASD and suggest ways to achieve it through an IEP. What do you need to keep in mind? How will you evaluate the effectiveness of an IEP?

Cognitive-behavioural therapy

Some individuals with high-functioning ASD need psychological support to face problems in their everyday life, as well as in their relationships with others and with themselves. Children and adolescents with high-functioning ASD report loneliness (with only 8 per cent having reciprocal friendships), specific phobias (44 per cent), various depressive symptoms (17–27 per cent) (Klinger and Williams, 2009; Reaven et al., 2009), as well as eating disordered attitudes (Kalyva, 2009). Cognitive-behavourial therapy combines two effective kinds of psychotherapy: cognitive and behavioural. Cognitive-behavioural therapy helps the individual weaken the relationship that exists between problematic conditions and his usual reactions, such as fear, depression, anger, self-destruction and self-defeat (Sze and Wood, 2007; Wood et al., 2009a). It allows the individual to understand that certain behavioural patterns cause unwanted symptoms and either make him feel anxious, depressed or angry without any apparent reason or lead him to wrongdoing (Attwood, 1998).

Cognitive-behavioural therapy starts with the evaluation of the nature and the extent of the emotional disorder, with the use of self-measures and clinical interviews. The next stage is emotional training with discussion and exercises to understand the connection between cognition, emotion, behaviour and the way in which people perceive their emotions and construct different situations. The final stage is cognitive restructuring, stress management, self-reflection and an individual activity schedule for the training of new cognitive skills. Cognitive restructuring corrects distorted conceptual perceptions and dysfunctional convictions. The individual is encouraged to establish and examine the evidence that exists in favour of or against his thoughts, and structure a new perception for certain events. Stress management is used to promote reactions that are incompatible with stress or anger. Self-perception activities help the individual identify his inner state, observe and consider his thoughts, and construct a new self-image. A graded individual activity programme is developed that allows the individual to practise new skills, which are suggested and observed by the therapist.

Cognitive-behavioural therapy and autism

Autism spectrum disorder is often accompanied by symptoms of depression and stress, especially during adolescence and adulthood. These problems are usually expressed in the way that individuals with ASD react when they experience difficulties. They may have a problem dealing with uncertainty, controlling their behaviour and their emotions, and they may have issues with alcohol or drug use. Cognitive-behavioural therapists believe that if an individual changes the way of thinking about himself and others (and what was happening in the past or what will happen in the future), then he is able to function better in his everyday life. Individuals with ASD, just as many other people, think in a way that stops them from dealing with daily situations, which is defined as cognitive distortion. Examples of cognitive distortions are:

1. 'All or nothing' type of thought (for example, I have to feel good all the time, without any exceptions).

2. Polarised thought (for example, people are either my best friends or my worst enemies).

3. Fatalistic thought (for example, things will get worse no matter what I do).

4. Inaccurate attributions (for example, someone else is always responsible for my problems).

5. Downplay of proof, when something is not confirmed about himself (for example, my teacher was wrong. I did not manage to answer the maths problem after all).

Children and adults with high-functioning ASD are susceptible to the development of secondary emotional disorders. This is linked to the level of awareness about the difficulties that they face in their social inclusion, as well as the identification and management of their emotions. Cognitive-behavioural therapy can change the way that an individual with high-functioning ASD thinks and reacts to emotions, such as anger, sadness or stress. The therapy addresses the cognitive deficit – the immaturity, the complexity and the ineffectiveness of thought – and the cognitive distortion – dysfunctional thought and erroneous assumptions.

Emotional training

The individual with ASD learns that emotions are experienced along a spectrum of intensity, personal experience and expression. He is then guided to learn to discern the degree of his feelings for himself and for others, from biological signs through to expressed behaviours. This treatment aspect is extremely valuable for individuals with ASD who have difficulty experiencing the spectrum and the continuum of emotional experience and expression. An educational programme is designed that focuses directly on a positive emotion or dimension that affects everyday life. The therapist must be certain that both she and the individual with ASD understand every word that is used to describe a specific emotional situation in the same way. The therapist could use a 'thermometer' of emotions, where the individual with ASD can report where he would place a word or a comment. An individual with ASD might use excessive statements, such as 'I will kill myself' to express a moderate level of emotional distress. There is training in common-sense skills – codes of social behaviours, problem-solving and friendship skills.

 Question for discussion

An adolescent with ASD is likely to feel depressed because he cannot form friendships. How could you use the thermometer of emotions to help him recognise the difficulties that he faces in creating and maintaining genuine friendships? Which other areas would you work on to improve his ability to make friends?

Cognitive restructuring

Cognitive restructuring allows individuals with high-functioning ASD to correct their erroneous, distorted and dysfunctional perceptions and beliefs (Attwood, 2004). This procedure includes challenging and questioning their thoughts with logical proof and rationalisation of their emotions. The first stage is establishing proof. Individuals with ASD can make erroneous assumptions about situations and outcomes, as well as others' intentions. They tend to interpret situations literally and an ordinary comment can be removed from its context and mis-interpreted. An example could be an adolescent girl with ASD who overhears at school some peers saying that a girl has to be thin in order to be popular. She could then starve in order to lose a lot of weight in an effort to gain acceptance from her peers. The therapist has to encourage the individual with ASD to acquire a more flexible thought and to ask for clarifications using 'rescue' comments, such as 'are you kidding?' or 'I do not understand what you mean'. Similar comments could be made to 'save' an individual with ASD who responded inappropriately to a comment (for example, 'I am sorry that I offended you' or 'excuse me, what should I do?'). Many indi-viduals with ASD have problems with attribution, since they may blame only others and fail to recognise their contribution to an event. They select some people that they consider to be responsible for every-thing that happens. They have a hard time understanding that they have also contributed to the realisation of an event. On the other hand, they could consider themselves to be responsible for everything and to experience low self-esteem, anxiety and guilt. The therapist could also help them expand their restricted repertoire of physical and verbal reactions.

Classic relaxation techniques can be used to help children manage stress. The greatest source of stress is usually socialisation, and the ther-apist has to determine, with the help of the child, the social situations where he feels more vulnerable. A common source of stress is at break time, where the child may resort to going to the library, to draw or to participate in an activity that pleases him – which does not improve, his socialisation. Children with ASD need more time to cognitively process explanations and new strategies. They need a clear structured approach with shorter but more frequent therapy and training sessions. It is recommended to provide the child with written or printed main points that he can use to see, practise and review at the beginning of every new session. The therapist has to be in regular contact with the child to ensure the accuracy and validity of the description of the events and strategies that he uses.

Hare (1997) reported that a 26-year-old individual with ASD who had severe depression and self-injurious behaviour attended 15 sessions. After the end of the therapy he managed to decrease the levels of depression and self-injury. However, it is not clear which aspects of the intervention caused the observed improvement. Reaven and Hepburn (2003) applied CBT to a 7-year-old girl with ASD who had obsessive-compulsive symptoms and improved dramatically six months after the end of therapy. Similar findings were also reported for a 12-year-old girl with ASD and obsessive compulsive disorder (OCD) (Lehmkuhl et al., 2008). Almost two-thirds of a group of children with ASD and anxiety disorders attending a family-based CBT programme did not meet the diagnostic criteria for an anxiety disorder after three months (Chalfant et al., 2007). Decreases in levels of anxiety following CBT were also reported by Reaven (2009) and by Wood et al. (2009b). Changes in the ability of children with ASD to exhibit specific social behaviours (for example, sharing) and social skills (for example, group participation) were also recorded following CBT (Lim et al., 2007). TEACCH has incorporated CBT in its programme, because the latter is considered to be extremely effective in dealing with emotional disorders when implemented by properly trained and sensitised therapists.

Denver Health Sciences Programme

The Denver Health Sciences Programme was started in 1981 by Rogers at the University of Colorado, and it places a lot of emphasis on using play to enhance interpersonal relationships, speech and language development, symbolic thinking, structure and routine in the class-room (Rogers and Lewis, 1989). It has a developmental focus and it is based on the principles of Piaget's theory and not on the principles of ABA. The programme for each child lasts approximately 22 hours per week for 12 months and the teacher–child ratio is 2:1.

Some studies have reported that children with ASD who participated in the programme showed developmental gains in many areas, such as language, play skills, and social interactions with parents (for example, Rogers and DiLalla, 1991). Rogers et al. (1986), Rogers and Lewis (1989) and Rogers et al. (2006) assessed the language, cognitive and motor skills of the children who attended this programme and reported sub-stantial developmental gains in the above areas of functioning. Another study by Rogers et al. (1987) showed that children's develop-ment was accelerated in the following areas: cognitive, language, social, as well as self-help skills. Vismara and Rogers (2008) and Vismara et al. (2009) reported improvements in social communication behaviours in children with and at risk of ASD.

Despite the fact that some of these studies use sensitive measures and testify to the strict adherence to the guidelines of the suggested programme, there are some methodological weaknesses that undermine the significance of the findings. Furthermore, most of the studies were conducted by the founder of the programme so there is also need for external evaluation.

DIR/Floortime method

In the past 20 years, Doctor Stanley Greenspan and his associates have published numerous papers on theories of child development. Greenspan and Wieder (2000) worked with children aged 1–10 years old who had several disorders, and created a developmental approach to early intervention, which has not been thoroughly studied by independent researchers. This method is based on six functional milestones that are a prerequisite for success in learning and development:

1. The dual ability of the child to express interest in sights, sounds and sensations of the world and to calm himself.

2. The ability to get emotionally involved with other people.

3. The ability to engage in dual communication, with gestures.

4. The ability to create complex gestures and combine a series of deliberate acts to resolve problems.

5. The ability to create ideas.

6. The ability to render ideas realistic and logical (Greenspan, 1998; Greenspan and Wieder, 2006).

The Greenspan method involves interactive experiences, which are targeted at the child, and take place in an environment with a few stimuli from an interval of two to five hours per day. It also addresses inclusion with peers at the preschool setting. Greenspan (1998) writes that interactive play, where the adult follows the child's lead, encourages the child to want to relate to the outside world. The therapeutic programme should start as early as possible, so that children and their parents can become involved in emotional interactions that use the emerging – but not fully developed – communication skills of children (initially more often with gestures than with language). The more time children spend without communicating and the less time parents spend bonding with their children, the more the latter are estranged and consumed in self-stimulatory behaviours (Cartwright and Beskina, 2007; Greenspan, 1992).

The intervention has to transform apathy into interaction, so that the child can acquire a purpose and learn to imitate gestures, sounds and games. Greenspan himself reported that he has worked with many children with ASD aged between 18 and 30 months, who can now communicate fully by using complex sentences and are creative, warm, tender and happy (Greenspan and Wieder, 2000). Solomon et al. (2007) argued that DIR/Floortime is a cost-effective intervention for young children with ASD. However, more independent scientific research is needed to verify the therapy's effectiveness.

LEAP – Learning Experiences: An Alternative Programme for Preschoolers and Parents

Hoyson et al. (1984) describe the effects of the LEAP programme that was funded by the state and was directed at children with ASD and children with typical development aged 3–5 years old. When it was created it was one of the first available inclusion programmes for children with ASD and their families (Kohler et al., 1996, 2005).

Kohler et al. (1996) presented the five basic principles that shaped the LEAP programme: all the children could benefit greatly for integrated inclusion settings; the intervention benefits are maximised when it is implemented at home, at school and in the community; the intervention is more effective when parents and professionals cooperate; young children with ASD can learn many important skills from their typically developing peers; and children with or without disabilities benefit from activities that relate to their developmental level.

The LEAP programme consists of four basic elements: (1) an integrated preschool setting with three classrooms that include 13 children each (10 typically developing children and three children with ASD), (2) a training programme in behaviour management techniques aimed at parents that includes effective strategies for teaching young children with ASD, (3) training initiatives in basic areas of development at international level (for example, creation of individualised teaching programmes, behavioural management, training in social skills, planning the transition from one educational level to the next), and (4) continuous research in teaching practices.

There is not enough research on the effectiveness of the LEAP programme. Some of its elements, such as interventions with the participation of typically developing peers, receive empirical support from case studies that took place before the creation of LEAP (Odom and Strain, 1984; Strain and Fox, 1981; Strain et al., 1977). There is also evidence that parent–teacher collaboration promotes the academic performance of children (Dawson and Osterling, 1997; Strain and Cordisco, 1994). Hoyson et al. (1984) reported that the behaviour of six children with autistic features who attended the programme improved. Strain and Cordisco (1994) claimed that 24 out of the 51 children attended mainstream classes, without providing any further information. Although some aspects of LEAP seem to be promising, the paucity of relevant research and the absence of controlled studies minimise the ability to draw valid conclusions on its effectiveness in treating ASD.

Miller method

The Miller method is intended for children with ASD who face problems with physical organisation, social interaction and communication at school, at the clinical setting and at home (Miller and Chretien, 2007). Each individual working with a child with ASD focuses on just one aspect of his functioning, while dealing also with other areas where he has difficulties. She is also in close contact with the parents and with other professionals who work with the particular child. A basic principle of this method is that the child learns better if he moves and comes into direct physical contact with objects and people. Greenspan and Wieder (2000) report that the Miller approach is 'semi-structured', because the therapists are guided both by the child's initiatives and by some developmentally organised interventions that are introduced either by the teachers or by themselves.

The Miller method is based on a cognitive-developmental systemic approach that links the work of Piaget (1948), Von Bertallanfy (1968), Vygotsky (1962), and Werner and Kaplan (1963) and is adjusted to the needs of children with severe developmental disabilities. It is a cognitive approach because it deals with the way that the children organise their behaviour, develop the concepts of space and time, resolve problems, and relate to other people. It is a developmental approach because it deals with the children's ability to move from functioning to communication and representation of reality through symbolic means. It is a systemic approach because it states that the formation and use of systems are essential in every form of human behaviour. More specifically, the goals of the Miller method are:

- to evaluate the child's ability to interact with people and objects, to adjust to change, and to learn from experience;

- to promote the child's awareness of his body in relation to people and objects;

- to guide the child in functional, social and communicational exchanges;

- to provide the necessary transitions from concrete to abstract symbolic functioning.

The Miller method employs two basic strategies to restore the processes of typical development. The first is taking advantage of the deviant child's systems in an attempt to ensure developmental gains; it is based on the assumption that all the organised behaviours – even deviant ones – can benefit the child in some developmental area. For example, the atypical behavioural systems of children with ASD (such as placing objects in rows or switching the lights on and off) can be transformed into functional and interactive behaviours.

The second strategy is the systematic introduction of skills that correspond to the child's developmental level (repeated activities in relation to objects and people) and contribute to the reparation of developmental gaps and the restructuring of developmental sequences. For example, children who have never experienced lifting and throwing objects or who have not learned that they can move an object by pushing it with one hand or with a stick, can be taught in a way that will help them fill in a developmental gap discovering – for the first time – their ability to act on their environment and to affect the objects and the events around them.

An equally effective strategy is for the therapist to narrate with signs and words what children do while they are doing it. There is a conviction that narration helps children associate words and signs with their actions. When this happens, they develop greater self-awareness and they start acquiring internal speech, which is very important for communication with the self and others. This procedure is facilitated with the elevation of the children above the ground. The children's elevation does not merely guide the behaviour through words and signs (because of better eye contact), but it also leads to greater self-awareness and social-emotional contact. They also use big swinging balls that extend the child's reality system.

Miller and Eller-Miller (2000) mentioned that children whose families are highly motivated and 'live' the programme by implementing it at home and working closely with the therapeutic staff improve significantly. The philosophy of the Miller method is that every child – no matter how withdrawn or disorganised he is – tries to find a way to confront the world. The therapist's job is to help the child use every skill he possesses to achieve this, and so the therapist evaluates and observes the way in which the child reacts or fails to react to some aspects of a situation.

The therapist reinforces the child's ability to generalise his learning by teaching him certain functions. For example, she teaches the child to hang cups from hooks. Initially, she helps him hang the cup by holding his hand until he can do it independently. Then the therapist steps away from the child, so that he has to turn first to her to get the cup and then to go to the hook and hang it. At the final stage, the child learns to perform this activity and to take cups of different shapes and colours from different locations and from different people. This learning, which takes place with the help of at least one parent, enables the child to perform similar activities at school, at home and in other settings.

Temper tantrums are often viewed as a failure or inability of the child to deal with people or objects in the surroundings and they tend to differ from child to child. A child may have a temper tantrum because he cannot handle the change of a situation and needs help, while another child may experience a sense of loss because the teacher looked away from him. Regardless of the cause, the temper tantrum is not addressed by putting the child in isolation, but there is an effort to fulfil the expressed need through ritualistic behaviours that help him recompose himself. Even if these efforts do not pay off, the adult holds the child and talks to him peacefully about what is going to follow in this specific setting.

According to the Miller method, speech is developed through directed actions towards objects or events, and when the children are placed on elevated platforms they become more aware of their bodies, they concentrate better and they can deal with any obstacles or demands that are placed before them. The therapists using this method say that many children who are not able to follow instructions when they are on the ground can do so when they are elevated. When they put obstacles in the way of children and 'narrate' what the children are doing as they climb or overcome obstacles, then the children develop a repertoire of messages that can easily be transferred to the ground. Since the narrations are accompanied by gestures and words that are associated with their actions, children are guided by the gestures and words through the activities that they have to perform (Smith, 1996).

Miller method and autism

Five basic factors determine the success of the Miller therapy on a child with ASD (Miller and Eller-Miller, 2000):

1. The child's age (the younger the child the better).

2. The neurological condition (children who do not suffer from epilepsy or neurological problems will develop better).

3. The child's relationship with his parents (children who have a close bond with at least one parent respond better than other children).

4. The child's characteristics (some children progress faster than others).

5. The balance of support and demands (parents with high support and high demands have children who progress faster in relation to parents with low support and low demands).

Cook (1998) carried out the only evaluation of this method, with the participation of three children with ASD who improved a lot in many areas related to daily functioning. Their skills generalised to other settings, and parental participation contributed positively to their children's progress. The lack of other studies on this method using a larger sample and more precise measures of assessment – preferably by outside researchers – limits the evaluation of its effectiveness.

Further reading

Anderson, M. (2007) *Tales Form the Table: Lovaas/ABA Intervention with Children on the Autistic Spectrum.* London: Jessica Kingsley.

Broderick, A.A. (2009) 'Autism, "recovery (to normalcy)", and the politics of hope', *Intellectual and Developmental Disabilities,* 47: 263–81.

Kearney, A.J. (2008) *Understanding Applied Behavior Analysis: An Introduction to ABA for Parents, Teachers, and Other Professionals.* London: Jessica Kingsley.

Mesibov, G.B., Shea, V. and Schopler, E. (2005) *The TEACCH Approach to Autism Spectrum Disorders.* New York: Springer Science and Business Media.

Skokut, M., Robinson, S., Openden, D. and Jimerson, S.R. (2008) 'Promoting the social and cognitive competence of children with autism: interventions at school', *California School Psychologist,* 13: 93–107.

Sze, K.M. and Wood, J.J. (2008) 'Enhancing CBT for the treatment of autism spectrum disorders and concurrent anxiety', *Behavioural and Cognitive Psychotherapy,* 36: 403–9.

Turnbull, H.R., Wilcox, B.L. and Stowe, M.J. (2004) 'A brief overview of special education law with focus on autism', *Journal of Autism and Developmental Disorders,* 32: 479–93.

2

Approaches for Developing Social Interaction

Chapter overview

Children with ASD face severe problems in social interaction with peers and adults, mainly due to their inability to read and comprehend social cues, social situations and other people's intentions (Bellini and Peters, 2008; Mundy and Stella, 2001). This chapter looks at ways to improve socialisation at home and at school, which in turn may reduce the experiences of social rejection and isolation, and promote social-emotional inclusion, which is as important as academic inclusion. I refer to two approaches that can be employed either at school or at home, Social Stories and the Circle of Friends.

Social Stories

Carol Gray (1994) developed an approach called 'Social Stories' in order to address the social and communicative problems of children with ASD, as well as their difficulties with theory of mind (Hutchins and Prelock, 2008; Iobst et al., 2008; Konstantareas, 2006). A Social Story describes a social situation that may be problematic for a child with ASD, while providing simultaneously clear indications and directions for the manifestation of the proper social responses. It offers a social scenario that the child with ASD can study in order to learn how to react to a situation that causes stress, insecurity, or aggression. More specifically:

> a Social Story is written to provide information on what people in a given situation are doing, thinking or feeling, the sequence of events, the identification of significant social cues and their meaning, and the script of what to do or say; in other words, the what, when, who, and why aspects of social situations. (Attwood, 2000: 90)

Since the difficulties that each child faces are unique, it is reasonable to assume that every story is individualised and adjusted to the child's needs and cognitive level. However, Livanis et al. (2007) argue that Social Stories could also be used as a group treatment for adolescents with high-functioning autism in schools. The story usually comprises two to five sentences (Simpson and Regan, 1998), which include:

Descriptive sentences that explain where the story takes place and who the main characters are.

Directive sentences that provide the proper behavioural response (the directions must be very clear, accurate, and consistent).

Perspective sentences that describe the feelings and the responses to other people in a specific situation (to develop the empathy of children with ASD so that they realise that their actions and their words influence the feelings of other people).

Affirmative sentences that express the beliefs that are shared by the child's cultural context.

Gray (2000, 2004) later proposed two more types of sentences:

Control sentences that describe similar acts and responses without using human characters, for example, a turtle moves slowly from one place to another (the stories that use animals as protagonists may be less threatening and more familiar to children, but not all will have the ability to understand the symbolism).

Cooperative sentences that provide information on who will help the child if needed and in what way, to make him feel safer and to provide a reliable reference point.

The Social Story may have the form of a book with a cover. Each page contains usually one or two sentences and a corresponding picture or image, but pictures are not necessary for children who understand written language. Although therapists tend to use all types of sentences, Gray (1994) suggests that sometimes you may omit directive sentences, because the child with ASD can interpret and respond accordingly to a situation with the guidance of the other three types of sentences. Hagiwara and Myles (1999) attempted to present a Social Story with the help of a computer so as to ensure that it would be delivered in exactly the same way every time. They also enriched the presentation with images and visual or auditory effects. The introduction of computers in schools facilitates the training of children with ASD to use computerised Social Stories, which can improve rates of social communication with the appropriate access to social reinforcement (Sansosti and Powell-Smith, 2008). Otherwise, you would take out the social element from the Social Story. The process of reading a story is also an opportunity for interaction between the child with ASD and a significant adult (for example, the mother), which is missed if you use a computer, so it might be better to use the computerised version only when you cannot devote time to teach each child individually. I take a similar stance on stories that are presented either through audio equipment or through videotapes (Charlop and Milstein, 1989).

The creation of a Social Story that can produce noticeable change in a child's social behaviour is an extremely challenging task. Therefore, Gray (1994) and Gray and Garand (1993) offer some guidelines for designing and implementing successful Social Stories:

1. Identify the problematic behaviour or situation that you wish to change by working together with the parents or other adults who spend a lot of time with the child with ASD and know where he faces particular difficulties. Then identify the social behaviour that must change in order to increase the child's positive social interactions, to create a safe social environment and to provide additional opportunities for social learning. It is important to ensure that you have understood the child's personality, so that you can adjust the Social Story to his specific characteristics or traits.

2. Collect information on the behaviour that you want to change, for an extended period of time so that you observe if it occurs under specific situations. You will need to know who is involved, how long the social situation lasts and which events signify its beginning and its end. Data collection usually lasts between three and five days, or longer if deemed necessary (depending on the frequency of the behaviour). Ask parents or other individuals who know the child to share their information with you.

3. Write a Social Story using descriptive and directive sentences that offer a perspective and a sense of safety. A good guideline for writing an effective Social Story is the creation of two to five descriptive, perspective or affirmative sentences for each directive sentence, that is, the basic social story ratio. Gray (1995, 2000) also recommended the complete Social Story ratio that resembles the basic ratio, but which also includes control and cooperative sentences. No matter which Social Story ratio is adopted, the aim of the story is to describe a social situation and not to direct the actions of the child with ASD. The stories will vary according to the cognitive level of the child, and this dictates the writing style, the vocabulary and the content of the story (Reynhout and Carter, 2007). The stories must be written in the

first person and either in the present tense (in order to describe a situation as it occurs) or in the future tense (in order to predict something that may happen). Include one to three sentences in each page. One sentence per page is ideal, so that the child can concentrate on the words and process their meaning. If there are more sentences per page, the child may experience overload and misunderstand some information. Make your choice according to the child's level of understanding. Gray (1994) proposes that you use photographs and sketches or printed pictures, as visual representations might help the child perceive the appropriate behaviour better. However, pictorial representations might not describe a situation adequately or accurately. It is difficult, for example, to depict visually the expression of an emotion that is not reflected in the facial expression or the bodily posture.

4. After writing the story, check its content with the parents or the educators of the focus child with ASD. Then read the story to the child and show him the desirable behaviour; alternatively, let him read the story on his own. You can encourage him to share the story with his family and peers, so that they all have a common understanding of the appropriate behaviour and can help him stick to the scenario. The child must not be distracted when he reads the story, especially the first time. It might be a good idea to ask some clarifying questions in order to make sure that he understood the story correctly (Chan and O'Reilly, 2008). Gray and Garand (1993) proposed that you could ask the child to role play the social situation in order to assess his comprehension of the story.

5. In order to explore whether the Social Story has brought about the expected changes, observe the child's behaviour and record his reactions. To ensure the desirable change, read the story to the child on a daily basis and reinforce him appropriately every time he exhibits the proper behaviour. If the desirable changes in behaviour are not observed within two weeks, then you must revise the Social Story – changing only one aspect at a time. Likewise, identify which part of the story was dysfunctional, change it and try again to use the modified Social Story. When you alter the desirable behaviour, you need to create a programme in order to maintain and generalise it, while you start gradually to withdraw the Social Story. Finally, if you realise that the child can communicate effectively, then encourage him to identify the social targets that he wants to change and help him construct his own Social Story.

Question for discussion

Identify a behaviour of your own that you would like to change. How will you choose it (based on how easy it is to change it, how much it bothers you, what others think)? Whom would you ask for help? What alternative behaviour would you choose? How would you reinforce yourself to endorse the change? If it were that easy, why have you not changed it before? Consider the answers to these questions when contemplating preparing a Social Story for a child with ASD.

Social Stories and autism

Gray (1994) and Gray and Garand (1993) mention that Social Stories are more appropriate for high-functioning children with ASD but also for those with other learning disabilities. Kalyva and Agaliotis (2009) used Social Stories to enhance the interpersonal conflict resolution skills of children with learning disabilities, and Schneider and Goldstein (2009) used them to improve on-task behaviours of children with language impairment. In the framework of TEACCH, they are also used with low-functioning children with ASD. Scattone et al. (2006) argued that the population that Social Stories can best serve has not yet been fully identified. However, the use of pictures facilitates children with ASD who react positively to visual representations (Crozier, 2009; MacDuff et al., 1993; Pierce and Schreibman, 1994).

Gray (1994) reported that Social Stories can be used to fulfil the following goals:

- to describe a situation by providing simultaneously clear indications for the child's appropriate behaviour and reaction in a non-threatening way;

- to personalise and individualise the teaching of social skills;

- to teach the child adaptive routines and to support him in an effort to change certain behaviours;

- to teach the appropriate behaviours in a realistic social setting so that the child can generalise them more easily;

- to help the child face a variety of problematic behaviours, such as aggression, obsession with keeping routines, stress, and anger.

Tony Attwood (1998) reports that Social Stories are extremely effective in helping the child with ASD realise how he should react in certain circumstances and identifying which behaviours he should avoid.

Rowe (1999) studied the influence of Social Stories on a 3-year-old child with high-functioning ASD who faced many difficulties in social inter-action and communication. Visual stimuli distracted him, while he reacted with aversion to specific sounds and reported that certain audi-tory stimuli caused him pain in the ears. Rowe (1999) followed this procedure in order to collect information for the child in question:

1. She identified the social situation that posed a problem and asked the teaching staff to define the conditions under which the child felt anx-ious and did not function properly; for example, he refused to go to the cafeteria to eat with other children.

2. She interviewed the staff in order to explore the nature of the problem, the exact response of the child, and the frequency of his reactions. She discovered that he shouted that his peers were disgusting and noisy and he put up a fight with the assistant who tried to take him into the cafe-teria. All the children were affected by this behaviour and the assistant wanted to quit.

3. The next step was to ask the teachers to brief her on the strategies that they had implemented in the past in order to solve this issue.

4. She then observed the behaviour of the child with ASD and kept detailed notes of the events that took place during lunchtime.

5. At the end, she asked the child to describe how he felt at lunchtime. It is very important to ask for the child's opinion and perspective, if he is able to communicate effectively. If he cannot talk, then you can ask him to draw the problematic situation.

Rowe (1999) wrote a Social Story entitled 'Lunchtime' in order to help the child cope with this situation. The teaching staff read the story to him just before he went to lunch. The first change in his behaviour was observed right after the introductory session, since he took his lunch basket, walked into the cafeteria, sat at the edge of the table and ate his lunch. He was under constant supervision for a period of approxi-mately 12 weeks during lunchtime and everyone made positive comments about his improved behaviour (Rowe, 1999). Gray (1994) believes that Social Stories are successful because they are visual, they offer accurate information, they describe the expected behaviours and they remove the social dimension in order to maximise learning.

The Social Story simplifies and applies the cognitive schemas that the child holds for each social situation, and is based on his existing knowledge base. The story tries to expand this knowledge base so that the child can accommodate more cognitive schemas – namely, new ways of response. You can also use the Social Story in order to create a new cognitive schema, so that the child knows how to react in novel situations.

Simpson (1993) mentions that Social Stories have been used success-fully to introduce changes and new routines at home and at school, to explain the causes of other people's behaviours or to teach new aca-demic and social skills. Although some children follow the scenarios immediately, other children react only after the introduction of addi-tional prompts and motives. Social Stories can teach the child how to control his tone of voice while singing together with other children (Fullerton et al., 1996); share his toys (Swaggart et al., 1995); learn new routines and respond appropriately to changes in his routines (Gray and Garand, 1993); develop his play skills (Barry and Burlew, 2004); overcome problems in sleeping behaviours (Burke et al., 2004; Moore, 2004); improve communication skills (Adams et al., 2004); increase positive and decrease negative behaviours in the classroom (Ozdemir, 2008; Spencer et al., 2008) or at school (Toplis and Hadwin, 2006); and promote independent behaviours in novel events (Ivey et al., 2004). Furthermore, Smith (2001) showed that Social Stories can be used to teach management of inappropriate sexual behaviour (Tarnai and Wolfe, 2008), as well as risky behaviour, and to address physical inac-tivity (Zimbelman et al., 2007).

Thiemann and Goldstein (2001) studied the effects of written text and visual cues on the social interactions of five children with ASD and social inadequacies, aged between 6 and 12 years old. They also included two typically developing peers as social partners of each child with ASD in order to form five triads. The intervention was applied twice weekly and included 10 minutes of systematic instruction with the use of visual stimuli, 10 minutes of social interaction and 10 min-utes of feedback through video. They found that the social skills of children with ASD were increased and generalised to other settings. Therefore, it is advisable to use visual directions to guide the social lan-guage development of children with ASD who interact with typically developing peers – for example, in the inclusion setting. Finally, Brownell (2002) explored the effectiveness of Social Stories that have been used as song lyrics and were accompanied by music, and con-cluded that they were as effective as Social Stories that had the form of a book. This could be explained by the observation that children with ASD respond positively to music.

Most studies that have examined the effectiveness of Social Stories have recorded positive changes in behaviour (Rowe, 1999; Simpson, 1993; Simpson and Regan, 1998; Swaggart et al., 1995). Cullain (2002) reported that Social Stories were effective in reducing the intensity of temper tantrums and anxiety levels experienced by the participants of her study. In order to reach the desired outcome, the story that was cre-ated for each child was read to him twice every day for a fortnight.

Feinberg (2002) claimed that Social Stories increased four desirable social behaviours: greeting behaviours; requests for participation in play activities; asking for the play preferences of another child and choosing another child as a play partner.

Kuttler and Myles (1998) conducted a study aimed at decreasing the temper tantrums experienced by a girl with ASD when she was studying in the morning and during lunchtime. These tantrums were accompanied by inappropriate verbal expressions and lying on the floor. The girl's behaviour improved and remained more positive after the end of the intervention, although the results were not spectacular. More specifically, according to Norris and Dattilo (1999), the girl did not manage to improve her behaviour while eating, but she did decrease her negative behaviour by 50 per cent. The fact that she stopped singing loudly or talking to herself probably made her a more attractive playmate.

Despite the encouraging results, I ought to point out that most studies on the effectiveness of Social Stories have methodological limitations or use incorrect story structures (Rust and Smith, 2006; Sansosti and Powell-Smith, 2006; Sansosti et al., 2004; Scattone et al., 2002). Simpson and Regan (1998) and Reynhout and Carter (2006) draw attention to the fact that studies assessing Social Stories are not strictly experimental and combine Social Stories with other interventions. They are usually done unofficially, in the school setting, and they are teacher-friendly, so that they can produce desirable changes that will help the participants achieve successful inclusion. Quilty (2007) found that paraprofessionals can be trained easily to write and implement Social Stories for children with ASD. Ali and Frederickson (2006) reviewed all the studies that were conducted on Social Stories between 1994 and 2004 and concluded that their effects show positive potentials. Sansosti et al. (2004) in a smaller relevant review reached a similar conclusion. Moreover, more recently, there have been a lot of studies that used experimental designs with a substantial number of participants and testified to the effectiveness of Social Stories (Crozier and Tincani, 2007; Delano and Snell, 2006; Dodd et al., 2008; Hutchins and Prelock, 2005; Quirmbach et al., 2009; Sansosti and Powell-Smith, 2006).

Lorimer et al. (2002) reported that the unwanted temper tantrums decreased during the implementation of Social Stories, but increased when the intervention ended. This could by explained by Staley's (2002) speculation that it is possible that it is not the Social Stories that are so motivating, but the reinforcers that are associated with positive behaviours. If the child does not discover a secondary reward in carrying out a certain behaviour, when the immediate reward that is presented in the Social Story is withdrawn, the child abandons this behaviour. Crozier and Tincani (2005) reported that maintenance probes that were conducted two weeks after the end of the intervention showed that the Social Story had become a regular instructional routine for a disruptive girl with ASD.

I strongly believe that Social Stories constitute an effective intervention that has the potential to help children with ASD overcome some of the difficulties they face, mainly in the area of socialisation. However, it is not possible to describe all the situations that may pose a problem in just one story. Social Stories can have even better results if they are combined with video modelling (Scattone, 2008).

 Questions for discussion

How could a Social Story help a child with ASD who is verbally abused by a peer on a daily basis and as a consequence gets very upset and refuses to go to school? What should the Social Story model – to respond in a similarly aggressive way, to ignore his peer or to seek adult help every time the incident occurs? Will this solve the problem permanently? How could the story target the emotional element of verbal abuse?

Now consider an adolescent with high-functioning ASD who experiences symptoms of depression because he has difficulty trying to create friendly or romantic relationships with peers. If this situation does not create tension, disputes or negative behaviours within the family or school setting, it is likely that it will remain unnoticed. The adolescent, however, will probably suffer since the difficulties that he faces seem unsurpassable and can lead him to depression. Therefore, the risk involved in a certain social situation is subjective and it is important to direct your attention to problematic behaviours that are not always overtly expressed. It is easier to discern and identify the behaviours that cause disturbance at home or at school, while you might often fail to locate the social conditions that cause internal turmoil or pain to the child with ASD experiencing them.

Another fact that I need to stress is that if you are not very careful, you risk creating children who depend on Social Stories to such an extent that the stories become stereotypical behaviour. They may reach a point where they need to use Social Stories in every aspect of their life in order to function effectively. It is therefore essential to ensure that once a child with ASD follows a Social Story and resolves the problematic situation, you help him generalise the skills that he has mastered in a variety of settings. As children with ASD tend to interpret speech literally, it would be interesting to try to teach them the meaning of metaphors or other abstract concepts through Social Stories in order to help them think more flexibly. If you take these points into account, you can create very effective Social Stories that will really help children with ASD overcome some social problems that they face.

Circle of Friends

One of the approaches that has been used to promote the inclusion of children with behavioural and emotional problems in mainstream schools is the 'Circle of Friends' (Newton et al., 1996; Taylor, 1997). It is a systemic approach 'that recognises the power of the peer-group – and thereby of pupil culture – to be a positive as well as a constraining or exacerbating influence on individual behaviour' (Newton et al., 1996: 42). The Circle of Friends has been proven highly effective, since it creates a supportive network in the environment of the child who starts to experience success and receive positive feedback from his peers.

It is possible to focus on a particular aspect of social skills that have not been mastered by the child or that the child did not have a chance to practise. Peers participating in the circle are taught how to handle the inappropriate behaviours exhibited by the child with ASD (Eccles and Pitchford, 1997; Norgate, 1998). This is the main reason why this method has been widely used with children who exhibit emotional and behavioural problems (Frederickson and Turner, 2003; Kelly, 1999). For example, it has been applied successfully to decrease bullying in the school setting (Taylor, 1997) with a 5-year-old child who was in danger of being expelled from nursery, because he had problems in forming and maintaining relationships with peers (Shotton, 1998; Smith and Cooke, 2000).

The aims of the circle are the following:

1. To create a setting where the child can come into regular contact with more socially able peers and receive their support.

2. To provide a framework that allows the teacher to focus on the social interaction deficits of the child.

3. To help typically developing peers recognise that the social impairment of children with ASD constitutes a fundamental and pervasive difficulty.

4. To address certain problems by introducing the notion of creativity to

the members of the circle and to promote understanding of peer culture in certain educational settings (Roeyers, 1995; Whitaker et al., 1998).

Elliot and Busse (1991) agreed that this intervention could assist the generalisation of some of the skills that children with ASD already possess. However, as they maintain, this can be achieved through teaching behaviours that are normally highly appreciated in everyday settings, establishing training across people and settings where the focus child spends most of his time, encouraging the natural occurrence of target behaviours, reinforcing practise and applications of learned skills to new and appropriate settings, and including peers in the training process.

Sitting in a circle and interacting with adult supervision

Circle of Friends and autism

The Circle of Friends is effective with children with ASD, because it uses the social networks that operate within schools to create an environment that supports the 'vulnerable' child. It helps children with ASD deal with the social deficits that impede their full inclusion. Gus (2000) has successfully implemented the Circle of Friends in order to explain the nature of the disorder to the peers of a child with ASD, and Whitaker et al. (1998) mentioned that the typically developing children who participated in the circle reported increased social and communication skills.

Each session begins with a warm-up activity that is kept constant during the whole intervention in order to signal its beginning. This ritual offers children with ASD an opportunity to feel safe, as they are in control of the situation. Each of the 12 sessions (one session per week) lasts for 30 minutes and usually takes place after the end of the educational day, so that the children who will participate in the circle have free time and the room is available. The teacher is asked to identify the typically developing children who would be suitable to participate in the circle. The criteria they use for this selection are the sensitivity of these children, the relationship that they have with the child with ASD, as well as the consent of their parents. The teacher briefs the typically developing children about the aim of the circle, and the way in which they can help the child with ASD interact with them. The teacher is usually in charge of the Circle of Friends and gives directions to the remaining members. Whitaker et al. (1998) mention that the teachers who participated actively in the circle reported that they felt more able to 'face' the child with ASD or to resolve a conflict.

Kalyva and Avramidis (2005) applied the Circle of Friends to nursery children with ASD for a period of three months with the help of one nursery teacher and four typically developing children from each school. The effects of the intervention were systematically examined by means of an observation schedule which recorded the number of responses and initiation attempts – both unsuccessful and successful – of all participating children with ASD during baseline, post-intervention and at the 2-month follow-up. The findings revealed that children in the intervention group had significantly fewer unsuccessful responses and better initiation rates at post-intervention and follow-up than children in the control group. Moreover, children in the intervention group had significantly higher successful response and initiation rates at post-intervention and follow-up than children in the control group. I believe that the increase of desirable behaviours – regardless of its level of statistical significance – has great practical value. In the area of special needs, even the slightest improvement can produce spectacular changes in everyday life, both for the child with ASD and his family (Wilson, 1995). In order to maintain these changes, the Circle of Friends could be implemented at home. A parent could act as the leader and siblings, friends and classmates could be the remaining members of the circle.

I should point out that 'circle time' is an activity that is part of the nursery curriculum and therefore the nursery teacher is familiar with it. This constitutes an important advantage of the Circle of Friends, since the child with ASD learns to participate in an activity that does not cease to exist after the end of the intervention. He is given a chance to practise, generalise and master the behaviours that were reinforced through the Circle of Friends. This point is also stressed by Fox and McEvoy (1993), who claim that the behaviours that are maintained and become part of the child's repertoire are those that occur often in his environment.

The children sit in a circle and have a set of similar objects in front of them which they use in order to participate in some activities. Alternatively, they take part in verbal games. It would be advisable to have another teacher or assistant in the classroom who would sit near the child with ASD and intervene in case something serious happened (for example, when the child exhibits stereotypical behaviour and does not pay attention to the circle). Typically developing children who are members of the circle are verbally praised for their involvement in the intervention.

Since the aim of the Circle of Friends is not to teach or practise language but to improve social interaction skills (Roeyers, 1995), children with ASD who do not speak could benefit from it as well. In this case, the activities of the circle should focus more around handling objects or performing motor activities.

 Question for discussion

How could the Circle of Friends be modified to allow mute children with ASD to be included?

A problem that can be observed is that many typically developing children who do not participate in the circle might express their dissatisfaction and ask why they cannot be active members of the group. Some of them may express feelings of rejection and ask persistently to remain in the classroom and observe the session (Kalyva and Avramidis, 2005). This problem can be solved with the creation of a parallel circle that operates during school hours without the inclusion of the child with ASD, or you could alternate the typically developing children who are members of the circle so that they can all have the opportunity to get to know the child with ASD. Likewise, the improvement of the provocative behaviour of the child with ASD will not be the responsibility of a small group of peers but of the whole classroom (Shotton, 1998). However, it is important to be extremely careful with the children with ASD who respond negatively to changes and cannot adjust to them easily.

It is worth mentioning that typically developing children seem to benefit from interacting with children with ASD or other disorders, since they learn to accept and support them (Guralnick, 1990; Hendrickson et al., 1996). They realise that the latter are usually not responsible for their inappropriate behaviours that seem to be out of their control. Frederickson and Turner (2003) claim that the Circle of Friends – when implemented properly – directs attention away from the child with ASD, thus decreasing the danger of stigmatisation, a concern that was also expressed by Shotton (1998).

It is also worth emphasising that the success of this intervention – as well as most approaches presented in this book – is due to the degree of interest and dedication expressed by both teachers and typically developing children. It is better to choose boys and girls of varying abilities to become members of the circle, so that the child with ASD does not stand out.

Moreover, children with ASD communicate more when they engage in activities that they are familiar with and which require less attention. Therefore, it is necessary to suggest activities that are known to the child with ASD, since the aim of the circle is not to teach new skills but to practise communication with peers (Taylor, 1997). This is a very significant challenge for the teacher; it is widely accepted that children with ASD are not easily motivated and cannot sustain their attention for long periods of time. So, it would be preferable to encourage the child with ASD to select the toys that will be used or the activities that will take place during the intervention. This will partly ensure their positive mood and their active participation in the circle.

Calabrese et al. (2007) examined with qualitative measures the benefits of the Circle of Friends for the social inclusion of students with disabilities, asking parents and professionals, and found that: (1) a decrease was noted in the degree of alienation and estrangement among parents of children with disabilities; (2) participants reported increased involvement that was labelled a transformative experience; (3) the intervention provided ecological conditions for the social inclusion of students with disabilities; and (4) additional resources for the Circle of Friends might actually manage to increase its sphere of influence.

An issue that warrants special attention is the fact that children with ASD do not often initiate contact with peers – even when they are high functioning and can communicate effectively. They have a problem approaching a peer and sustaining the interaction (Lewy and Dawson, 1992; Prizant and Wetherby, 1987). Therefore, it is likely that the Circle of Friends represents for these children the framework that they need in order to take the initiative and communicate with another person. The structure of the circle may signify a safe and predictable environment, where children with ASD are given the opportunity to observe and imitate the behaviour of their peers, who act as behavioural models. However, it is imperative to make sure that the acquired skills are generalised to other people and settings.

This concern has also been expressed by Sapon-Shevin et al. (1998), who suggested that techniques such as the Circle of Friends do not adequately address the social deficits of children with ASD. The relationships that are created are not reciprocal, since the child with ASD receives continuous support and help from his peers, so not enough attention is paid to the general educational framework (McDonald and Hemmes, 2003). You also need to consider that even if typically developing peers who are part of the circle learn to interact effectively with the child with ASD, other peers will still not know how to behave.

Another significant parameter that I must stress is that the focus children with ASD might get upset if the circle stops as abruptly as it started. They may feel that they are being punished for doing something wrong by losing all the 'friends' that they made recently. Therefore, the teacher or the therapist who is in charge of the intervention should explain to the child why the circle must stop and to reassure him that he will have the opportunity to interact with his friends in other settings – for example, during circle time or during the break. The sudden and inexplicable interruption of a routine may be extremely problematic for children with ASD who depend largely on prediction of the surrounding environment (Jordan and Powell, 1995).

Frederickson et al. (2003) reported that a disadvantage of the Circle of Friends is that it does not devote enough time to teaching cognitive and academic skills. However, the curriculum should place more emphasis on the social aspect of development, which is equally important. Children with ASD have the ability to learn and practise social skills that will help them become more popular and less isolated, aggressive and withdrawn (Beckman, 1983; Cogher, 1999; Koegel et al., 1992; Oke et al., 1990). Therefore, it is essential to include training skills programmes in preschool and primary education.

The Circle of Friends is an intervention that does not aim to create friendly relationships – despite its 'misleading' name – but to develop and improve the communication skills of children with ASD who may grow to acquire friends (Whitaker et al., 1998). James and Leyden (2008) wrote that the Circle of Friends can help a closed and isolated or withdrawn child to open up and to engage in social interactions with peers. The studies by Whitaker et al. (1998) and Kalyva and Avramidis (2005) showed the effectiveness of the intervention in improving the social skills of the children with ASD who participate in the Circle of

Friends. However, Barrett and Randall (2004) said that more studies are needed to detect its effectiveness. Future studies should include more participants and stress the generalisation of acquired social skills across settings. For example, Frederickson et al. (2005) assessed the effects of the intervention on other settings after it ended.

You must also know that the main aim of the Circle of Friends is to help the peers understand the social difficulties that are experienced by the child with ASD; if you modify this environment, the children will be able to meet its demands. However, you must at the same time reinforce the social skills of children with ASD, so that they can function even in settings where people are not sensitive to their condition. Since it is not always possible to inform and prepare the environment to accept a child with ASD, you must equip the child with the basic skills that he needs to face the social challenges that he will encounter. Finally, I ought to stress that the Circle of Friends must be applied either before or straight after the inclusion of the child with ASD in school, so that he does not experience negative feelings and is not stigmatised by his peers. Prevention is better than intervention. In the past decade, there have been limited studies on the Circle of Friends in comparison to Social Stories, for example. This may also be due to the fact that there are other similar interventions that use a different name (Gutierrez et al., 2007) – for example, Carter et al. (2004) called it the friendship club.

Further reading

Gray, C.A. (1994) *The New Social Story Book*. Arlington, TX: Future Horizons.

Kalyva, E. and Avramidis, E. (2005) 'Improving communication between children with autism and their peers through the "Circle of Friends": a small scale intervention study', *Journal of Applied Research in Intellectual Disabilities*, 18: 253–61.

Ling, J. (2010) *I Can't Do That! My Social Stories to Help with Communication, Self-care and Personal Skills*, 2nd edn. London: Sage.

Sainsbury, C. (2009) *Martian in the Playground*. London: Sage.

3

Approaches for Developing Alternative Communication

Chapter overview

Many children with ASD develop speech and language later and use it less functionally than typically developing peers, while others show no signs of speech (Frankel et al., 1987). It is, therefore, essential to find a way to help them communicate at least their basic needs. Programmes such as ABA and TEACCH make certain suggestions about the way in which adults can reinforce the communication and the development of speech of children with ASD. However, there are also two alternative communication methods that can be implemented independently or in combination with other educational programmes: PECS and sign language. Both systems have advantages and disadvantages, which I underline later in the chapter, and great differences in their effectiveness have been observed. Parental preferences together with the training of the educators or the therapists who work with the child usually determine the choice of the alternative communication system that he will eventually use (Anderson, 2002).

Before I describe and critically evaluate these two approaches using evidence from scientific research, I would like to stress that they do not constitute a remedy for autism. They may help some children learn how to ask for certain things and to fulfil some of their basic needs (such as drink water or use the toilet), but they do not teach them the meaning or the importance of communication that they find hard to master. The example of some children with ASD who show a picture to an adult who has her back turned to them or make signs in an empty room is indicative. Therefore, these children have not understood the basic principle of communication that requires the active engagement of both parties. So it is essential that readers understand that the approaches described do not teach communication to children, but the basic skills that they need in order to learn how to ask for certain things. These approaches do not automatically teach the child with ASD to initiate a discussion, to share his interests, thoughts, experiences and feelings with people around him or to decode the non-verbal stimuli that 'frame' communication.

PECS

The Picture Exchange Communication System (PECS) was developed in 1994 by Bondy and Frost as a specific training package to reinforce alternative communication that is addressed to children with ASD and adults or people who are non-verbal or lack other communication skills that enable them to initiate communication (Sulzer-Azaroff et al., 2009). It is designed for educators, tutors or parents of children with ASD, so it can be used in many different contexts. The Picture Exchange Communication System's ultimate aim is for children to learn to make comments or answer questions directly. The relevant book by Lori Frost and Andrew Bondy provides all the necessary information for the effective implementation of PECS; it takes the readers through six training stages and example sheets for recording data and the child's progress. This system has been used to teach blind young people with ASD to make requests using appropriate symbols (Lund and Troha, 2008).

The Picture Exchange Communication System basically teaches a child how to exchange a photograph of a desired object with an adult, who directly responds to this demand. Since photographs may distract with detail, sometimes symbols are better. Verbal prompts are not used, so that the initiation of the interaction can be immediate and independent. Then, the child learns to distinguish between various symbols and to put them together in order to structure simple 'sentences'. He is also taught to make comments or to ask directly for what he wants. It is not clear how the adult can figure out by just looking at the photograph whether the child asks for something or whether he just makes a comment (Bondy et al., 2004). The founders of this programme suggest that many preschoolers who use PECS finally develop speech, but they do not provide sufficient scientific evidence to support their claim. It is also probable that certain children develop speech because they grow up and not because they use an alternative communication system. Bondy and Frost (1994) state that PECS can be particularly effective if it is combined with elements of ABA. The Picture Exchange Communication System is commonly used in combination with other interventions, such as TEACCH, which has been using pictures for many years to help non-verbal children and which, in fact, constitutes the cornerstone for the development of PECS.

The Picture Exchange Communication System teaches basic communication skills to address fundamental self-help needs, such as asking for food. One of its basic principles is the integration of theoretical and practical aspects of both ABA and speech and language pathology. Adults who want to implement PECS have to discover first the appropriate reinforcers that will motivate the child to communicate. It is extremely important to ensure that the child learns to approach his communication partner spontaneously from the beginning of the session.

Training in communication tackles basic issues that are pertinent to the very nature of ASD, so in order to understand communication it is important first to define and to distinguish it from other actions. For example, a girl enters the living room, switches on the television and watches it. In this particular case, there is no form of communication – the girl just acted upon an aspect of her environment and achieved the desired outcome through her own actions. Your ability to interpret her actions does not alter their nature. Alternatively, the girl could have gone to her mother and said 'TV' and then her mother would probably switch on the television so that her daughter could watch. Now there is evident intention for communication because the girl turned to her mother, rather than to the television. The mother's role was to identify and satisfy her daughter's demand.

Another basic type of communication occurs when the girl, while watching television, shouts 'doggie! doggie!'. She may keep repeating this word until her mother says: 'Yes, you are right. I can see the doggie.' In this case, she does not ask her mother to give her a dog. She communicated the need for her mother's attention. So, when teaching functional communication to children with ASD, it is important to consider that they may respond to diverse rewards or reinforcements.

One more crucial aspect of effective communication is the context in which a word (or a picture, a notion or a symbol) is used and not the word itself. For example, a boy may say the word 'milk' because: (1) he saw his mother standing next to a bottle and asked for it, initiating spontaneously the communicative interaction; (2) he answered his mother's question as to whether he wanted something, responding to a certain prompt (the question); or (3) echoed his mother's suggestion to offer it. The word was the same in all three cases, but the communicative intent differed enormously. An even more important step is to teach the child to look for his mother and to ask her for the milk that is not next to her. This constitutes real communication, because in example (1) there is a bottle of milk 'reminding' the child that he wants to drink. So, it could be the case that he does not communicate, but just asks for something that he detects in the environment and that in fact he may not even want.

Question for discussion

Can you think of ways to engage children with ASD in effective communicative acts? Would you consider using their interests/rituals as a basis for interaction? How would you decide if the communicative act is successful?

Bondy and Frost (1994) suggest that the first lesson should focus on teaching the child with ASD how to ask spontaneously for certain things or activities. Therefore, the first step is to detect what the child wants. No training in compliance or 'readiness' is needed. It is sufficient to find out which reward constitutes a strong incentive. Since the primary goal is to teach the child how to be spontaneous, adults should avoid using direct verbal prompts, such as 'What are you doing? What do you want? Give me the picture'. The presence of two adults is the most effective way to initiate the training. The first adult tempts the child with the desired reward, while the second adult sits behind the child, waits for a movement towards the reward and physically helps the child to take the picture and give it to the adult who has the reward. The physical prompt should be removed and extinguished as soon as possible. When the adult takes the picture, she directly rewards the child and makes an appropriate comment about the object (for example, she names it).

When a child can exchange pictures effectively, the training is modified to promote spontaneity, persistence and generalisation. The child is taught to walk longer distances to reach his partner or the desired picture and to look for different rewards in different settings (for example, different rooms and contexts) with different people. During the first stages, the child is not expected to distinguish between different pictures. Such training begins once the willingness to communicate has been established. Typically developing children also learn first to approach their parents, to look at them and to nod or make gestures to get what they want before they are able to speak. The third stage of training involves decision-making regarding symbols. Some children are extremely good at visual discrimination (they can match objects or symbols), while others need intense training. Silverman (1995) argued that even children who have difficulty distinguishing between several symbols are able to use them within a structured communication context. But even so, this does not mean that they have learnt to communicate spontaneously and to initiate meaningful reciprocal interactions. For example, Carre et al. (2009) studied whether training in PECS can generalise at home and school and concluded that even when PECS training is designed to enhance generalisation, it can be extremely difficult to achieve – if it ever does.

Once children can distinguish between symbols, they are trained to structure a sentence. Very young typically developing children in the process of acquiring language use intonation and other means to help adults understand whether the word 'ball' is a demand or a comment. So, adults need to teach children with ASD to demonstrate whether they present a picture as a demand or as a comment. When children ask for something, they should use a simple sentence consisting of a picture which represents 'I want' and a picture of the desired object. They place (both) pictures in order and give them to the person who will satisfy their demand. This training helps children respond to the simple question 'What do you want?' Bondy and Frost (1994) suggest that adults should try to motivate children to ask spontaneously for the desired object, otherwise they just learn how to act mechanically in order to get what they want without understanding the meaning of communication.

Then the child learns how to make more complicated sentences. For example, a child who always prefers red sweets can be taught to ask for them using the appropriate adjective (for example, I want red sweets). At this stage of training, more definitions can also be added – for example, size, amount, location, relative place, and so on. Instead of asking the child to touch something or to show something – for example, 'show me a big box' – adults can motivate him to show them something that he wants – for example, 'I want the large piece of chocolate', as long as in the latter case the reward is direct. The training in communication begins when the child's speech becomes more complicated. Adults place in front of him an object that is attractive or interesting and ask him to tell them what he sees. Adults add in the PECS book a picture that represents the verb 'see' and teach the child to form the sentence 'I see a biscuit'. At this point, the adult changes his response and instead of giving the child the biscuit, she makes a comment such as 'I also see a biscuit'. Then the training on generalisation begins, so that the child does not develop established patterns of objects that he comments on. Since the goal is for the child to develop spontaneous speech, adults need to gradually withdraw the question 'what do you see?' or other indirect prompts (for example, 'Oh, look'). Other senses (for example, hearing, feeling, smelling) in combination with other sentences (for example, 'the towel is soft') are also used. Even if the child learns to comment on an object spontaneously – which is extremely hard to achieve – the comments are limited mainly to objects that intrigue him and not to ideas, thoughts or feelings. Moreover, it is likely that the child 'comments' on an object because he wants to get it and not because he wants to communicate, as suggested by the advocates of PECS. Therefore, any 'dialogue' would be specific, 'structured' and far from the level of abstract thinking as discussed by Piaget (1948).

Exchanging a card for an object

PECS and autism

Autism is characterised by difficulties in communication, which include the exchange of messages between people, the expression of needs, and the sharing of ideas, thoughts and feelings. Communication is usually expressed through written language or speech. People use communication in a social context and derive joy from mutual conversation. Children with ASD have difficulty in discovering the power and joy of social communication, while they tend to learn through visual means which can help them understand and use the process of communication. Temple Grandin (1995) explains that she thinks through images and that the words seem to her like a foreign language. Individuals who think visually are aided by visual support and TEACCH encourages the use of visual structure for the reduction of stress and the promotion of learning for people with ASD rendering the environment more comprehensible. Visual spurs can help people with ASD understand the world and other people, as well as some aspects of the communication process.

Visual means can be utilised in order to accompany or enhance speech and to help the child with ASD understand verbal information. They can also help the non-verbal child learn how to express his needs by asking for what he wants. The selected visual means, which are determined by each individual's needs are objects, pictures, visual symbols and written words. The simplest developmental visual mean is the relative object itself, which is three-dimensional. But since it is impossible for a child to carry with him all the objects that he wants or needs, he may sometimes use pictures, symbols and words. Since individuals with ASD pay more attention to details than to the whole and have difficulty with generalisation, they may get confused if the picture used does not clearly depict the real object. Thus, it would be better to use pictures that depict the actual objects found in the child's environment (for example, the family's car and not the picture of any car) (Angermeier et al., 2008). Moreover, you can use the labels or the packages of objects that the child likes (for example, the wrapper of biscuits or chocolate) instead of using pictures.

I need to stress that since some children with ASD can identify written words more easily than spoken words, it is recommended to use visual symbols with an accompanying written word printed in small letters. This can help both the child with ASD and the rest of the people to understand the symbol. It is crucial that you all use the same name when you refer to an object so as not to confuse the child who has not yet generalised his knowledge (for example, the 'cat' should not be called 'kitty'). Most people can easily perceive and understand visual symbols (especially if they are accompanied by a written explanation) in contrast to signs which are used effectively only by those trained in sign language.

Initially, the child with ASD should relate the visual symbol with the represented object through the process of 'name giving': the connection of a symbol to the object or the place that it represents (for example, 'chocolate' or 'toilet'). As soon as the child can relate the symbol with the real object (or place), a similar object can be presented a short distance from the real object, so that the parent or the caregiver can show the symbol and at the same time tell him what to fetch or where to go. So, the symbol can be used away from the actual object it represents. The pace at which new symbols are introduced varies from one person to another, but it is important that you first use objects that constitute a motive for the child with ASD and wait for definite signs of understanding before you present the new symbol. If you introduce a lot of symbols at the same time, you may cause overload and the child may confuse them and not be able to use them properly.

 Question for discussion

If children with ASD cannot realise that other people might not understand what they want, why would they bother communicating their desire or need? How could you try to make them understand this basic principle of communication using PECS?

Children with ASD find it difficult to understand how communication works. This is the most difficult thing that you should teach to the child with ASD and you cannot achieve it merely through using pictures or symbols. For example, Ganz et al. (2008) reported that children with ASD who mastered PECS did not manage to produce intelligible words. The Picture Exchange Communication System is easy to use and does not require expensive equipment or training (Chaabane et al., 2009; Schwartz et al., 1998). You may sometimes see children carry their picture book with them in public places in order to express and fulfil their desires and needs but not necessarily to communicate fully.

You can use PECS to introduce the concept of choices – for example, with food. When you establish the understanding of the connection of symbols to food, then you can use them to show the available choices and to encourage the child with ASD to communicate the desired choice. You can use tables of choices for play or for recreational activities and you can encourage the child to choose an available activity (instead of him remaining passive or insisting on the same activity). In this way you show the child that he can have some influence and control over the environment, thereby increasing his sense of self-confidence and safety. Since learning how to choose is instrumental in understanding the concepts of denial and affirmation, it should be mastered in the early stages of development.

Children with ASD, whether verbal or non-verbal, may benefit from the use of visual symbols in individual programmes that depict the sequence of daily routines. In this way you can avoid temper tantrums, as well as encourage the independent completion of certain activities, such as dressing. You can adapt the charts in order to use them at home, at school, at the workplace or in a place of independent living. Visual symbols render the world organised and predictable, and encourage desirable behaviour. You can also reinforce the understanding that something is 'over' and it is important to proceed to the next activity (Janzen, 1996). Once the child with ASD completes an activity that he has chosen, then he can learn to place the respective symbol in a box and continue with the next activity. It should be noted at this point that most of these elements are borrowed from TEACCH.

Bondy and Frost (1994) noticed that 60 per cent of the children aged up to 5 who used PECS for more than a year finally developed speech. The percentage of preschoolers who developed independent speech before the completion of the first year of using PECS was significantly smaller (approximately 10 per cent). Moreover, they noticed that certain children initially used speech only in combination with PECS. Ganz and Simpson (2004) mentioned that PECS helps children with ASD to increase the number of words they say and use a more complicated grammatical structure. Some other children improved their speech – for both the number of words and the complexity of communication – through PECS (Frost et al., 1997). Bondy and Frost (1994) recommend that PECS is maintained as a means of communication support until the child is able to communicate equally effectively without it. The child's progress will determine the decision whether to use PECS or not. These claims are quite arbitrary, since it is not known whether children with ASD developed speech because of PECS or because of other educational programmes that they attended simultaneously, or simply because they grew up and started communicating more effectively. Carr and Felce (2007a) reported that children in the PECS group showed concomitant increases in initiating or responding to communications by staff after intensive training, while only one child in the control group demonstrated similar minimal increase.

Charlop-Christy et al. (2002) studied the impact of PECS on three boys aged 3–12 with ASD, and tested its efficacy in the development of speech during play and in academic contexts. All three boys improved their ability to talk, while their communicative behaviours increased and their problematic behaviours decreased. Kravits et al. (2002) studied the contribution of PECS to the increase of spontaneous communication skills of a 6-year-old girl with ASD at home and at school. She started to develop spontaneous speech when she used PECS and her efforts for social interaction increased. Liddle (2001) stated that PECS was tested with 21 children with ASD who showed progress in their communication ability. Other recent studies report that children with ASD trained in PECS show improvement not only in language, but also in play (Anderson et al., 2007; Jurgens et al., 2009) and in communicative initiations and dyadic interactions between students and teaching staff (Carr and

Felce, 2007b). Yokoyama et al. (2006) argued that with PECS training non-verbal children with ASD replaced their prior mode of communication, which consisted of grabbing, crying or reaching, with appropriate picture-exchanging behaviours.

Cummings and Williams (2000) studied five boys aged 3–5 with ASD, who were receiving daily behavioural therapy at home. All of them had learnt how to match objects to objects, objects to pictures and, finally, pictures to pictures. Then, four of these children learned to properly respond to PECS and they soon started to imitate simple sounds. In this case, the researchers were quick to attribute this improvement in learning to PECS, whereas the contribution of ABA, which shares a lot of common elements with PECS, was not fully recognised. Moreover, it is not known whether these children finally acquired communicative speech or whether they were content with the use of pictures and, as a result, imitated and made sounds instead of producing completed words and sentences. There has been a lot of expressed concern about the use of PECS (or other visibly oriented communicative systems) as well as about the consequences that it may have in the development and use of speech. Reliance upon a non-verbal means of communication might jeopardise the efforts of both the child with ASD and his family to develop speech. It is also unclear to what extent children with ASD can adequately understand the principles of communication, in order to use PECS consciously and effectively, since it is in essence a communication system. Howlin et al. (2007) conducted a group randomised controlled trial and concluded that no increases were found in ADOS-G ratings, frequency of speech, or language test scores. Any improvements disappeared once the active intervention ceased.

To sum up, if you use PECS supportively, you can teach a child with ASD to develop certain communicative skills – mostly to fulfil his basic needs (Magiati and Howlin, 2003). You can teach him to ask for an object or to carry out an activity, but it is difficult to explain to him how he can share his ideas, feelings, thoughts or experiences. Moreover, instilling the need for communication with the environment around him is even more difficult. This may be the reason that even those children with ASD who have learnt to use PECS effectively do not usually spontaneously initiate interaction with someone else, and they depend to a large extent on the prompt from others in their environment. This is also reflected in the act of showing the communication cards to the intended recipient without ensuring first that she is paying attention to them, thus leading to disappointment. They did all that was needed, but they did not get the desired outcome. However, it should be pointed out that PECS may substantially help parents of non-verbal children with ASD to identify at least their basic needs. As a result, children with ASD will exhibit less tantrums and frustration and their parents will feel more confident and effective in their parenting skills. On the whole, you must remember that PECS does not constitute a remedy for autism, but when used appropriately and in combination with TEACCH, ABA or other effective approaches, it could enhance the expression of basic needs.

Sign language

Sign language (SL) is used predominantly for communication by non-verbal individuals. There are several sign languages – which are used even within the same country – and this fact hinders the study of their effectiveness. Moreover, people who understand and use SL sufficiently are usually limited within the families and the trainers. Therefore, the number of people who can interact and communicate through SL is very small in comparison to the number of people who can use and understand photographs or pictures. On several occasions, it is the parents, professionals and educators who are called on to decide which technique will be the most effective as a communication means for non-verbal individuals with ASD (Anderson, 2002). However, the basic problem is that SL is a language with its own rules. If children with ASD were capable of mastering SL, then they would be equally able to acquire verbal or written language, as well as non-verbal communication. Also, ASD is characterised by difficulty in understanding the meaning of communication and not by speech problems. So when you help children with ASD to learn how to ask for something through signs, you do not really teach them how to communicate.

Sign language and autism

Older studies have shown that a lot of children with ASD are able to learn and produce signs – which vary from 5 to 350 (Bonvillan et al., 1981) or 400 signs (Kiernan, 1983). There is also sufficient evidence that even children with low-functioning ASD are able to learn how to communicate their basic needs by using signs (Lewis, 1987; Stull et al., 1980; Webster et al., 1980). Yet, this does not mean that they have learnt to communicate. They have just connected the forming of certain signs with the fulfilment of their desires (for example, when they form the sign 'chocolate' they eat chocolate); they have not necessarily understood that they can also communicate in this way, because they do not understand the meaning of communication. It is therefore difficult for children with ASD to be taught to communicate through signs and not just to copy them (Ricks and Wing, 1976).

Certain researchers support the view that children with ASD can be taught to use SL in a creative way (Goldstein, 2002; Koegel et al., 1982a) and spontaneously (Benaroya et al., 1979; Bonvilllan, et al., 1981; Konstantareas et al., 1979; Layton, 1988; Shimizu, 1988; Von Tetzchner, 1984; Webster et al., 1980) and thus improve their communication skills (Konstantareas et al., 1980; Stull et al., 1980) and generalise them in other contexts (Bonvillan et al., 1981; Casey, 1978; Webster et al., 1980). Most of these studies were conducted almost three decades ago and have not used scientifically sound research methods. When these children, who were unable to express their basic needs, learned to use a sign, it was reasonable to assume that they were making progress; but this does not equal communication. Moreover, it is probable that children who learn signs may use them constantly as practice, while adults in their environment may perceive them as intention for communication and therefore report improvement in communication skills which is actually misleading. Moreover, the fragmentary use of signs does not mean knowledge of SL.

Some researchers view training in SL as contributing to the reduction of self-stimulation and disruptive behaviour that are usually observed in children with ASD (Bonvillan and Nelson, 1976; Carr et al., 1978; Rutter, 1965; Sato et al., 1987; Shimizu, 1988). It is difficult to ascertain whether the claimed changes are 'generated' by the training in SL or by the application of other structured interventions. The most probable explanation is that when a means of communication of needs is provided, certain behavioural problems subside (Kiernan, 1983). So, when the child uses the appropriate sign to ask for water, he gets what he wants and there is no reason to get frustrated or mad and manifest aggressive behaviour.

 Question for discussion

Consider what will happen if the child confuses the signs, uses the wrong sign and as a result does not get the water that he wanted. Moreover, what will happen when he wants to communicate something that it is not tangible, such as a feeling, an idea or an experience? Do you think it is probable that the child will manifest undesirable behaviours, since his needs are not fulfilled?

A recurring concern is that children with ASD who use signs may stop trying to develop speech. There are, however, some scientists who argue that many children with ASD who initially learn to communicate by using SL finally manage to acquire verbal speech as well (Bonvillan et al., 1981; Kiernan and Reid, 1984; Lewis, 1987; Shimizu, 1988), because the teachers and therapists say the words and make the respective signs simultaneously. They think that simultaneous communication facilitates the development of speech because: (1) the signs that the children remember serve as reminders for the words they have forgotten and vice versa, and (2) the signs help children to discern where a word starts and where it ends – especially when words are difficult or homophones. Bebko (1990), Bonvillan et al. (1981) and Casey (1978) suggest that even the children who are verbal profit from the programmes of simultaneous presentation of signs and speech.

The relevant literature review shows that there are a lot of methodological issues that have to be taken into consideration when assessing the effect of SL on improving the communication problems of children with ASD. First, children with ASD may exhibit substantially different symptoms. Researchers do not usually clarify the diagnosis or the specific traits of the children who participated in their studies, so it is not possible to verify that all of them had ASD. It is therefore important to improve the definition criteria of the participants' characteristics and to collect data through tasks that are related to differential diagnosis (Kiernan, 1983).

Furthermore, the majority of studies that 'advertise' the positive results of SL basically refer to the use of isolated signs and not to communication. Children with ASD can learn to use certain signs effectively in order to fulfil some of their basic needs, but they have not understood or put into practice the basic principles of communication. This fact is reinforced by the recording of incidents where children use signs when there is nobody in the room to see them or they use various signs consecutively waiting for the adult to satisfy their demand at some point. Moreover, there is no evidence on whether a child with ASD could communicate effectively with a deaf child who uses SL. I believe that they will use sign language in a different way. The child with ASD will make single signs or combinations of two or three signs because he cannot communicate, while a deaf child will substantially and effectively use sign language. I must also point out that several children with ASD find it difficult to correctly form signs with their hands, because of problems with their fine motor skills (Oxman and Konstantareas, 1981) and as a result they do not manage to achieve their goal. Moreover, given the fact that the majority of people cannot identify signs, it might be preferable to train a non-verbal child to use pictures or photographs to express his needs. The goal and meaning of communication can be taught only within the context of a structured educational programme and not with fragmentary solutions dictated by current needs. The paucity of published research in the use of sign language in ASD in recent years testifies further to the limitations mentioned previously.

Further reading

Matthews, B. (2003) *Review of a Picture's Worth: PECS and Other Visual Communication Strategies in Autism*. New York: Informa Healthcare.

Preston, D. and Carter, M. (2009) 'A review of the efficacy of the Picture Exchange Communication System intervention', *Journal of Autism and Developmental Disorders*, 39: 1471–86.

Tincani, M. (2004) 'Comparing the Picture Exchange Communication System and sign language training for children with autism', *Focus on Autism and Other Developmental Disabilities*, 19: 152–63.

Approaches Based on Play

Chapter overview

Children with ASD lack varied, spontaneous pretend or social imitative play. The American Psychiatric Association (APA, 2001) reports that children with ASD play in their own unique ways, since they do not move away from the early infancy stage of occupation with objects. I felt compelled to refer to play in more detail, because although it should be one of the main occupations of children with ASD, it is often omitted from many educational or therapeutic interventions. It is usually treated as an activity that takes place during the breaks and when it is taught in the framework of a behavioural approach, this is done in a highly structured way using mainly the therapist as play partner. But in this chapter, I present some approaches that are implemented at school or at home with the participation of peers and promote not only autonomous play, but also inclusion in group activities and in the wider social context. I place more emphasis on teaching social play, which poses one of the greatest challenges, since it requires the participation and cooperation of more individuals than just the child with ASD. It is an essential step to enable the child to learn and practise in a relatively safe environment all the skills that he needs to become integrated into society. The play-based approaches that I present are non-directive play, pivotal response training and integrated play groups.

Play is an activity that is not imposed or directed by others, is free from external rules, with, usually, no specific goal that needs to be met and the child is pleased just because he is playing (Jordan and Libby, 1997; Scarlett, 2004). These features differentiate play from other activities and make it particularly popular and accessible. Bekoff and Byers (1981) define play as all the motor activities that take place after birth and seem to have no purpose, at least no obvious purpose. As time goes by and the toddler develops cognitively, these motor skills are often enriched by motor patterns and other reference points with altered time sequence. Children start including in their repertoires movements that they first observe, record and imitate from their environment and then modify according to their current skills (Restall and Magill-Evans, 1994; Scarlett, 2004).

However, the play of children with ASD is differentiated substantially from the definition that I just provided. They lack varied, spontaneous pretend or social imitative play according to their developmental level. The APA (2001) reports that children with ASD play in their own unique ways, since they do not move away from the early infancy stage of occupation with objects. They like to savour different senses – such as tasting, smelling, rocking or revolving their bodies. However, while the toddler with typical development progresses, imitates and explores, becomes involved with others, and learns how to use the objects and his bodily movements in pretend play, toddlers with ASD are limited to a small number of solitary activities. They prefer these activities that offer them pleasure and so they repeat them again and again (Beyer and Gammeltoft, 2000; Bruckner and Yoder, 2007; Holmes and Willoughby, 2005; Honey et al., 2007; Moore and Russ, 2006).

Some children with ASD enjoy 'rough and tumble' play, which gives parents and caregivers the ability to share the joy of playing with them. This can help establish a mutually enjoyable relationship that includes the exchange of experiences and constitutes a form of communication. However, rough and tumble play and play with objects are characteristic of younger children. Children with ASD have a hard time trying to incorporate it spontaneously into pretend play (Rutherford et al., 2007; Stanley and Konstantareas, 2007; White, 2002).

Several children with high-functioning ASD acquire certain advanced play skills, such as putting together the train tracks and moving the trains around making the appropriate noise, completing a puzzle or building bricks. But the typical child with ASD does not evolve these activities and is not happy to share them with others. So, play seems to get stuck, be solitary and repetitive. Children with ASD do not usually play spontaneously in uncontrolled environments, because they have trouble playing effectively (Beyer and Gammeltoft, 2000; Holmes and Willoughby, 2005; Prendeville et al., 2006; Stahmer, 1999).

You may wonder why it matters if children with ASD cannot play like their typically developing peers. Besides, all people are different and maybe it is pointless to try to force children with ASD to play in ways that do not come naturally to them and probably do not offer them any pleasure. However, it is extremely important to teach children with ASD to play appropriately in order to enhance their cognitive skills (Boucher, 1999). Sensorimotor play teaches young children about their bodies and the objects in their environments. Manipulative and exploratory play teaches older children about objects' properties and the ways in which they can influence the world around them. 'Rough and tumble' play and energetic physical play teach toddlers motor skills and the interaction of their body with others and with objects in the environment. Social play begins with the first social exchanges between babies and their caregivers during feeding, bathing and nappy change. It continues with more complex interactions among elementary children who play cops and robbers. Social play teaches children social relations and the way to engage in them, as well as the cultural rules of their society. Pretend play, either social or solitary, teaches children how to distance their thought from the experience that they have at that moment and how to use symbols and representations to achieve this way of thinking (Boucher and Lewis, 1990; Mastrangelo, 2009).

Another argument for the importance of facilitating play for a child with ASD, is that the lack of play skills isolates him even further and makes him stand out from his peers. One could say that the child's job is to play. Moreover, play is or should be fun. Typically developing children want to play not because they learn, but because they like to play. Part of this pleasure derives from the fact that children continuously evolve their skills, achieve something more and experience the positive emotion that comes with increased skills. If children with ASD who improve their play skills feel more accomplished, pleased and motivated, this is a big step in itself. Play for children with ASD is valuable because it is a means of expressing themselves. Adults can learn a lot about a child just by watching him play; if children have thoughts and feelings that they cannot express verbally, then maybe they can express them through their play (Boucher, 1999).

Social as well as cognitive factors can account for the poor pretend play of children with ASD. Pretend play is closely linked to social activity. A prerequisite for the conventional use of objects, which forms the basis of functional play, is that children can observe adults and older children. Children with ASD may engage in less functional play because they are less synchronised with the actions and interests of other people. Furthermore, when they observe others, they tend not to interpret their behaviours in relation to accompanying emotions, attitudes and beliefs. A second tie to social activity is that the functional and symbolic forms of play are usually performed with dolls or other people. Children with ASD, however, tend to avoid initiating social contact – with dolls or with people – and so they may get involved in less functional and symbolic play (Sherratt, 2002).

Children with ASD tend to show poor symbolic play because it demands the kind of cognitive skills that they do not possess. Engagement in pretend play has as a prerequisite the ability to overcome the literal meaning of situations. But it is known that literal understanding constitutes one of the main problems of children with ASD. In order to pretend that a brick is a car, they have to create a different, additional level of reality. Pretence means that they have to be able to act as if the brick were a car, keeping in mind at the same time that the brick is actually a brick. They have to do more than just attribute imaginary properties to objects; they also have to understand that other people can do that as well (Jordan, 1999b; Sherratt, 2002).

The main social achievement of a child is his ability to cooperate with a social partner. When children communicate messages, they understand how to play a particular game. The sign or the invitation to initiate a game (for example, eye contact), the sign to reverse the roles (for example, it is my turn) and the way to show that they share this knowledge enable children to play a range of games (Howes, 1988). Peers play a very important and multidimensional role in this whole procedure and they constitute a basic component of the social and academic inclusion of children with ASD. Peers can help them develop some social skills by:

1. *Reinforcing the desirable behaviour.* Children at the age of 4 praise and share more with their peers than children at the age of 3. Reciprocation is common practice even in kindergartners who tend to reinforce the peers who reinforce them. When adults train the peers of a child with ASD to pay attention only to specific behaviours (for example, cooperative and auxiliary) and to ignore other behaviours (for example, annoying and aggressive), then this reinforcement programme can bring about significant changes in peers' behaviour. I explained before that this constitutes an important element of the philosophy of the 'Circle of Friends'.

2. *Acting as role models of positive and adaptive behaviour.* Children with ASD learn new social skills through imitation, which leads to more sophisticated forms of play, such as social play. In many cultures, siblings are the primary caregivers and this allows young children to learn from interactions with peers of different age groups. This is why, as I have

mentioned about ABA and TEACCH in Chapter 1, therapists must actively involve the family – and especially siblings of children with ASD – in the therapeutic process.

3. *Contributing to the development of self-concept.* Peers help children with ASD develop their self-image and their self-esteem, as well as their self-perception. In the first years of primary school, children show a remarkable increase in the use of social comparison and the peer group acts as a means of self-evaluation. If academic inclusion is not smooth and with the proper support, then it is likely that the child's self-esteem will decrease, because he will receive negative comments from his peers (who may not be familiar with his condition).

The play-based interventions that I present are used with children with ASD and differ in terms of the age groups that they target, their goals, their methods and their theoretical backgrounds. For example, non-directive therapy that was introduced by Cogher (1999) has been designed for children with severe communication difficulties, such as children with ASD who have not yet mastered the early stages of pre-verbal social interaction and communication. It offers enhanced opportunities and support to guide the child through the basic stages of language development. In non-directive therapy, the therapist works with the child on a one-to-one basis using ordinary play material. The intervention is led by the child, it is not intrusive and it does not have a very clear and abiding structure.

Pivotal response training, developed by Stahmer (1999), is designed for children with ASD who are able to work on a one-to-one basis with a therapist or a parent on activities that have been designed to enhance certain play skills and to increase their motivation to play. This intervention is led by the adult and is highly structured, and is based primarily on behavioural techniques. The integrated playgroup project (Wolfberg and Schuler, 1999) involved preschoolers who are capable of starting to play with peers. The short-term goals of the intervention are to improve the child's level and quality of play, while he is taught to participate in social play in the context of smaller groups. The long-term goal is to decrease the effects of social isolation on the child's overall development and is based on Vygotsky's theory of the importance of supportive social interactions in the enhancement of typical development.

 Question for discussion

Which information would you need to collect, and from whom, in order to decide which of these play-based approaches best suit the needs of the focus child with ASD?

Children at play

Non-directive play

Non-directive play is used to enhance the development of social inter-action and the perception and expression of language. The role of the therapist or the parent is to follow the child's interest. Non-directive play works on a systemic level and focuses on the individual skills of every child, emphasing the development of language and communica-tion. It aims to equip the child with experiences of language and communication strategies that are dynamic and effective, so that he can use them in every possible context. The basic teaching principle of non-directive play is the layout of the environment that should increase the child's motivation and opportunities to respond to diverse environmental stimuli (Koegel et al., 1999).

This technique involves playing with the child in an environment that can be structured by parents, teachers or therapists. The child participates in an activity, while the adult plays next to him, imitates his actions and makes a verbal comment that is appropriate either to the child's verbal level or to the context's level. If the child wants to play more effectively, he has to be able to communicate, to deter-mine a point of joint attention or common reference, to get involved in play routines and to respond appropriately to language. These are the basic elements of non-directive play:

1. The adult engages in joint attention by following the child's example.

2. The adult challenges slightly the child's learning level, by imitating initially his behaviour or actions and then showing him a way to change or expand them.

3. The adult responds consistently and adaptively to the child's attempts to communicate.

4. The adult creates contexts and opportunities for the child to develop his play.

5. The adult comments on the object or the activity that the child attends and is interested in.

 Question for discussion

Many children with ASD engage in stereotypic play behaviours (such as spinning objects). How could you join in this kind of activity and expand it? How do you think the child might react?

Harris (1992) mentions that it is essential to make sure that the comments are synchronised and relevant to the child's activity. Tiegeman and Primavera (1987) showed that imitation led to higher percentages of exploratory play, while Dawson and Adams (1984) discovered that imitation resulted in more diversified play patterns. Many children with ASD lack spontaneous play ideas, which have to be taught to them (Drew, 1996).

Non-directive play can be used at any assessment or intervention stage with children with ASD or different communication difficulties. It can be implemented either individually or in a group format and in public places or at home with a higher or lower intensity level. The adult creates a safe environment for the child with toys that she has chosen either randomly or on purpose. During the session, the adult spends a lot of time next to the child and every time he carries out an activity, the adult imitates it and/or makes an appropriate accompanying comment. Enderby and Emerson (1995) stress that this technique has not been adequately researched, but there are some studies that underline its individual benefits. For example, Kenny and Winick (2000) used non-directive play therapy with an 11-year-old girl with ASD and reported increased social behaviour and compliance at home, as well as decreased irritability.

Moreover, I should emphasise that despite the fact that one of the intervention's goals is to enhance language, there is no testimony to it. There seems to be an improvement in the child's ability to interact with peers, but not to communicate.

Pivotal response training

Pivotal response training is an intervention designed for individuals who live or work with children and adolescents with ASD – namely, therapists, teachers, parents, siblings and peers (Terpstra et al., 2002). The intervention can be implemented in a variety of settings, such as the school, the home, or the wider community. It uses a pivotal behaviour to change another behaviour. The pivotal behaviour can be effective in many developmental areas (for example, communication and social interaction). Several researchers have expanded the use of pivotal training to increase language (for example, using words), to initiate interactions in the context of play and to increase the amount of time that children with ASD play to enhance joint attention skills (Jones et al., 2006; Koegel and Koegel, 2006; Pierce and Schreibman, 1995; Trevisanello and Gremigni, 2008). The amount of time that children spend in positive social interaction increases because of social and dramatic play that is taught through pivotal training (Thorp et al., 1995). Stahmer (1995) mentioned that after the implementation of pivotal training, children with ASD engaged in significantly more symbolic play.

Typically developing children should be trained to use pivotal response training through role play, role models and instruction (Pierce and Schreibman, 1997). Then the peer applies the strategies that she has learnt to the child with ASD in a context where the teachers can supervise the whole process and make constructive comments on the use of the strategies. The training lasts for as long as is deemed necessary for the typically developing child to master the most effective interaction strategies.

After the training, peers were also able to implement the intervention in classroom setting. Stahmer (1995) applied pivotal response training to teach reciprocal symbolic play skills to children with ASD and discovered that the teacher needs to offer a setting that motivates them to engage in symbolic play. The teacher initially has to observe the child with ASD if she wants to identify what motivates him. Then she will be able to determine the activities and the materials that he prefers, the children and the adults that he approaches more often, as well the types of reward/reinforcement that are more effective in his case. The focus on a pivotal behaviour during the instruction of certain activities increases the child's desire to engage and to learn the new skill.

 Question for discussion

If you were asked to select a peer to train, what criteria would you use? How would get informed consent from the peer and his parents? How would you explain your choice to the selected peers and to the other classmates?

Thorp and his associates (1995) argued that socio-dramatic play can be taught through pivotal response training, which can be modified and adjusted by a teacher or a parent in order to implement it in class or in a play group. These are the steps to foster socio-dramatic play:

1. The adult gives the child a toy that he prefers according to his interests.

2. The adult waits and takes turns to play with the toy and to promote appropriate socio-dramatic play. This is repeated until the child starts responding.

3. The adult should reinforce proper responses and attempts to respond properly.

4. The adult should actively encourage the child and act as a role model to reinforce the appropriate socio-dramatic play and to develop socio-dramatic themes.

Children with ASD who participated in pivotal response training programmes were able to engage in high levels of interaction, in varied play with objects, and in conversations after the intervention ended (Bellini and Peters, 2008), while their skills were generalised to different contexts, stimuli and peers (Pierce and Schreibman, 1995, 1997). The interactions that form an integral part of pivotal response training represent more naturalistic parent–child interactions and are more pleasant for parents (Schreibman et al., 1991). Thorp et al. (1995) used pivotal response training to help their participants conceptualise better social roles and social events. Pivotal response training focuses on the enhancement of the motivation to learn, allowing children with ASD to choose, reinforcing the attempts to respond properly, using sufficient role models, and offering naturalistic consequences (Bryson et al., 2007). Positive changes in play, language and social skills were reported, whereas there was limited generalisation to other people and other settings. This improvement could be due partly to the sensitisation of the environment to the child's needs and not so much to the increase of his positive behaviours. It should also be taken into account that many children with ASD react to change and may not welcome the interference of a third person who will interrupt their game and try to modify it.

Integrated play groups

Integrated play groups offer children with ASD the possibility of engaging in play with more able typically developing peers in natural settings, such as home, school, recreational areas or neighbourhood parks. Each group consists of three to five children who have advanced social skills (siblings or peers), and are experienced players, and the child with ASD who is a novice player. Children participate in small groups organised around a game or an activity that corresponds to their developmental level and is supervised by an adult (professional or parent) who has been trained to construct interactive games with peers; these interactions are non-intrusive and focused on the child with ASD (Hall, 2009). 'Matching persons with equal development and then placing them together in dyads or groups to help each other learn, leads to the development of intensely powerful emotional bonds' (Gutstein and Sheely, 2002: 29).

The integrated play groups model is based on sociocultural theories and on principles of 'guided participation'. Children participate actively with the guidance, support and invitation of their peers who differ in terms of their skills and social status (Rogoff, 1990). Developmental changes are expressed initially in the context of social interactions with adults and other more able peers, who can adjust their help to facilitate and teach the more inexperienced and novice players. Given that children with ASD respond well to routine and structure, the groups are set regularly two or three times a week for 30 minutes to an hour. There are individualised visual schedules or diaries that help the players predict the future play sessions. There should be rituals for opening and closing every session – for example, a brief plan or review of the events or a song. The toys and the space should be organised in such a way as to be accessible, visible and categorised by activities or by topics. In order to organise and define the activities that will be carried out by the group, first adults need to assess the skills of the child with ASD – in isolation or together with other children (Wolfberg, 2005, 2006a, 2006b, 2007).

The strategies that are employed to guide play vary from orientation (observing peers and activities) to mirroring (imitating a peer's actions) to parallel play (playing next to another child using the same space and similar materials) and, finally, to joint attention (sharing and taking turns in an activity), joint action and role playing (Wolfberg and Schuler, 2006; Wolfberg et al., 2008).

Wolfberg and Schuler (1999) evaluated the effect of this model on the social and cognitive dimensions of the play of three children with ASD. They found a decrease in solitary and stereotypical play and an increase in interactive play. Positive changes were observed in the attitudes, beliefs and knowledge of typically developing peers as a result of their participation in an integrated play group (Lantz et al., 2004). Initially, they viewed themselves as helpers who would work together with children with special educational needs, whereas later they started enjoying their roles. They developed more balanced and mutual relations and some friendships that extended beyond school – at home and in the community. Boucher and Lewis (1990), Charman and Baron-Cohen (1997) and Jarrold et al. (1996) reported that children with ASD can engage in and understand symbolic play when they are given additional supportive infrastructures. But, can they generalise the acquired skills and function effectively when the support from the environment is removed? If not, then children are not essentially independent and they have not learned to play and enjoy the game. It should also be pointed out that the principles of this intervention agree with those of TEACCH.

 Question for discussion

What are the similarities and differences between this intervention and the 'Circle of Friends' described in Chapter 3?

All the interventions presented here have been implemented for some time and tested to a satisfactory extent. In some cases, the interventions were evaluated officially and the authors referred extensively to their benefits, as well as to their restraints. Play-based interventions are quite fascinating, successful and promising, but they are not widespread and applied. You should also explore to what extend their gains could be generalised and attributed to a change in the child or to modification in his environment. To be able to answer these questions, you should bear in mind that:

1. You need to realise that play has an educational role and is not just an excuse to take a break or to give the child a way to spend his time.

2. You have to set one target at a time for every activity that the child has to master.

3. You should not exclude from play children with low-functioning ASD or non-verbal children.

4. You should try, at least initially, to take the child's interests into account.

5. You should develop pretend, imitative and social play.

6. You should teach the child how to play with dolls and puppets.

7. You have to teach the child how to follow a script, to add to it gradually new elements and, finally, to make his own script.

8. You should gradually introduce more people to play (preferably siblings or peers), who were previously instructed how to approach the child with ASD and what to expect from him (please note that Roeyers, 1996, showed that it was more successful in terms of generalisation if peers were facilitated rather than trained).

9. You must be certain that the child can play creatively on his own and generalise his play to other objects, people and environments.

The interventions to teach social play analysed here are not the only ones, but they are some of the few that have been studied. A general observation is that the only skill that seems to be developed is the social interaction skill and not language or basic communicative principles. Most important is to realise that play should be incorporated in all the educational or therapeutic programmes and not be viewed as a simple activity that has nothing to offer. Many therapists use play just to occupy the child while taking a break or preparing the materials for their next task. The play of children with ASD should not be limited to a repetitive stereotype, but should become a productive opportunity for learning and socialisation.

Further reading 📖

Baker-Ericzen, M.J., Stahmer, A.C. and Burns, A. (2007) 'Child demographics associated with outcomes in a community-based Pivotal Response Training program', *Journal of Positive Behaviour Interventions*, 9: 52–60.

Harper, C.B., Symon, J.B.G. and Frea, W.D. (2008) 'Recess is time-in: using peers to improve social skills of children with autism', *Journal of Autism and Developmental Disorders*, 38: 815–26.

Philips, N. and Beavan, L. (2007) *Teaching Play to Children with Autism: Practical Interventions Using Identiplay*. London: Sage.

Sherratt, D. (2002) 'Developing pretend play in children with autism: a case study', *Autism*, 6: 169–79.

Thomas, N. and Smith, C. (2004) 'Developing play skills in children with autism spectrum disorders', *Good Autism Practice*, 5: 53–7.

Wolfberg, P.J. (2003) *Peer Play and the Autism Spectrum: The Art of Guiding Children's Socialization and Imagination*. Shawnee Mission, KS: Autism Asperger Publishing.

5

Sensorimotor Approaches

Chapter overview

Some children with ASD may experience either excessive or inadequate sensory stimulation in comparison with most typically developing peers (Cheung and Siu, 2009; Dawson and Watling, 2000). They may have trouble perceiving environmental stimuli and responding to them appropriately. Based on this theory, some ritualistic behaviours, such as rocking, and some self-injurious behaviours can be interpreted as attempts made by the child with ASD to mediate the quantity and the level of the received environmental stimuli (Green, 1996a). This principle informs the basic sensorimotor therapies that I present in this chapter. I have chosen those therapies that were studied more thoroughly and can be used jointly with other interventions to address the needs of children with ASD. I start with music therapy and then move on to sensory integration training and facilitated communication, and also refer briefly to Higashi school or Daily Life therapy.

Music therapy

Music therapy (MT) has been a useful supportive intervention for individuals with ASD since its introduction into the UK in the 1950s and the 1960s by therapists such as Juliette Alvin, Paul Nordoff and Clive Robbins. It is a holistic approach that aims to promote balance between the child's emotional, physical, cognitive and social development. It differs from musical education, music classes and the purely recreational purpose of music, in terms of its emphasis, approach and goals – although there could be some things in common. The goals of musical education and MT are considered to be complementary. Musical training is specialising in acquiring musical knowledge, skills and appreciation of music, while MT is used to achieve goals that are not directly linked to music (Christie and Wimpory, 1986; Daveson and Edwards, 1998; Freundlich et al., 1989). It should be emphasised that MT does not teach the child with ASD how to play a musical instrument.

Music therapy offers a unique range of musical experiences that cause changes in behaviour and develop social skills through activities that correspond to the child's developmental level. It involves the use of behavioural, developmental, educational, humanitarian and/or other approaches. Music improves quality of life and fosters a positive relationship between the child with ASD, his family and the therapist (Trevarthen, 2002), which is construed and evolved through elements of music. Music therapy brings together musical elements, such as rhythm, melody and harmony, with certain therapeutic goals. Reid et al. (1975) suggest that since MT is a non-verbal therapy, it possesses the unique capacity to open up new horizons of self-awareness and self-expression that lead to improved functioning. Music therapy does not teach a set group of behaviours, but it includes many basic elements of social interaction – self-awareness and awareness of self in relation to others. Therapy stimulates and develops the communicative use of voice and pre-verbal dialogue with another individual, while establishing simultaneously the meaning of language development. The child with ASD can also benefit from increased tolerance of sounds, dual interaction and practice in joint attention (Aldridge, 1996).

Music therapy is an energetic process that follows a predetermined course and involves playing instruments (which does not require any talent or special training), singing, listening to music and moving to its rhythm. Therefore, individuals of all ages and all abilities can attain important life goals through music (Wheeler, 1995). When children start MT, they are assessed for a period that is determined by the therapist in a place that is especially designed to lack distractions and make them feel safe. If it is proven that MT is an appropriate intervention for the child, then the educational context is agreed. The therapist determines the time and the duration of sessions, the individual or group instruction format and the therapeutic goals. Sessions may be videotaped to provide the therapist with the opportunity to develop musical elements that are important for the child's progress on a weekly basis. This material is usually private, but it can be shared with parents or other professionals for therapeutic purposes (Berger, 2002; Wigram and DeBacker, 1999).

There are different approaches to MT, the most popular being improvisation music that allows the child with ASD to take over. The therapist uses percussion and stringed musical instruments or his voice to respond creatively to the noise that the child is making, encouraging him to construct his own music language. The instrument and the kind of music that are chosen must be simple and cause a pleasant reaction to the child, so that the therapist can use them flexibly and adjust them to his clinical and developmental needs at any given time. The therapist can respond to the child's voices, screams and movements, which have rhythm and volume and can be organised musically. These sessions are turned into discussions through music. A second type of MT uses modified music. Children listen to music and their reactions are recorded. Then, the music is modified and only the sounds to which the child responded positively are retained. The session's goal is to make MT pleasant for the child and therefore more effective (Darnley-Smith and Patey, 2003). The most frequently used interventions with children with ASD are interactive instrument playing, musical instrument instruction, interactive signing, instrument choice and song choices (Kaplan and Steele, 2005).

The creation of a supportive, trusting and creative relationship between the therapist and the child with ASD is central to MT, since it enhances the development of social skills. The therapist aims to help the child develop self-awareness and interact with other family members. She achieves this by copying his movements, music, verbal utterances, voices and actions. The realisation that sounds are produced and understood is instrumental for the establishment of a rapport between the therapist and the child. The therapist should record sounds that are not threatening, since some children may prefer the drum, while others might consider it unbearable or annoying and prefer the sound of another musical instrument (Bunt, 1994). Music-supported interaction (Christie and Wimpory, 1986; Prevezer, 1990) differs from MT in that the therapist does not develop a relationship directly with the child but instead facilitates (through live music) a relationship between the child and a key worker or parent.

The role of music therapists can be either purely therapeutic or counselling. They work either individually or in small groups using various kinds of music and techniques in order to motivate children with ASD to get involved. They encourage children to sing, to listen to music, to dance, to play some instrument and to participate in predetermined educational goals. They create a familiar musical environment that promotes positive interpersonal interaction and gives children the freedom that they need to discover and express themselves (Pavlicevic, 1997). Music therapists must have professional training in using clinical music interventions in order to address the needs of children with ASD. They must be dextrous musicians with creativity, understanding, ethos and many other skills. They should be familiar with a variety of therapeutic musical applications and relevant research data, be adequately informed about the characteristics of children with ASD and capable of adjusting the therapy to each child's needs. They should also be skilled to create a therapeutic environment, to motivate the child to participate in the therapeutic process and, finally, to communicate with children, their parents, other experts and the general public (Brunk, 1999).

 Question for discussion

In relation to the other approaches presented in this book, MT allows more freedom to make choices about the nature of the interaction with the child with ASD. How confident and trained should the therapist be to achieve this? Could this be a limitation to the effectiveness of the implementation of MT?

Music therapy and autism

Kaplan and Steele (2005) examined the effectiveness of MT on 40 individuals with ASD, aged 2–49 years old, who attended a two-year programme. The primary goals that all the participants met were: language/communication (41 per cent), behavioural/psychosocial (39 per cent), cognitive (8 per cent), musical (7 per cent) and perceptual/motor (5 per cent). Whipple (2004) conducted a meta-analysis of studies assessing MT and concluded that all music interventions were effective. In the literature there are many statements regarding the effects of music on the development of children with ASD in the areas which follow in the next sections (Agrotou, 1988; Brown, 1994; Duffy and Fuller, 2000; Fuggle et al., 1995; Wigram and Gold, 2006).

Interrupting isolation patterns and social withdrawal and enhancing social-emotional development

Social withdrawal and isolation are some basic characteristics of ASD together with lack of eye contact, lack of physical response, lack of relations with peers, stereotypical occupation with objects and maintenance of uniformity in the environment. Individuals with ASD, especially in the first stages of relationship formation, reject physically or ignore the attempts of other people to interact socially. Music therapy uses a musical instrument as a 'mediator' for the creation of a social interaction. The shape, the sound and the texture of the musical instrument do not threaten the child, while they could actually be intriguing (Thaut, 1984). A trained music therapist could construct the whole experience from the beginning, so as to decrease the motor stereotypes or sensory overload that can make the child shut down. Kern and Aldridge (2006) used embedded MT interventions to support outdoor play of youngsters with ASD. They reported that although their social interactions did not improve significantly, the intervention facilitated their play and involvement with peers, since they were attracted to sounds.

Auditory experiences can offer additional tactile and visual experiences. They help the child become aware of the sound and of the fact that there is another individual present, who makes the specific sound. Alvin (1975) used music to create a series of relations between the child with ASD and his musical instrument, the child and the therapist's musical instrument, the child and his music, the child and the therapist's music, the child and the therapist, the child with ASD and other children with or without ASD, and so on. As soon as obstacles are removed and interaction is established, then the music therapist can follow a range of structured musical experiences that continue to provoke the child's interest and take him out of his inner ritualistic world. Although the whole process can be slow and demanding, MT constitutes a unique, pleasant and flexible tool that can be adjusted to the child's changing needs (Nolan, 1989). Music is by nature structured and includes a sense of security and familiarisation with the context of MT, encouraging the child to try new things and to experiment. Taking for granted that several children with ASD have inherent music talent, MT gives them a chance to experience success. Their strengths surface and can be used later on as motives and rewards (Dempsey and Foreman, 2001).

As the child progresses and starts interacting, MT is an effective way to teach social skills as well. Schmidt et al. (1976) discovered that music can contribute substantially to shaping and reinforcing appropriate social behaviours. Wimpory (1995) studied a girl with ASD and reported that MT enhanced her interpersonal contact and joint attention, by combining live music with adult–child interactions. So, she concluded that MT facilitates planning actions that can be generalised beyond the therapeutic setting. Reid et al. (1975) found that music helped teach social skills, which in turn facilitated the socialisation of a child with hyperactivity who used to distance himself from social situations. Moreover, they discovered that behavioural changes that were linked to music were also generalised to settings that were not musical. Nelson et al. (1984) stated that MT may address the social deficit successfully, because it depends mainly on the quality of environmental experiences. Kim et al. (2009) conducted a randomised controlled study with 10 children with ASD and concluded that MT can promote their social, emotional and motivational development. Moreover, Katagiri (2009) reported that background music can constitute an effective tool to increase emotional understanding in children with ASD, thus enhancing their social interactions. It is refreshing to note that some researchers combine elements from different approaches to help children with ASD. For example, Pasiali (2004) followed the structure of 'Social Stories' and developed lyrics, which were adapted and set to the tune of a favourite song of the child with ASD and some positive changes were noticed in their social interaction skills.

Facilitating verbal and non-verbal communication

Music is a 'universal language' that provides bridges of communication between children with ASD and the environment in a non-threatening context. It facilitates interpersonal relations, self-expression and communication. The techniques of MT in the area of communication target perception, symbolism and understanding. The music therapist tries to support and facilitate the desire or the necessity for communication. Children with ASD may perceive sounds easier than verbal approaches, and awareness of music and of the relationship between music and children's actions can mobilise communication (Thaut, 1984). Music therapy enables those who do not have language to participate in social interactions and to express themselves non-verbally. It can lead to the increase of interpersonal synchronisation and reciprocal joint play, turn-taking, listening and responding to another individual. So, children learn to change and adjust to the way in which they communicate (Buday, 1995). Kim et al. (2008) reported that after attending improvisional MT, children with ASD exhibited significantly more and longer occasions of eye contact and turn-taking sessions.

Music therapy sessions usually consist of parallel musical activities, which support the goals that the therapist, the parent or the teacher set for the child. The therapist could observe, for example, a child's need for social interaction with others. To foster this relationship, she can use games, such as musical chairs or circle time with music. She can also encourage eye contact by clapping hands or shaking an instrument near the child's face. It is preferable to choose music that the child likes in order to reinforce many cooperative social behaviours, such as sitting on a chair or staying in the circle together with peers (Baker, 1982). Music therapists usually work with children with ASD because their positive reaction can also be directed to goals that are not related to music. Since there are some children with ASD who sing but do not talk, music therapists can work on language systematically through verbal activities that have a music style. The speech of children with ASD can be supported through songs with simple words, repeated phrases or even repeated syllabi with no meaning. The sentences and the songs that have some meaning are presented in combination with visual or tactile stimuli to further facilitate the whole process (Clarkson, 1994).

The advocates of MT note that some children with ASD have managed to minimise their repetitive speech by singing, but without providing convincing evidence from scientifically sound studies. Since it is difficult for the therapist to compose special songs, she uses songs that already exist and includes repetitive words or expressions from primary school books. All the opportunities that are provided to a child with ASD to sing are considered precious, especially when the songs are presented slowly, clearly and direct the child's attention to the specific activity. Nordoff and Robbins (1985) argue that the idea of a child with ASD who leaves his classroom quietly humming all the lyrics of a song is very pleasant. Moreover, the idea of the same child who attempts to use these words in a conversation outside the classroom testifies to the contribution of music to the development of his language skills. However, there are no published case studies that verify this description.

In the case where the child starts expressing communicative intents and responses – either verbal or non-verbal – music can reinforce speech and sound utterances. Alvin (1975) suggests that learning a wind instrument is somehow equal to uttering speech. It can also reinforce the awareness and the functional use of lips, tongue, jaw and teeth that must be used to produce speech. She also noted that there is a significant improvement in speech comprehension from the use of music in the educational environment, although she did not make specific suggestions on how to integrate music in the school setting. She also stressed that music creates an important communication channel and a model for interaction between parents and children. She does not clarify, however, how parents learn to communicate with their children through music and if they need to attend some seminars or to be trained to implement the therapy correctly.

Music therapy is said to decrease speech that lacks communicative intent. Bruscia (1982) reported remarkable findings when he used MT to assess and to make use of echolalia. He actually mentioned that the echolalia of his participants decreased from 95 per cent of total utterances to 10 per cent regardless of the context. Another finding of his study was that the skills and the abilities acquired through MT can be generalised to many other settings and environments. However, it is not clarified how echolalia was measured and how the generalisation of skills to other settings was recorded.

Decreasing the behaviours that characterise disturbed perceptual and motor development and functionality

Music therapy techniques aim at reducing unwanted behaviours and interrupting patterns of stereotypic movements. Rhythmical activities and moving according to music – apart from the characteristic rocking – could also help. Soraci et al. (1982) observed that music with certain rhythmic characteristics can reduce stereotypic behaviours. When the child with ASD is 'disorganised' from the events in his environment, he is likely to engage in stereotypic behaviours. When these behaviours are reduced or suppressed, then the child can be motivated to engage in productive learning processes. The music therapist can structure a music experience that ensures that motor responses to music are adjusting and not repetitive. Even in this case, MT is not effective on its own, but should be used in combination with an appropriate educational approach.

Kostka (1993) examined whether music in the context of a primary school could influence certain aspects of the behaviour of a 9-year-old child with ASD. She observed and recorded the duration and frequency of hand-flapping and rocking, as well as appropriate participation behaviours in the classroom (for example, to lift his hand to participate in class). She found that the unwanted behaviours decreased when there was a musical activity in the classroom. Buday (1995) also observed that the memory of children with ASD who were taught language together with music in the classroom improved.

 Question for discussion

How is it possible to have music in a mainstream classroom when some tasks require concentration? What happens when music disturbs the other children in the classroom?

Rocking to the rhythm can contribute to the integration of tactile/kinaesthetic and auditory perception and to differentiate the self from others (Thaut, 1984). The songs that are accompanied by movements can be beneficial for the development of auditory-motor coordination and the awareness of body image (Alvin, 1975). Music therapy techniques can be adjusted to the child's developmental level, to break stereotypic behavioural patterns, and to help integrate different sensory experiences and appropriate motor reactions (Toigo, 1992).

Facilitating the creative expression of the self and the promotion of emotional satisfaction

Since many children with ASD respond in a relatively positive way to musical stimuli (Alvin and Warwick, 1997), the fact that music is used to motivate and encourage them is not surprising. Their positive emotional reactions reinforce their participation in other activities that have been designed to promote social, linguistic and perceptual-motor functions. Moreover, music can provide a useful framework with which to develop curiosity and interest in exploration that provides sheer pleasure. The context of MT allows the child to discover and express himself in a way that he has chosen on his own. It constitutes a means of communication and expression that is not threatening, gives pleasure and promotes a sense of emotional satisfaction. Trevarthen (2002) describes the contribution of MT to the improvement of cognitive functioning, the ability to learn and the motor coordination of children with ASD, but without providing sufficient proof.

Music therapy does not aim simply to decrease the child's weaknesses, but it is a process of perfecting and improving his individual virtues. Children with ASD who respond positively to music discover a socially acceptable area where they can express their skills and abilities and learn to interact with safety. Learning a song or a musical instrument could have long-term benefit even for a child who faces many severe problems in both speech and social functioning (Mahlberg, 1973; Myers, 1979).

Supporting families of children with ASD

Supporting a child with ASD through MT could improve the quality of life of the whole family. When the child masters more skills, he can become more independent and able to interact and communicate with other people in his environment. Music therapy can provide several opportunities for positive interaction and for the creation of supportive relationships between the family members and the child with ASD. The family can choose, for example, to go out to places where there is music (Pavlicevic, 1997).

Music therapy can teach family members new forms of interaction, socialisation and communication, while it promotes the generalisation of skills to sessions outside the house. Furthermore, participation in MT allows family members to see their favourite child from a different perspective, to identify his abilities and his weaknesses, and even to

TOURO COLLEGE LIBRARY

observe new responses that have not been recognised until that time. Music therapy can give hope for the future and instil faith in the abilities of the child with ASD (Allgood, 2005; Wimpory, 1995). It is essential, however, to make some necessary preparations so that the family can accept and interact effectively with the child who has learned to communicate through music.

Diagnosing and assessing ASD

Wigram (2000) stresses that MT can contribute to the diagnosis and assessment of children and adolescents with pervasive developmental disorders. Most professionals use standardised tests to assess cognitive, speech and language skills, as well as neurological tests. The assessment that is based on MT reveals strengths and weaknesses in basic areas, such as social interaction and communication. A 9-year-old child was assessed by using Bruscia's Improvisation Assessment Profiles (1987) and the assessment supports the diagnostic criteria for ASD. It is important to construct valid and reliable standardised assessment measures with the use of MT. However, these evaluations are quite subjective and raters have to be very well trained to apply the assessment profiles. This is an interesting alternative assessment suggestion that needs a lot of work to become standardised and widely used.

Some researchers argue that MT can be particularly effective in addressing some characteristic behaviours of ASD. Boso et al. (2007) claimed that active MT sessions could contribute to the improvement of autistic symptoms of low-functioning young adults with ASD. Thaut (1984) suggested an intervention that has been designed to support language, emotional, cognitive and motor deficits. Controlled studies by Edgerton (1994) and Aldridge et al. (1995) have stated that improvisational MT can increase the communicative intent of children with ASD, which is also generalised to other settings. However, these findings have not been empirically supported and there are a few studies that have examined the effectiveness of MT – a fact that is recognised by the professionals who practise this intervention. It is also essential to develop reliable measures of the changes that might occur during the intervention (Wimpory, 1995). Some reports are based on case studies (Monti, 1985), while other studies do not specify the therapeutic procedures that they followed and the participants' characteristics that may have influenced significantly the therapy's outcomes (Toolan and Coleman, 1994). Hairston (1990), for example, assessed the effectiveness of art therapy and MT in four children with ASD and four children without ASD who had severe learning disabilities. She assessed behaviour, socialisation, communication and academic skills. The results showed that during therapy the children who did not have ASD gained more than children with ASD in the four areas of development, but without explaining in detail the procedure that was followed. Kern et al. (2007) used an embedded song intervention to help a young boy with ASD to take care of himself (for example, to wash his hands and to clean up).

It is indisputable that owing to individual differences in the ASD, it is impossible to apply universal rules about appropriate behaviours. Although one child can respond positively to a specific technique, another child may regress or fail to respond. Music can break the patterns of isolation by creating alternative relations to musical stimuli. However, musical stimuli can create stereotypical moves or even sensory overload, so they should always be carefully controlled and structured. Alvin (1975) reports several controversies that can be presented during the therapy of a child with ASD. She stresses that music could also become an obsession, which reinforces isolation and self-stimulation.

In conclusion, music cannot cure ASD like a drug can cure an infection, but it can improve the child's life to some extent. Music therapy teaches and reinforces skills that are very important for the child and constitute the basis for future learning and therapeutic experiences. Accordino et al. (2007) reviewed studies on the effectiveness of MT with individuals with ASD. They argued that although most reviewed studies have provided limited empirical support of its effectiveness, they have used a range of creative techniques to assess MT. It is recommended to apply MT in the context of a therapeutic programme that provides an enriched educational environment for the development of communication and other aspects of the personality of the child with ASD.

Sensory integration

Dr Jean Ayres (1972) developed more than 30 years ago the therapeutic method of sensory integration (SI) (see also Schaaf and Miller, 2005). It is based on the hypothesis that SI is basically a neurobiological process (Hatch-Rasmussen, 1995; Oberman and Ramachandran, 2008) and that children with ASD and other developmental disabilities experience dysfunctions in the integration of sensory data from the brain (Grossman et al., 2009). Smith and Bennetto (2007) studied 18 adolescents with high-functioning ASD and documented that their deficits in audiovisual speech integration and lip-reading can lead to difficulties in speech comprehension and consequently in delayed language development. Fisher and Murray

(1991) describe SI as 'a neurological process and a theory about the relation that exists between the neurological process and the behaviour'. Fisher et al. (1991) present the basic principles of SI: the central nervous system is flexible; the process of SI is realised in the context of a developmental sequence; brain functions compose a complete whole that consists of hierarchically structured systems; adaptive behaviours promote SI; and individuals have the inner drive to develop SI through participation in sensorimotor activities.

Arendt and her colleagues (1988) suggest that although Ayres's theories regarding the hierarchy of the nervous systems and neural flexibility are valid, he has not incorporated them into the theoretical model that he created. Goldstein (2000), on the other hand, proposes a different approach and suggests that the theoretical background of SI is considered to be unfounded and outdated.

The therapy starts with the assessment of the child with ASD through play in a quiet and warm environment that has been designed to make him feel more confident. The therapists collect all the supplementary information that they need from parents. They also create a complete sensory history that provides valuable information for diagnosis, since it allows therapists to focus on specific areas of the child's functioning and to interpret and measure his progress with greater accuracy (Ayres, 1979).

Experts and parents need to analyse the child's sensory patterns in order to understand why he acts in a certain way. So, an unnatural or obscure behaviour can become understood and justified if the child's efforts to overcome certain difficulties are realised. It is also likely that a child perceives the world in a way that differs drastically from the conventional perception of most people. For example, a child who spins objects all the time or spins around himself may be trying to stimulate a system or a sense that does not function adequately, since it is common knowledge that most people are stimulated through movement. However, it is also plausible that the child who has some organic difficulties needs a greater quantity and force of strength that is accelerated through spinning. When you realise the causes of a behaviour, you try to find a better way to help the child discover the stimulation that he looks for in other ways and so to stop behaving in a seemingly inappropriate way.

Then, experts decide if the SI programme suits the child with ASD who was assessed and start to prepare an individualised plan. Of course, parents are not obliged to follow a programme just because their child was assessed, but only if they agree with the whole process. What experts have not clarified is whether the SI programme fits everyone or whether it is not recommended for certain cases. Advocates of SI claim that it is designed for children or adults with sensory integration disorders, auditory information processing problems, pervasive developmental disorder and autism, attention deficit disorder, learning disabilities and dyslexia, as well as speech and language difficulties.

Sensory integration therapists claim that they can help children who go to school, who have problems with their behaviour and their social skills, and have difficulty learning to read, write and understand mathematical concepts. They also suggest that they are able to help children who 'slip' from diagnostic centres because they have not been diagnosed with a specific disorder, such as children with dyspraxia, cerebral paralysis and genetic disorders such as Down syndrome, Beckwith-Wiedemann syndrome and Fragile-X syndrome. It is surprising that one treatment can be suitable for such diverse populations with so many different disorders and such different symptoms. These statements are not supported by scientific evidence, since most studies have been done on children with ASD. Zollweg and his associates (1997) studied children with multiple disabilities, Yencer (1998) examined children with problems in auditory processing and Mason and Iwata (1990) studied children with severe learning disabilities, but in all these cases SI was not proven to be particularly effective.

Sensory integration and autism

Sensory integration is a therapy that has been applied extensively to individuals with ASD to help them overcome some sensory difficulties. This conclusion is drawn by Watling et al. (1999) who evaluated the practices, the theoretical approaches, the intervention techniques and the preferred preparation methods of occupational therapists who were experienced in working with children aged 2–12 years old with autistic features. They reported that the most common practice that they used was SI (99 per cent), followed by the reinforcement of positive behaviours (93 per cent). The most popular theoretical approaches that they had adopted to approach ASD were SI (99 per cent) and behavioural therapy (73 per cent). They actually mentioned that they apply SI therapy to improve the perceptual processing abilities of the brain. Another study by Case-Smith and Arbesman (2008) refers to SI among other interventions used by occupational therapists to treat children with ASD.

To perceive the improvement observed in the characteristic behaviours of ASD, it is important to collect data on self-injurious behaviour, the ability to learn new information, eye contact and motor abilities before and after the implementation of the therapeutic approach (Smith,

1996). King (1987) actually suggested that in order to meet the thera-peutic goals, the chosen activities are really pleasant for the child with ASD because they involve movement, as well as visual, auditory or tac-tile stimuli. It is not clear, however, how King concluded that the children consider the activities to be pleasant, since there is no relevant research. It is also likely that some of the machines that are used upset or stress the child who cannot express his feelings.

It is known that children with ASD differ significantly in their skills. Some children face serious problems in their fine and gross motor skills (for example, climbing, using tools, buttons and zippers), while other children as young as 2 years old are able to operate with ease a PC or a DVD player. Grandin (1996) underlines the need for more research in the areas of sensory processing, shifting the focus of attention and incorporating information from different sensory organs of children with ASD.

Children with ASD may exhibit different types of sensory processing impairments (Tomchek and Dunn, 2007) and may have an under- or over-sensitive tactile system. Some children who cannot tolerate even the slightest touch have problems with daily hygiene, since even washing their hands can be a very painful experience. Similar fluctuation in sensitivity levels is also apparent in the visual system of children with ASD. They may be impressed with certain visual stimuli that are constantly moving and spinning (for example, spinning wheels) or remaining stable (for example, letters and numbers). It is also likely that their visual memory is extremely developed and they can memorise and do a complex puzzle that they have seen only once.

 Question for discussion

A father once told me about his son with ASD: 'My child does not turn around when I stand behind him and call him, but he rushes down the stairs when he hears his favourite song from the radio in the base-ment.' Do you believe this is something that the child can control? Can this response make the father believe that his son is indifferent or disobedient?

There are some noises (for example, a vacuum cleaner) that upset some children a lot, while quite a few cannot be present in environments that are very noisy (for example, birthday parties), something that can lead to social withdrawal, since most places where children go are usu-ally noisy. The concerns and the sensitivities that were mentioned above are also apparent in typically developing children, but not to such a degree that they hinder development in other areas, such as communication and socialisation. Families of children with ASD have described to me adventurous family outings that make the family feel ashamed or embarrassed because children can suddenly have a temper tantrum. I have to note also that parents of children with ASD complain often that their children do not respond to their hugs, which are likely to cause physical discomfort.

The brain functions better when it can incorporate all the information that it receives through the senses in order to create abstract concepts. The integration of information helps the child perceive initially the concept of red, of hard and of round, and then develop the concept of apple and the ability to identify the photograph of an apple. Later on the child can recognise and link the written symbols APPLE that mean apple. Then the process becomes even more abstract and the child may be able to understand the expression 'an apple every day makes the doctor go away'. There are, however, many children with ASD who have difficulty making the transition from symbolic to abstract thinking and so they are 'trapped' in the lower level of thinking that is attached to the present. They may spin the wheels of an aeroplane, but not be able to pretend that they make it fly in the air. This difficulty hinders children from developing cognitive and language structures that are essential for communication, such as the opposite terms: dirty/clean, up/down, in/out, black/white.

 Question for discussion

Having read this information about the causes of social skills deficits of children with ASD, how could you incorporate it in the approaches based on play presented in Chapter 4?

Therapists (for example, Jung et al., 2006) suggest that children with ASD attending SI therapy respond differently according to their degree of sensitivity to sensory stimuli. The child who is extremely sensitive becomes quieter, while the alertness of a child who is passive is increased. Children focus more on the behaviour that will bring about the positive outcome and less on random or incidental behaviour, and they become more caring, their eye contact improves, their interest in their parent's faces and their own reflection in the mirror increases, they imitate sounds and movements with more ease and they start observing things that they were indifferent to in the past. They do not explain, however, how it is possible that a single intervention can cause two completely different reactions, either an increase or decrease in sensitivity to sensory data.

The advocates of SI claim that a child with no language skills is likely to start naming more objects and to make sounds that are not part of his repertoire until the given time. He may have a clearer accent and pronunciation, develop more complex sentences, repeat words more easily and start using expressions spontaneously. He is more willing to interact and communicate with people in his environment and to understand better and fuller the oral directions that are given to him. Many parents describe a new opening to the world, since their children understand better the way that things function and they start to engage in symbolic play for the first time. There is also change in their emotional expression, since they show more interest in the world and greater tendency for interaction. They develop the vocabulary that helps them communicate with the people around them, control the environment, and develop a sense of autonomy and independence that makes them happier. The people who are responsible for most SI programmes argue that since the changes that were observed differ from child to child, they are not able to predict the exact changes that each child will exhibit. However, they claim that they can use specific ways to observe the child's progress, though without defining the nature of these methods. Evidence on the effectiveness of this therapy is based mainly on testimony from parents, who are asked to cooperate closely with therapists in order to generalise the behaviours and the skills that their children have mastered. It is not easy to understand the process by which exposure to a sensory experience can result in so many and drastic changes in the behaviour of a child with ASD. The advocates of this method have not presented convincing evidence for the way in which the reported changes that seem to be assessed subjectively are caused (Cook, 1991).

An example of SI therapy that became the focus of attention during the past decades was the programme of Glen Boman and Carl Delacato (Delacato, 1974) which was designed initially for children with brain damage, but has been used with children with different disorders. Carl Delacato suggested in his book that individuals with ASD experience terrifying or distorted sensations. His method contains activities that stimulate the brain of children who have suffered brain damage. A team of experts assesses each child and creates a programme that corresponds to his needs. The programmes focus on the normalisation of the senses and have been designed so that parents can implement them at home. They include facilities for massage, auditory and visual training, and tasks for smell, taste and movement. All the tasks last 2 to 5 minutes, so that the child does not get bored and the exercises can be repeated if deemed necessary. It is not known whether and to what extent this specific method can help children with ASD improve and overcome some of their difficulties. Cummins (1988) evaluated this programme and concluded that most studies had serious methodological flaws (for example, lack of a control group, non-random selection of participants) that limit the ability to make assumptions about the effectiveness of this approach (Goldstein, 2000). The rationale of this intervention is ambiguous, since it requires family members to make significant financial and time commitments, which may impede the family's functioning. The same criticism applies to most SI programmes that have been presented up to this point or are presented later in this chapter.

Some studies suggest that SI therapies are effective and I present them here – pointing out the questions that come out of their evaluation. Mary Brown (1999), an occupational therapist who implemented the SI therapy in two brothers with autism aged 5 and 3½ years old, reported that there was improvement in balance, alertness and sensory adjustment, language and speech, eye contact and attention. She does not explain, however, how much time passed for this improvement to be noticed and how it is possible that both children – who definitely had diverse characteristics – showed improvement in the exact same behaviours. It is also unclear whether these children were offered another treatment that could have caused the observed changes. Case-Smith and Bryan (1999) explored the effectiveness of SI in five preschoolers with ASD, using videotaped clippings while they were playing freely at the school's playground. It was observed that after the end of the intervention, four children spent more time engaging in an activity and a game that had a specific goal, without increasing, though, the frequency of their interaction with peers. But they do not clarify how SI can result in improved socialisation.

Larrington (1987) reported that the use of an SI programme helped an adolescent with ASD decrease his self-injurious and aggressive behaviours. Although the reported progress in these areas was remarkable, the evaluation of the intervention was retrospective and so it may contain significant omissions or mistakes. It is also likely that these behaviours decreased because of the maturation progress and not because of the implementation of the specific therapy. Moreover, Ray et al. (1988) revealed that SI increased the word utterances of a child with ASD who acquired 13 new words. However, it was not clear whether he used the words that he had also mastered in other settings. Dawson and Watling (2000) note that only one study used more than five participants (Mudford et al., 2000) and no study had included a control group (Burns, 1988; Green, 1996a; Ottenbacher, 1982).

In most studies, the therapy lasts for a limited period of time – although any substantial change in a child's behaviour requires a lot of hard work. Moreover, the effectiveness of SI was based mainly on subjective reports and non-systematic observations. Most scientifically sound studies conclude that SI therapies are either ineffective or as affective as alternative therapeutic treatments (Grandin, 1996; Hoehn and Baumeister, 1994; Kaplan et al., 1993; Shore, 1994) and do not constitute a comprehensive therapeutic option, but they could be used to complement an effective educational approach. A study by Fazlioglu and Baran (2008) that also used a control group to examine the effects of SI therapy on children with ASD reported that children in the intervention group exhibited significantly less sensory problems than control children. However, this finding cannot be perceived as a difference in the general level of functioning that is the desired outcome of most interventions.

Auditory integration

Auditory integration (AI) is considered to be a form of SI that refers specifically to sensitivity to auditory stimuli. It became popular in the 1990s and it was based on the hypothesis that the extremely sensitive hearing of individuals with ASD contributes to the appearance of behavioural problems and hinders learning in educational settings. AI is recommended for individuals with ASD (Hayes and Gordon, 1977) who have difficulties in three developmental areas: auditory processing (issues of attention, concentration and communication), motor coordination (issues of coordination, fine and gross motor skills) and SI (extreme or inadequate auditory and visual sensitivity) (Randall, 1999). The two most popular methods of AI are those of Alfred Tomatis (1978) and Guy Berard (1993), but they are so different that they could be viewed as two separate therapies, thus posing questions about their theoretical background and effectiveness.

Dr Alfred Tomatis (1978), a French otolaryngologist who studied the connection between the ear and communicative ability, discovered that the ear is not just a passive recipient of sound, but the centre of the body's sensory control. Tomatis (1996) suggests that hearing and communication starts during the foetal period. The ear is the first basic organ that is developed during the first weeks of gestation and its formation is completed by the fourth month. When babies are born, they are 'prepared' and 'pre-programmed' to communicate. Tomatis (1996) believes that in the gestational period different traumatic events may take place that cause problems to hearing and so the child loses first his interest and a bit later his ability to use his ear as an organ that allows him to communicate with his environment. This interruption in the auditory process can also cause later difficulties in other areas, such as acquiring speech, concentrating or learning new information. Tomatis (1996) believes that autism is the most extreme example of 'cutting off' hearing and of 'non-hearing'. He does not explain, however, in what way the functioning of the ear of a child with ASD and a child with hearing problems differ or how it is possible that a child with ASD who has 'cut off' his hearing can understand the language that he hears in his environment. He also fails to clarify why the child with hearing problems does not exhibit the same extreme symptoms as the child with ASD. There must be something beyond the functioning of the ear that differentiates them and cannot be restrained to auditory sensitivity or ability.

Auditory integration is based on the simulation of the main phases of the development of the child's hearing and communication. It also suggests that language development follows a predictable undifferentiated sequence of steps. The programme of auditory simulation is based on some basic principles, but each child has his own programme that addresses his unique needs (Collins, 2000). In order to be more effective, AI is implemented in combination with other supportive therapies, such as techniques of SI, motor activities, verbal-motor and visual-motor stimulation. It is not specified how the individual needs of each child are assessed and addressed, since it seems to follow a very specific and strictly predetermined process.

The initial training programme consists of three groups of therapeutic sessions, each followed by a break of four to six weeks. The first group lasts 15 days with daily two-hour intensive meetings and includes auditory stimulation and activities of AI. The children's parents and the therapists meet at the beginning and at the end of the first cycle, which is followed by a one-month break until the beginning of the second cycle, which consists of eight days of intensive two-hour sessions. The children attend sessions of auditory training and can start working verbally with a microphone. After a break of one or two months, the third cycle starts that lasts, again, eight days with two-hour sessions. Each child follows an individualised programme. Therapists meet with parents for the last time to give them some instructions, while the intervention is repeated if deemed necessary or some sessions are added. However, it is not clear what children do in the meantime and to what extent the interruption of the therapy can be disruptive, if the two-hour session is tiring for the children, and when the therapy is inadequate or has to be repeated. Moreover, there is no information on how the therapy is assessed, so as to establish which part is not effective and how it will be modified to bring the desirable results.

During the first phase of the programme, the child listens to the recorded voice of his mother that has been cleared from the lower frequencies and simulates the noise that he hears when he is in the womb; Mozart music that has been filtered in a similar way is also used. This specific phase is called the 'phase of prenatal memorisation'.

 Question for discussion

Does the idea that the causes of ASD lie in the problematic relationship with the mother sound convincing? If the mother's voice can act as a remedy for ASD, then why would the child react differently to his mother's voice when he was listening to it constantly from the womb or from birth until the beginning of the therapy?

The child's reactions to this phase of the programme are (Fisher et al., 1991):

1. The child expresses more emotions and laughs and cries more, often for the first time in his life. He expresses more affection – mainly towards his mother – by approaching her more, kissing her, hugging her or nestling in her arms. However, he may not yet be able to accept her attempts to express love and affection. It is not known whether these observations come from therapists or from parents – and in which context. Is it that simple for a child with ASD to overcome the problems that he faces in communicating and in expressing his feelings?

2. Children with ASD who have not developed speech start to make continuous sounds with high intensity that are gradually modified and turn into babbling. They look more at people around them – although eye contact is not continuous – and they manage to concentrate for a longer period of time. Parents usually report that their child can sit quietly for longer and participate in some simple activities and games. They observe a decrease in stereotypic rhythmical rocking movements and self-destructive behaviours. At the same time, the child can better handle some social situations and so starts asking for the companionship of other children instead of remaining isolated in a corner of the classroom. The periods of 'autistic withdrawal' are decreased in intensity and frequency. When the child listens to the filtered music of his mother, he seems to start being more interested in communication. Much more can be accomplished if the parents are also actively involved and the child starts to accept communication from others. Parents participate in counselling sessions and learn how to support and reinforce their child's opening to communication and how to respond to his initiatives. Each

parent can have access to some means that will help her accelerate her child's progress when he is ready to communicate successfully with others. This second stage of development is achieved easier and faster in children who have speech, but lack the intention to communicate. Still, it is very difficult to instil in children with ASD the intention to communicate – especially when using just an audiotape as a tool. It is equally difficult to believe that all the behaviours that constitute chronic problems can suddenly be resolved. It is positive for the parents that they try to interact with their children because this enhances their self-confidence, but they need to be persistent and consistent to achieve positive results – which may never appear.

3. Children use speech more appropriately and they start using personal pronouns (for example, I or you) or even their first names. They respond more to the efforts of others to interact with them, while looking in the eyes of the person that they talk to. They observe, for example, their mother singing or reading a bedtime story to them. It is difficult to believe that AI can contribute to the improvement of the social skills of the child with ASD. Moreover, the fact that the child looks at his mother is not the most objective indication of communication and social ability, unless he can use and develop it further.

4. In some cases, children participate in the energetic phase of the programme, where they listen to – and repeat if they want – short songs and small words or sentences. This activity encourages speech utterances and allows children to hear their voice better. The programme involves 150 to 200 hours of auditory stimulation that take place in a special centre for a period of 6 to 12 months. The people in charge report that the degree of improvement varies according to the characteristics of each child and comes up to almost 80 per cent of the children who attend AI. They do not report, however, the characteristics of the children who do not respond to the programme, how the reported improvement was measured, if the skills that were acquired were generalised to other settings and were maintained after the intervention ended. There are many children with ASD who know songs and echo verses or advertisements, but cannot communicate even their most basic needs.

The basic principles of AI are the daily briefing of the parent, the regular meetings between parents and therapists, as well as the periodical examination of the child to determine the therapy's course and effectiveness. Dr Tomatis in the late 1950s and 1960s manufactured the Electronic Ear, a device that was designed to re-train the ear by stimulating the muscles and replicating the sounds that the child listens to in the womb. The Electronic Ear enhances the normal auditory functioning of the ear (Tomatis, 1991). Auditory stimulation constitutes an important part of the process of AI. Listening is the ability to focus on selected sounds and interpret their meaning. Listening differs from hearing because many people with perfect hearing have a hard time listening and understanding. Listening is taking place in the brain and not in the sensory organs of hearing. Moreover, Tomatis's method uses the energetic listening therapy and a microphone to further improve the connection between ear, brain and voice. I am not aware of studies that provide scientifically sound evidence for the effectiveness of the Electronic Ear in dealing with symptoms of ASD.

Berard (1993) is the other pioneer of AI who suggested that problems with auditory processing can lead to different disorders that are caused when the individuals perceive sounds as abnormal. He actually suggested that if an individual can hear some frequencies better than others and perceive sounds in distorted ways, then he can develop behavioural disorders (such as ASD, learning disabilities, depression and aggression). Berard used auditory diagrams to choose the children who would participate in AI training. He does not clarify, however, which were the criteria that he used and which therapy he suggested for the children who could not benefit from AI. Berard believed that auditory distortions can be addressed successfully with the practice of the muscles of the middle ear and the auditory nervous system in a way similar to physiotherapy that can heal a traumatised elbow. He actually suggested that, after the end of therapy, the auditory diagrams that had 'peaks' and 'hollows' that corresponded to over- and under-sensitive areas are 'flatter', revealing that auditory distortions have minimised and therefore the problems that were observed in behaviour have improved. However, he still does not clarify how auditory distortions can be corrected and the reported improvement sustained.

Auditory integration and autism

It is clear that more studies must be conducted to examine the effectiveness of AI. There seem to be some individuals with high-functioning autism who are affected by over- or under-sensitivity to environmental stimuli – a fact that contributes to the appearance of problems in their behaviour and socialisation (O'Neill and Jones, 1997; Toigo, 1992). There are some indications that there is a relationship between visual sensitivity and rigid behaviour, echolalia and visual distortions experienced by individuals with ASD (Ayres and Tickle, 1980; Baranek et al., 1997).

Berard used AI with more than 8000 individuals with hearing problems in his clinic in France. Out of the 48 patients with ASD (Berard, 1993), it was reported that one was cured of autism after attending AI therapy (Stehli, 1991). First, it is common knowledge that no one can be 'cured' of autism as if it were flu or a virus. Moreover, it is hard to believe that the improvement that was reportedly observed in just one individual is due to AI alone and not to external factors. Approximately 98 per cent of the patients with ASD had no change in behaviour.

Rimland and Edelson (1995) measured the effectiveness of AI in eight individuals with ASD aged 4 to 21 years old over a period of three months. In comparison to the control group, their behaviour improved, but sensitivity to sound was not reduced. The researchers do not specify who participated in the control group and which were the observed areas of improvement, since an individual's behaviour has different aspects. Even if there was an improvement, it could be due to the fact that they attended a therapy, whereas they were not receiving any before. Moreover, a study conducted without a control group (Rimland and Edelson, 1994) and a controlled study (Edelson et al., 1999) that presented the benefits of AI did not provide convincing arguments to support even the smallest improvement.

Most conducted studies do not report any benefits from attending AI therapy. Link (1997) followed the progress of three boys with ASD who used the device of Berard (1993). No beneficial effect was detected in behaviour and there was no observed change in their sensitivity to sound. Moreover, four well-controlled studies were published (Bettison, 1996; Gillberg et al., 1997; Smith, 1996; Zollweg et al., 1997), which did not document any benefit from AI. Rimland and Edelson (1998) responded to the negative findings of Gillberg and her colleagues (1998) regarding the ineffectiveness of AI in nine children with ASD and argued that both the statistical analysis and the visual inspection of the findings 'showed clearly positive effects'. This observation, however, did not change the impression that AI is not that effective, as also highlighted by Patricia Howlin (1996). Rimland and Edelson (1998) responded to the negative evaluation of Howlin (1996) and said that she based her comments on their pilot study and not on their main study.

So, the few studies that support the effectiveness of AI are based on parental narrations and provide minimum information on behavioural measurement techniques, as well as the statistic measures to evaluate the reported results. Although the initial enthusiasm for a new therapy provokes general interest, it is not sufficient to consider the therapy effective. There is a need for scientifically sound studies, which will provide the necessary evidence – this is not the case for AI (Murray and Anzalone, 1991). The writers of some articles that were published about the method of AI have expressed their concerns about its methodological weaknesses – like the statistical analysis of data, the low number and the sampling procedures of the participants, as well as the interpretation of results (Bettison, 1996; Goldstein, 2000; Gravel, 1994; Rimland and Edelson, 1992, 1994, 1995, 1999). Moreover, the auditory diagrams that are used to assess the progress of children with ASD are not always accurate, as reported by Klin et al. (1992), since there are often small variations from activity to activity even in typically developing children. It should also be noted that a change in auditory diagrams cannot be connected arbitrarily with a change in behaviour.

Another important parameter that makes researchers sceptical towards AI is that it is based on theories that are not congruent with contemporary knowledge about the auditory system (Berkell et al., 1996). Rimland and Edelson (1994) who are the warmest advocates of AI claim that the essence is that it is effective and not whether it has a sound theoretical background or not. However, the theory on which a therapy is based is essential for its effectiveness. Some products that are necessary for AI have not been approved by official state bodies (Tharpe, 1999). Moreover, AI is introduced by doctors who may not be familiar with some basic psychological, emotional and behavioural characteristics of autism – and many children with ASD do not have auditory problems. This information does not allow experts to conclude that AI is an effective treatment for ASD.

Visual therapies

Several children with ASD have tried numerous visual therapies that include eye movement exercises, contact lenses and coloured filters, which aim to improve visual processing and spatial perception that could be linked to some characteristics of ASD (for example, unusual visual stereotypes, coordination problems, strabismus and attention problems). There are individual reports about the effectiveness of visual therapies, but scientific studies measuring their effectiveness for children with ASD are very limited. There are only three studies that have been conducted from the same group of scientists and examine ambient lenses (Carmody et al., 2001; Kaplan et al., 1996, 1998), but they have reached different conclusions – perhaps due to differences in the participants' ages and in the methodological design. There is a need for more long-term studies by independent researchers who will use well-designed research plans that will be carried out in naturalistic settings. However, it is difficult to establish that apart from an improvement in the function of the optic nerve and the eye–hand coordination, corrective lenses can treat problems such as lack of communication, imagination or socialisation.

Facilitated communication

Facilitated communication (FC) started in Australia in the 1970s, when Rosemary Crossley who worked with individuals with severe multiple handicaps helped a woman with brain paralysis to communicate through a computer by supporting her (Crossley and McDonald, 1980). It is important to differentiate between FC and other methods of augmentative and alternative communication – where people with handicaps handle independently different keyboards to communicate and their credibility and effectiveness is not questioned scientifically (Jacobson et al., 1995). Individuals with ASD seem to enjoy interacting with a computer, because the stimuli that they receive are stable and can be controlled. So, a lot of programmes have been created either by parents of children with ASD or by experts, which can be used at home so that they have enough time to complete the activity that they are performing. These programmes do not aim to teach communication, but to teach cognitive skills such as naming objects – so they are differentiated from FC.

Facilitated communication uses a communication tool (usually a keyboard) in order to support an individual that has a severe communication problem. The degree of facilitation that is required varies from person to person: some people need just a touch on the shoulder that will enhance their self-confidence, while others need help to isolate and to extend their index finger in order to show something or to press a button. A basic principle of FC is that choices are made by the user and not by the facilitator. The direction of the movement is controlled and determined by the user, so he must be stronger than the facilitator (Mulick et al., 1993). However, there is a lot of scientific evidence that questions the facilitator's objectivity in the process.

Training in FC allows individuals with severe communication problems to use communication tools with their own hands. I should clarify that individuals with ASD do not have an issue with using communication, but with understanding its necessity. A communication partner is present at training to help and facilitate the user to overcome neurological and motor problems, such as impulsivity and poor eye–hand coordination, and to learn to point effectively. The immediate goal is to enable the user to make choices and to start communicating in a primitive and effective way. He is encouraged to practise on a board with photographs, on a synthesiser or on a keyboard that can increase his physical skills and his self-confidence and help him become more independent from the facilitator. As his skills and confidence improve, the quantity of offered facilitation decreases. The ultimate goal is for the user to use independently the communication tools of his choice (Crossley, 1994). This was achieved in very few cases, since it has been found that when the facilitator is absent the user's performance starts deteriorating suddenly.

Facilitated communication is not designed for individuals of a specific age group. It has been used with individuals with autism, Down syndrome, brain paralysis and acquired brain damage. The founders stated that it was appropriate for individuals with no or minimal functional speech, who do not have an alternative communication strategy, cannot learn sign language easily, have difficulty making a clear and unhesitant choice and do not have sufficient direct or indirect access to other means of communication (Mulick et al., 1993). They have not clarified, however, how they reached this conclusion and how it is possible that individuals with severe deficits and documented inability to use language can suddenly write words and messages.

When the therapists decide that a person fulfils the unspecified criteria to follow FC, then it is important to: (1) assess the nature of the problem that hinders the successful access to communicative means; (2) select the appropriate therapeutic strategies; (3) estimate which system of alternative communication is the most appropriate for the potential user (objects, photographs, diagrams with pictures, written words, letters); and (4) teach key workers in the user's environment the way to use communicative prompts.

The next stage is to assess other areas, such as writing, reading and fine motor skills. If the user can form words in the initial assessment, then he needs to improve his abilities in the next assessment. If he does not manage to form words, then he must attend a special literacy programme. Word formation constitutes the most reinforced communication strategy for individuals who cannot speak or use sign language with accuracy. Individuals with ASD who are not able to master literacy should be taught a wider range of vocabulary through photographs and symbols. Regardless of the system that they will choose, all users must learn acceptable ways to attract attention and to select the place where they will sit in relation to the people with whom they communicate. It is recommended to train several communicative partners, so that they do not depend on only one person. The level of supplied facilitation must be revised regularly in order to reduce it as soon as possible (Crossley, 1994). These are the basic principles of FC, but it is not known to what extent they are applied in practice.

Crossley (1994) reports that the specific approach can be particularly useful for people with communication problems who are not able to write or use sign language. They must have access to prompts that can be carried easily and can contain pictures, words or letters. The user chooses some of them to communicate without needing to practise or coordinate his fine motor skills. So far there is no substantial differentiation from PECS, presented in Chapter 3. Unfortunately, there are many users who do not possess the necessary skills to show or choose such communicative prompts effectively. Facilitated pointing can produce permanent improvement in the hand's functioning, which is part of a structured educational programme (Shane, 1994). Even when a child has learned to point or to use a picture, this does not mean that he has learned to communicate. There have been several reports of children who point persistently at something they want although there is no one present to see his action and to satisfy his demand.

Margolin (1994) argues that the time that a child needs to be able to use the communicative prompt independently is influenced by several factors, such as the frequency of the use of the communicative prompt, the severity of the problem that each individual faces when using FC, his self-confidence, and the presence of skilful and compassionate facilitators. Children who attend public school and are offered continuous support from their teachers and peers usually progress well. However, not all schools have the appropriate infrastructure and peers are often too overloaded to care for their classmates with ASD. It is also reasonable to assume that the more time someone uses a communicative prompt, the better he becomes at it – but this does not render it automatically effective.

Crossley (1994) reports that many children feel and express the need for emotional and physical contact beyond what is required for therapy and this should be respected. Otherwise, the child may withdraw and stop communicating, in which case all the progress that was achieved will disappear. So, she suggests introducing and reinforcing verbal encouragement that does not interfere with the whole process and is socially acceptable. It is surprising that children with ASD who are not inclined to express tenderness to familiar faces – such as their parents and siblings – express such a pressing need for physical contact with their facilitator. The connection between physical contact and communicative intent is not supported by literature.

Crossley and McDonald (1980) argue that the child's need for support varies according to his mood and his physical condition. He may be sick, tired or agitated, so the facilitator should adjust the help that she provides in each situation. When a child starts working with a new facilitator, he may regress until they become familiar. This is expected, since children with ASD have difficulty generalising their knowledge to different contexts and different people, and so they resist changes. The speed with which a child responds is very important and is assessed at school and improved with practice. Crossley (1994) declares that the provided support does not aim to develop reading or typing skills, but the basic aim is to teach the child to make choices in his everyday life. It is not understood how a child learns to choose when the facilitator interferes too often in the process.

Since the child needs to be able to extend his index finger in order to press the buttons or to point to a picture, the facilitators suggest some activities that should be performed to improve his fine motor skills:

- make holes in balls of clay;
- make holes in a plastic membrane that is stretched over a bowl;
- press a balloon with his finger trying not to burst it;
- draw with his fingertips on tables or big surfaces;
- use toys with buttons or controls;
- play 'educational games' that require him to exert pressure to make a choice;
- make holes in the ground to plant seeds;
- point to photographs or parts of pictures;
- point to puzzle pieces to show which goes where;
- play lotto or domino, pointing at the right piece;
- play piano or other musical instruments with just one finger;
- draw shapes in wet sand;
- make drawings and shapes on coarse paper;
- perform a series of daily activities (for example, turn the lights on and off, change channel, put on music, dial, turn on different appliances).

However, as pointed out elsewhere, even if the child manages to learn to point or to press a button, this does not mean that he has learned to communicate or to make choices, as supported by Crossley (1994).

Facilitated communication and autism

Green (1994) argues that some individuals with ASD possess a 'hidden stock of literacy' that they can express as soon as they overcome their motor deficits. They have problems initiating, maintaining or interrupting an action, as well as stopping engaging in obsessive behaviours. The deficits that they have in speech or fine motor skills could become a serious educational setback if they are not addressed adequately. Although this is valid, it is not clear how FC can contribute to speech development, since even Crossley (1994) herself mentions that this therapy aims only to teach the ability to make choices.

Crossley (1994) has identified the problems that FC can address: inadequate eye–hand coordination; low or high muscle tone; hand tremor; isolation of the index finger and problems in extending it; persistence of choice; the use of both hands when only one is required; problems in initiating an action; instability of the child's trunk and shoulders; and impulsivity.

 Question for discussion

When looking at the problems that FC can help overcome, how is it different from occupational therapy or physiotherapy?

The range of services that FC is supposed to offer causes confusion. The spectacular results that are promised in the area of communication have inspired many families – and particularly parents – of children with ASD who had not shown any signs of communication up to that point and started suddenly sending written messages saying 'I love you' or participating in sophisticated dialogues. It was only natural that many families implemented this therapy in the exaggerated hope of getting the expected benefits (Mostert, 2001).

The effectiveness of FC is based on descriptions and personal testimonies of parents and some therapists, while all the other scientific methods of evaluation of this method were automatically rejected (Crossley, 1994). The children's skills before the beginning of the treatment were not recorded in order to evaluate whether there has been some actual progress. Crossley (1994) argues that the facilitator is solely responsible for failure of the programme, either because she is not trained or because she does not believe in the implemented therapy. She also refuses to have a controlled independent evaluation of FC. Moreover, Biklen et al. (1992) do not provide adequate information on the way that children respond to their parents' attempts to function as facilitators (Schopler, 1992). Green (1994) claims that the approximately 700 individuals with ASD who participated in controlled studies, did not perform as expected because either their self-confidence decreased or because they refused to cooperate. However, she did not explain why they did not do well even in the studies where they cooperated well with the facilitators that they were familiar with. It should also be noted that when in 1988 the Intellectual Disability Review Panel asked to evaluate this intervention, it could not identify a sample.

All the potential participants were clients of DEAL Communication Centre, which refused to cooperate because it preferred a more qualitative methodology that would include naturalistic observation.

In order to evaluate the effectiveness of an intervention, researchers use 'blind' studies, where the access of children to information is limited. Researchers record the children's and not the facilitators' responses to the stimuli that they are exposed to. Kerrin et al. (1998) studied facilitators who operated under the three following conditions: they could see normally, they wore sunglasses or they could not see at all during the therapy session. The findings showed that children with ASD responded more accurately when the facilitator could see normally – even though the facilitator did not believe that she influenced their responses and did not intend to do so. Sheehan and Matuozzi (1996) found that when the facilitators are not familiar with the content of the information, then children with ASD have difficulty passing over the message. Howlin (1997) reviewed 45 controlled studies of FC with more than 350 individuals with ASD and only 6 per cent showed truly independent communication. In almost 90 per cent of the cases, it was found that the responses were definitely influenced by the facilitator.

Another method to examine the effectiveness of FC is to transfer a message, where the child sees a photograph or an object, manipulates or uses an object or carries out an activity when the facilitator is absent. When the facilitator returns, she runs a session with the child who has to describe the object, the photo or the activity that he just saw. Caban (1994) found that 95 per cent of children with ASD responded correctly only when the facilitator also knew the answer and only 19 per cent of the responses were correct when the facilitator did not know the answer. Wheeler et al. (1993) conducted a study where the participants were asked to type the name of daily objects that were presented to them in cards. They typed under three conditions: (1) the facilitators did not see the cards, (2) the facilitators did not assist in typing, and (3) the cards were presented to both children and facilitators, but in such a way that sometimes they saw the same cards and other times they saw different cards. The participants typed the correct word only in the condition where they saw the same card as the facilitator. Moreover, in cases where they had seen different cards, the participants typed the card that the facilitator saw. This study clearly demonstrates that facilitators are the source of typed information. Schiavo et al. (2005) confirmed that individuals with ASD provide more accurate answers when the facilitator knows the information. However, they argued that some independent answers were also correct and this is essential for people who communicate mainly through manifesting behavioural problems.

Since in reality the help of the facilitator is not removed on time, it could influence the outcome. This procedure is believed to produce the 'unexpected literacy' that is revealed from the context, the syntax and the fluency of communication (Biklen, 1992, 1993). The main scientific question is whether FC can 'unlock' the hidden cognitive ability of a child and unveil his potential or whether the facilitator chooses unconsciously the letters that make up the message. Zanobini et al. (2008) examined the authorship of written texts produced by three boys with ASD and argued that core exclusive words used by them testify to their authorship, and are indicative of some level of knowledge of mind and emotions. Since it is practically impossible to determine who types the message, it is worth questioning the findings when:

1. It is believed that the child is illiterate or does not have the necessary cognitive skills to create such a message.

2. The child cannot type messages without the facilitator.

3. The child communicates only with certain facilitators.

4. The message becomes pointless when the facilitator does not know what the child will type.

5. The created messages are hard to believe.

6. The message's content requires life changes.

7. The child has a hard time to create messages under experimental conditions, where the facilitator does not know the answers to the questions that are posed to the child.

There are more scientific studies that do not support the effectiveness of FC in treating ASD (Mostert, 2001). More specifically, Myles et al. (1996) explored its educational purpose and its effectiveness in teaching and evaluating children with ASD on basic academic skills: letter recognition, sound/symbol correspondence, number recognition, as well as words and concepts that involve motion. The results showed that FC cannot be used as an academic tool. Myles and Simpson (1996) concluded that FC seems to have no effect on the behaviours and the social interactions of children with ASD.

Konstantareas and Gravelle (1998) explored the kinds of support that were offered in the context of FC to 12 individuals with ASD aged 7.6 to 21.7 years old who did not use language. In order to assess the literacy skill, they used tests that were progressively more difficult and included reading letters, understanding words, naming objects and completing sentences. The support had three forms: physical, emotional and cognitive. Although children with ASD performed extremely well in all the tasks with full support, emotional and physical support on their own did not have any effect. Therefore, the outcome of FC is determined mainly by the cognitive support that the facilitator provides to the child. This happens regardless of the task difficulty and the required motor complexity and shows that the specific technique cannot address motor, emotional or literacy problems. Finally, Simpson and Myles (1995) conducted a study that lasted 15 weeks with the participation of 18 children and adolescents with ASD and their teachers who acted as facilitators. The children were able to perform simple tasks and respond only to the questions that were known to the facilitators. Although FC is not a treatment for ASD, it could be a communication choice for some children with ASD (Duchan, 1993).

It should also be mentioned that in the USA five major professional bodies (for example, American Association of Mental Retardation, American Academy of Child and Adolescent Psychiatry) have officially rejected FC as a valid way to promote the communication of individuals with handicaps. Moreover, Jordan et al. (1998) reviewed some educational approaches to treat ASD and concluded that there is no reason to continue studying and researching FC. Finally, Probst (2005) conducted a review of 37 controlled clinical studies of FC, taking into account socio-cultural aspects, and concluded that the facilitator significantly influences the outcome and there is no evidence of unexpected communicative skills. Moreover, he brings attention to some ethical issues, which are also highlighted by Kezuka (2002) and by Wehrenfenning and Surian (2008).

Higashi school or Daily Life therapy

The approach that is known as Higashi school or Daily Life therapy was introduced by Dr Kitahara (1984a, 1984b, 1984c) and is based in Japan, but there is also a branch in Boston and in the UK. These schools are designed for people with ASD aged 3–22 years old. They do not accept individuals with multiple disabilities, severe learning disabilities, emotional disorder or epilepsy. This means that they choose to train children who are more likely to improve because there is no co-morbidity and they have a normal IQ. Moreover, even if there is some improvement, it can be attributed to the child's dynamic and not to the therapy that he follows at school.

 Question for discussion

Do you believe that the choice of the children who will receive an intervention can affect the reporting of its effectiveness?

Daily Life therapy includes elements for training children with ASD, but it also places special emphasis and attention on physical activity. It uses behavioural techniques that provide support for teaching new skills and decreasing inappropriate behaviours either by ignoring them or by encouraging simultaneously another appropriate behaviour (Rimland, 1987). This holistic approach incorporates the essence of humanism and reflects the sensitivities, the cognition and the aesthetics of all people in order to achieve harmony in all aspects of life, as supported by its founder. The goal of this educational approach is to raise children with ASD who are as close as possible to typical physical, emotional, cognitive and social standards. There is a fully equipped centre with computers that are used for the development of language and speech. The teachers design academic activities that enhance the abilities of every child and correspond to the curriculum of mainstream schooling, so that it promotes inclusion wherever feasible (Peacock, 1994; Quill, 1989). It is not clear, however, how they promote inclusion and adjust the curriculum to every child's needs.

The curriculum focuses on academic skills, physical education, professional training and arts. Physical education and intense physical training are used to reduce stress, improve physical condition and establish rhythm and routine, based on the philosophy of sensory integration (Quill, 1989). There is also a programme for children who live at school that teaches self-help and social skills, but supporting at the same time daily academic work. So, the children learn gradually to integrate into the wider community in order to stay there on a long-term basis and not spend their life in the controlled school setting. The daily programme works 217 days per year and the open-house programme functions 304 days per year. An extra provision of this school is the seminars and the training for parents that occur through regular meetings. However, it should be noted that there are differences in the ways that each school is run.

Larkin and Gurry (1998) reported that three children with ASD who attended the Higashi school improved. Moreover, the parents of 19 children with ASD who were not Japanese but attended the school in Japan declared through the completion of a questionnaire that the school was very helpful and had exceeded their expectations (Rimland, 1987). However, the participants were not chosen randomly and might not be representative of the parents who participated in the programme. After entering school, all the students participate in practical training in the community so that they can ultimately find a job. However, the percentage of students who might benefit from the specific therapy is not known (Edwards, 1995; Elgar, 1989; Martell, 1996). This method could even lead to the development of more stereotypic behaviours (Upton, 1992).

Further reading

Larocci, G. and McDonald, J. (2006) 'Sensory integrations and the perceptual experience of persons with autism', *Journal of Autism and Developmental Disorders*, 36: 77–90.

Mulick, J.A. (2005) *Controversial Therapies for Developmental Disabilities: Fad, Fashion, and Science in Professional Practice*. Mahwah, NJ: Lawrence Erlbaum Associates.

Whipple, J. (2004) 'Music in intervention for children and adolescents with autism: a meta-analysis', *Journal of Music Therapy*, 41: 90–106.

Biochemical Approaches

Chapter overview

In this chapter, I first discuss pharmacotherapy, since some drugs can be effective in addressing some aspects of the behavioural and neurological profile of some individuals with ASD, and then I refer to several biochemical therapies and diets that have limited documented effectiveness. Pharmacotherapy and biochemical therapies have gained increased popularity because of the commonly accepted view that ASD is a neurological disorder, the popularity of psychotropic medication in psychiatry, and the popularity of homeopathic drugs, vitamins and 'alternative medicine' (Golnik and Ireland, 2009; Levy and Hyman, 2008).

Pharmacotherapy

Drugs are often prescribed to children with ASD, with 83 per cent of those studied by Oswald and Sonenklar (2007) having at least one drug claim in the course of one calendar year. Esbensen et al. (2009) found that 81 per cent of the 286 adolescents and adults with ASD they examined over a period of 4.5 years took at least one medication. Similar findings are presented by Langworthy-Lam et al. (2002) who reported that out of 1,538 children with ASD, a total of 703 took psychotropic drugs, 191 took antiepileptic drugs and 86 took supplements for ASD. They had prescriptions mainly for antidepressants, antipsychotics and stimulants, which were administered primarily to older children with severe ASD (Aman et al., 2005). These percentages are alarmingly high, especially given that only risperidone has Food and Drug Administration approval for treating children with ASD and therefore more longitudinal validation studies are urgently needed to identify potential side-effects (Scahill et al., 2007; West et al., 2009).

Several studies of the pharmaceutical treatments of ASD (AACAP, 1999; Aman and Langworthy, 2000; Campbell et al., 1996; Gillberg, 1996; King, 2000) confirm that although *drugs do not cure ASD*, they enhance the individual's ability to benefit from educational and behavioural interventions (Kolevzon, 2009; Nickels et al., 2008; Tsakanikos et al., 2007). For example, adolescents with HFA may become depressed when they realise their social deficits and their inability to maintain peer relationships. An antidepressant could help them cope with depression while an expert works with them on the cognitive and emotional level. Antipsychotic drugs and tranquillisers are used to treat aggression, self-injury, agitation or insomnia. Again, the ultimate goal is to address the behaviours that are potentially threatening, either to the children themselves or to the people around them, and to replace them with more desirable or acceptable behaviours through some complementary educational intervention (Frankel et al., 2007).

In order to test the effectiveness of a drug, researchers usually randomly assign children with ASD to a group that receives the drug and a group that receives a placebo (for example, sugar) (Broadstock et al., 2007). Potential differences in the behaviour of the children who took the drug indicate its effectiveness (Akhondzadeh et al., 2008; Erickson et al., 2007; Wisniewski et al., 2007). The few drugs that have been properly tested, but not extensively, with children with ASD are:

1. Haloperidol – more effective than placebo in addressing the social isolation, the stereotypic behaviours and the hyperactivity of some children with ASD (Anderson et al., 1984; Campbell et al., 1996; Locascio et al., 1991; Posey et al., 2008), although long-term administration can cause dyskinesia (Campbell et al., 1997).

2. Fluvoxamine (McDougle et al., 2000), fluoxetine (Cook et al., 1992; DeLong et al., 1998; Fatemi et al., 1998; Hollander et al., 2006) and chlomipramine (Gordon et al., 1992, 1993) – effective in treating some characteristic behaviours of ASD, but some severe side effects have been recorded, such as epileptic seizures, weight increase, constipation and lethargy (Brodkin et al., 1997; Hazell, 2007), especially in children but less so in teenagers or adults (Brasic et al., 1994; McDougle et al., 2000; Sanchez et al., 1996).

3. Antidepressants – ineffective; Marrosu et al. (1987) observed deterioration in hyperactivity and aggression after the administration of benzodiazepines (McCormick, 1997; Ratey et al., 1989; Realmuto et al., 1989).

Parents resort to pharmacotherapy mainly when their child manifests destructive behaviours – either for himself or for the people around him – or has co-morbid organic problems, such as epileptic seizures (Tuchman, 2004). Drugs are also administered to children who do not have access to alternative supportive services, in order to suppress some unwanted behaviours. However, since drugs do not treat ASD and could have severe side effects, it is recommended to offer at the same time appropriate cognitive, behavioural or emotional training and support (Anyanwu, 2007; Carlson et al., 2006; Handen and Lubetsky, 2005; Matson and Dempsey, 2008; Scahill, 2008).

 Question for discussion

A child with ASD and attention deficit is given stimulants to improve his concentration skills. Will there be any difference in his behaviour? What will happen if he stops taking the medication? Does he need to receive behavioural training at the same time? Will this cure his ASD?

Secretin

Secretin is a polypeptic hormone that serves as a message carrier from the upper small intestine to the pancreas and liver and has been used for regulating gastric functioning for the past 20 years. The secretin that is administered intravenously is either porcine natural or synthetic. Secretin made the headlines in the USA in 1998, when a mother of a boy with ASD who was given secretin to deal with a gastrointestinal problem observed that his ability to concentrate improved substantially. The relevant articles attracted the attention of Dr Bernard Rimland (1998), who conducted numerous studies on the effectiveness of secretin. In one of these studies, the father of a child with ASD who took secretin reported that in just three weeks his child who knew only two words had acquired an extensive vocabulary of hundreds of words, including short sentences (Beck and Rimland, 1998). This parent's testimony was very promising, but also hard to accept by people who know the difficulties that children with ASD face in speech and communication.

After the USA, secretin became widely known in the UK when Billy Tommey was administered secretin and his father observed that after the injection there was a dramatic improvement in his concentration, his alertness, his social interactions, his eye contact and his bowel control. There is no information on the time period that these improvements lasted and how often he had to be injected in order to maintain them. Despite the fact that parental testimonies were fragmentary and subjective, without providing sufficient information on the course of secretin administration that was not approved by the relevant bodies, they created a wave of excitement that swept over parents and professionals who were rushing to get it. Still, a lot of questions remain unanswered; for example:

1. It is not known which child with ASD is the most appropriate candidate for secretin. Initially, it was assumed that some categories of children with ASD would benefit more, but to date this has not been proven. It is suggested that children with diarrhoea respond better to secretin – possibly because it treats their gastrointestinal problems (Kern et al., 2002).

2. The recommended dosage is not known, and so one might get to the point of administering very high doses in regular intervals and cause severe side effects. Some suggest that there must be a five- to six-week interval between injections, but this is just speculation and is not based on scientific evidence.

3. The benefits that parents have reported in the areas of eye contact, self-awareness, sociability and speech have been evaluated with subjective criteria and are not supported by independent researchers (Goulet et al., 2001). It is also very naive to believe that fundamental problems, such as those of communication and sociability, which need many years of systematic work to improve, are 'fixed' with an injection.

4. Although initially no side effects were reported, it became known that some days or weeks after the injections, there were symptoms of increased hyperactivity and aggression. Since there is no control group, it is difficult to estimate which are the exact side effects and if the reported problems are caused by secretin or by autism. Dr Reichelt (1998) expresses his concerns because this hormone has not been tested experimentally, even on animals. There is also a danger that secretin may wear off gradually and cause allergic reactions.

In an attempt to address these questions, some controlled studies were conducted to provide a more substantiated view. Horvath et al. (1998) administered intravenous secretin to three children with ASD, who were relieved from their gastrointestinal symptoms after five weeks. The researchers mentioned that there was an increase in their eye contact, in their alertness and in their speech. However, this finding should be viewed with caution, since the participants were few and information is incomplete on their diagnosis and the ways their behaviours were measured. Lonsdale and Shamberger (2000) also talked about a significant improvement in 39 out of the 49 participants in their study, both in their behaviours and in their bowel control, without presenting the necessary evidence. If one accepts that secretin affects gastrointestinal function, it may have influenced bowel function that in turn limited the discomfort that children feel, but this does not constitute a substantial behavioural change. Toda et al. (2006) reported that seven out of the 12 children who were administered intravenous secretin showed improved performance in ADI-R, while two showed deterioration. Even if improvement was observed in 58 per cent of the cases, the deterioration in symptoms observed in 17 per cent of the children should not be overlooked.

Apart from the few systematic studies that presented some ambiguous results, most studies have concluded that secretin does not affect the behaviour of children with ASD (Carey et al., 2002; Chez et al., 2000; Dunn-Geier et al., 2000; Handen and Hofkosh, 2005; Owley et al., 1999; Posey et al., 2008). Coniglio et al. (2001) administered only one dose of intravenous secretin to 60 children with ASD and assessed them behaviourally and neurologically before the injection and three to six weeks later. The assessment of language skills and behaviours did not reveal significant differences between the control and the experimental groups. Sturmey (2005) reported that none of the 15 double-blind randomised controlled studies that he reviewed concluded beyond doubt that secretin is effective in treating ASD.

One additional factor that hinders the evaluation of the effects of secretin is that there are three kinds of secretin that can cause different reactions: porcine secretin (Kern et al., 2002), synthetic secretin (Molloy et al., 2002) and homeopathic secretin (Robinson, 2001). Unis et al. (2002) attempted to compare the effectiveness of two different kinds of secretin in 85 children with ASD who were randomly divided into three groups – one receiving porcine secretin, one receiving synthetic secretin and one control group. The researchers, the parents and the teachers recorded the behaviour and the language skills of the children one week before and four weeks after the administration. It was found that the two kinds of secretin did not decrease the participants' autistic characteristics.

Since the injection is quite a painful process that scares a lot of children and intravenous injection may cause more severe side effects, some have experimented with epidermal secretin. It has to be mixed with a substance called DMSO that allows its absorption through the skin (MacNeil, 2001). Although there have been only limited studies on this method, Lawson (2001) argued that a 2½-year-old with aphasia and ASD who received daily injections of secretin showed increased and prolonged developmental progress. However, this study included only one child, the alleged progress was not defined accurately and the substance DMSO may allow the absorption of other substances, such as body creams and perfumes.

The studies in this section have many methodological weaknesses and have failed to answer the following questions:

1. If the first and second administrations do not bring the expected results, is it worth repeating the process? Apart from the financial cost, which is a barrier for many families, could it endanger the child's health?

2. How much time goes by before any benefits of secretin are discontinued? Some claim that the benefits appear two weeks after the injection and last for three to four weeks, but these claims are subjective and unsubstantiated.

3. If one assumes that there are some benefits apart from relief from gastrointestinal problems, is it possible that they all appear and disappear simultaneously? What happens if the bowel control is maintained and the ability to concentrate is lost? Do adults keep injecting the child? If yes, what will be the consequences?

 Question for discussion

If the parents of a child with ASD tell you that they want to try out secretin, what would you advise them to do? What evidence would you present to support your opinion?

Although, as stressed repeatedly, the findings of studies on secretin are negative and discouraging, it seems that the first enthusiastic parental testimonies that were made public keep alive the interest of some families for secretin – even though overall interest has decreased substantially (Esch and Carr, 2004). Although so far there has been no report of serious and extensive side effects from the administration of secretin, most studies have used only one dosage and the possible side effects of long-term use are still unknown. In conclusion, the use of secretin has not been proven effective in the treatment of ASD and it could cause severe side effects (Molloy et al., 2002).

Other biochemical therapies

Biochemical therapies are based primarily on non-scientific observations. Dr Bernard Rimland, who has a child with ASD, is an advocate of most biochemical therapies that he has tested in small groups of children with ASD, but without providing adequate information on their characteristics, the administered dosages and the exact changes that were observed in their behaviours. He has not referred to the side effects that were recorded and were due either to the use of external substances or to the removal of substances from the diet at a crucial age. For example, McAbee et al. (2009) reported permanent visual loss in an adolescent with ASD due to dietary vitamin A deficiency following a restrictive diet. Although the evidence on the effectiveness of these studies is disputed, they are briefly presented so as to inform those who will hear or read about them in an often uncontrolled environment (Green, 2007; Green et al., 2006; Regehr and Feldman, 2009).

Casein and gluten-free diet

There is an assumption that ASD might be caused by a missing or dysfunctional digestive enzyme leading to inefficient digestion of proteins (for example, wheat, cow's milk, corn, sugar). It is reported that some children also exhibit certain physical problems that are almost unnoticed, such as excessive thirst, excessive lack of body temperature control, redness in the face and/or ears with black circles under the eyes. Some support the idea that the digestive process that converts proteins into amino acids (which cells can use) stops at the intermediate stage of peptides, which (if they manage to pass through the gut wall and the blood-brain barrier) can mimic (and so interfere with) brain neurotransmitters (Buxbaum et al., 2006; Comoletti et al., 2004; De Jaco et al., 2008). Gluten is a mixture of proteins that is found in products of grains, such as bread, while casein is a protein that is found in milk. There are several non-scientific reports (for example, Adams and Conn, 1997), claiming that some individuals with ASD who consume milk, bread or similar products exhibit increased negative behaviours. Therefore, they suggest that these substances should be removed from their diets (Kvinsberg et al., 1996; Whitley et al., 1999). However, most researchers did not find data to support these claims (Irvin, 2006; Levy et al., 2007).

If the parents of a child with ASD intend to subject him to such a diet – which is very strict and restrictive – they need to consult a doctor or a dietician. Depriving the child of these foods might cause problems with his development or some significant side effects, such as stomach ache, stress and bad moods. Reichelt (1981) and Rimland (1996) report that parents noticed an improvement in their child's behaviour within a few hours or days. However, Harrison et al. (2006) argued that parental reported improvements in some ASD symptoms are not validated by scientific data. Children who respond better (according to parental reports) usually have a history of ear infections, they cannot be consoled when they cry, they do not sleep enough, and they have an extreme desire for milk and dairy products. The same researchers claim that this intervention is quite harmless, and so they recommend that all children should try it to see how they will respond to it. Seung et al. (2007) tried to conduct a retrospective double-blind clinical trial, but did not find that a gluten-free and casein-free diet was effective in treating ASD. Finally, it should be mentioned that the ketogenic diet has recently received some attention, but findings are inconclusive (Evangeliou et al., 2003; Kossoff et al., 2009).

 Questions for discussion

How can the parents of a child with ASD teach him to follow a diet? How easy is it to monitor what he eats? What happens when he is at school and away from parental control? How can he learn to identify the gluten or casein that is not visible in some products?

Therapy with vitamins (B6 and C)

Some parents of children with ASD reported that their children's condition improved after taking vitamins, and Dr Rimland and other researchers developed a therapy with vitamins and minerals that they considered to be particularly effective for certain individuals. They suggested taking B6 in combination with other vitamins and minerals in order to help the body metabolise B6 and magnesium. Adams et al. (2006) concluded that vitamin B6 is abnormally low in individuals with ASD and this might explain the benefits of high-dose vitamin B6 supplementation in some children and adults with ASD. The reported improvements are observed usually in: speech, sleep, irritability, attention span, self-stimulation and overall health. In some cases, the improved behaviour appears in just a few days. However, this vitamin must be taken for 60–90 days in order to bring about any results. Smith (1996) mentioned that there are at least 15 studies that support vitamin B6 in combination with magnesium can help children with ASD to a satisfactory extent. However, there are many other studies showing that vitamin B6 had absolutely no positive effects on children with ASD (Findling et al., 1997; Tolbert et al., 1993).

Vitamin C deficiency can cause depression and confusion, which are symptoms often encountered in individuals with ASD. Rimland (1997) administered vitamins B5, B6 and C to children with ASD, but the dosage of vitamin C was too low and so it was difficult to study its effects. The second relevant study was conducted by Dolske

(1993) on 18 children with ASD and showed that the higher the administered dosage, the more favourable the observed effects. He concluded that vitamin C can be taken in high dosages without causing severe side-effects, but it can cause diarrhoea – in which case it should be discontinued. The critics of therapies based on vitamins mention that the main methodological flaw of most studies is that they were based on personal accounts of parents and staff, and not on evaluations by independent observers (Smith, 1996). They also raise some questions about the administration of high dosages of these substances. For example, a possible side effect of high dosages of B6 is damage of the nervous system, while extreme dosage of magnesium can decrease the heart rate and weaken the reflexes (Deutsch and Morrill, 1993). Extreme caution should be exercised in prescribing the dosage. Autism Research in the USA (www.autism. com) provides some instructions for the therapy of B6 and magnesium, and it includes a detailed description of the therapy, a diagram for dosage and extended relevant literature. In conclusion, it is not recommended to give vitamins to children with ASD without any control just because they are generally considered to be harmless and they can be bought without a doctor's prescription.

Iron deficiency

Iron contributes to the initial stages of brain development (Oski, 1993) and its deficiency may cause psychomotor problems (Lozoff, 1988; Moffatt et al., 1994; Walter et al., 1989) since it affects more than 200 enzyme functions, such as energy consumption, hormonal balance, muscle function and physical activity (Dallman, 1986; Enwonwu, 1989). Iron deficiency can be treated with relative ease, but its negative effects may be irreversible (Idjradinata and Pollit, 1993). Latif et al. (2002) did blood tests in 96 children (52 with ASD and 44 with AS) and discovered that a significant amount (almost 15 per cent) had iron deficiency, which can affect cognition, emotion and concentration. They also argue that more relevant studies are needed to validate the effect that iron deficiency may have on the aetiology, and possibly on the treatment, of ASD. But given that many children with ASD (the remaining 85 per cent) do not have low iron – and an equal number of typically developing children have iron deficiency – it cannot be stated that one cause of ASD was detected. This deficiency can be treated in order to decrease possible physical consequences, but not ASD.

Further reading 📖

Beck, N.H., Cataldo, M., Slifer, K.J., Pulbrook, V. and Guhman, J.K. (2005) 'How can parents teach their children with ASD to swallow pills? Teaching children with attention deficit hyperactivity disorder and autistic disorder how to swallow pills', *Clinical Paediatrics*, 44: 515–26.

Gillberg, C. (1996) 'The psychopharmacology of autism and related disorders', *Journal of Psychopharmacology*, 10: 54–63.

Schall, C. (2002) 'Consumer's guide to monitoring psychotropic medication for individuals with autism spectrum disorders', *Focus on Autism and Other Developmental Disabilities*, 17: 229–35.

Smith, T. (1996) 'Are other treatments effective?', in C. Maurice, G. Green and S.C. Luce (eds), *Behavioural Intervention for Young Children with Autism: A Manual for Parents and Professionals*. Austin, TX: PRO-ED. pp. 45–9.

Other Approaches

Chapter overview

In this chapter, I briefly present two psychoanalytic therapies that are based on inaccurate theories (namely, a problematic relationship between the child with ASD and his mother). Psychoanalysis uses communication – either verbal or non-verbal – an area where it is documented that children with ASD face great challenges. So, it is difficult to understand how a child who is not able to grasp the meaning and the basic principles of communication can interact effectively with the psychotherapist and resolve his 'problematic' relationship with his mother. Even the American Academy of Child and Adolescent Psychiatry reported in 1999 that different forms of psychotherapy are not effective in dealing with ASD and therefore they should not be applied. However, since some parents and professionals opt for these treatments, I am going to present them in a critical prism. The two most popular forms of psychoanalysis that have been used with children with ASD are: psychoanalytic psychotherapy and holding therapy. I also present Son-Rise programme or Options, which was set up in opposition to psychodynamic views of autism and is not based on psychoanalysis, any more than it is based on ABA, although there may be some common elements to both.

Psychoanalytic psychotherapy

Psychoanalytic psychotherapy has been advertised as a means of treating children with ASD (Beratis, 1994; Bromfield, 2000), since the problems they face are wrongly attributed to parental (and mainly maternal) rejection. If parents come to adopt this erroneous assumption, then they will feel guilty and they may not be able to act effectively as parents. Ana Alvarez (1992) claims that modern psychoanalytic theory can be used to shed new light on ways of understanding children with ASD. Psychotherapists try to correct the dysfunctional relationship that supposedly exists between children with ASD and their parents in order to help them overcome their difficulties. They have not clarified, however, how this can be achieved and there are no scientifically sound studies that assess and support the advertised benefits of psychoanalytic psychotherapy. Many psychoanalysts claim that the only way to evaluate the accomplished gains is through qualitative means, but they have not employed them yet. Another reason why psychotherapy may prove extremely challenging for children with ASD is that the session is not structured – a fact that may cause distress to these children who feel safe in a predictable environment (Smith, 1996). Psychoanalysis cannot work with low-functioning children with ASD who are not able to interact with other people. So, there is no published scientific evidence that a child with ASD could benefit from attending sessions of psychoanalytic psychotherapy. This is also reflected in the lack of relevant studies in the specific approach as a method for treating ASD in recent years.

 Question for discussion

How could you engage a child with ASD in meaningful psychoanalytic psychotherapy? How would you try to overcome any communication barriers?

Holding therapy

Holding therapy was described by Martha Welch (1989) in her book *Holding Time*. She is a child psychiatrist from New York, who started using holding therapy to work with children with ASD believing that ASD is caused by the children's inability to create a bond with their parents. The therapist or the parent forcefully holds the child until he stops resisting or until a specified amount of time elapses. During holding therapy, the parents try many ways to come into contact with their child; they try to console the child if he looks upset, and they hold the child for long periods of time even if he resists the hug (Welch, 1998). The child sits or lies down looking at the face of the parent who tries to maintain eye contact and to verbally share her feelings throughout the whole holding session. The parent seems calm, relaxed and in control of the situation, while she responds tenderly to the child when he finally stops resisting (Richer, 1991, 1992).

Questions for discussion

How could a child with ASD restore his relationship with a parent who holds him against his own will? How could a parent remain relaxed when holding down her screaming child?

Sometimes, the parent is advised not to free the child, until he starts developing eye contact. I still fail to understand why eye contact is deemed so important in restoring the parent–child bond, especially since it is associated with negative feelings caused by the violent hug. Despite the fact that this technique was designed initially for adults with ASD, it has also been used with children, adolescents and young people with 'attachment disorders' – although it has not been scientifically proven that children with ASD experience attachment difficulties with their parents. Even though holding therapy is not that popular any more, those who practice it defend it and claim that it can 'be good'. However, the same excuse has been offered for the use of other harsh discipline measures that professionals do not endorse. It should be emphasised that this therapy 'defies' the basic principle of parent–child attachment, that is, mutual trust. The child with ASD will have difficulty restoring the genuine trust towards the parent who was holding him violently, even if she meant well.

Timbergen and Timbergen (1983) claim that holding therapy is a variation of sensory integration and that it helps the child with ASD adjust to and overcome the sensory overload that he experiences. Some high-functioning individuals with ASD who are able to share their thoughts and experiences have protested against holding therapy, which they characterise as 'traumatic'. Temple Grandin (1995) has stated that the mother must not hold her child against his will, because she will provoke negative feelings. Holding therapy is violating the child's human rights, since the release of forbidden and suppressed feelings cannot be achieved in a violent way. Children with ASD deserve the same respect as other individuals with or without special needs.

The child experiences intense fear, confusion, helplessness, anger and betrayal as he tries to escape from the adult's arms. Even if an emotional catharsis could be achieved, the emotional cost that the child would have to pay would be too great. It is also difficult to estimate the potential future implications; it is very dangerous to teach children to tolerate violate hugs. They become familiar with behaviours that may even lead to sexual abuse and exploitation. In conclusion, this therapy has not been proven effective in dealing with ASD and it may even cause serious problems in the often fragile parent–child relationship. Again, there is no published scientifically valid research on this method, explaining its limited effectiveness and application.

Son-Rise Programme or Options

Son-Rise Programme or Options was created in 1983 by Barry Neil Kaufman and Samantha Lyte Kaufman in their attempt to teach their son Raul, who was diagnosed with autism. Later the Kaufmans wrote a book entitled: *Son-Rise: The Miracle Continues* (Kaufman, 1994) and founded the Option Institute in Massachusetts, which aims to educate families who want to follow the suggested programme at home with their children. The institute delivers a variety of programmes and seminars for people of all ages. The programme lasts from one week to six months. It is designed to teach parents, professionals and supportive staff how to implement at home the programmes that are based on Kaufman's learning theories. It includes a preliminary, an intensive and an advanced training programme. The preliminary programme is a group seminar lasting five days, where the programme's basic elements and principles are presented. The intensive programme is a one-week-long seminar that offers 40 hours of one-to-one interaction with a trained therapist and a child with ASD. The advanced educational seminar is essentially a re-evaluation system following the implementation of the programme (The Option Institute and Fellowship, 1997).

Options emphasises the need for parents and families of children with ASD to accept and understand their behaviour. If adults realise why children with ASD act in a certain way, then they can work out how to help them. The intervention is based on reinforcing desirable behaviours, while negative behaviours are acknowledged and altered. In essence, some behaviours are deliberately ignored, while others are welcomed with enthusiasm. This treatment is very intensive and parents are asked to organise and execute a demanding programme for an extensive period of months or even years (Gerlach, 1993; Williams and Wishart, 2003). Parents are normally expected to work with their child in a room that is especially designed for one-to-one instruction (Kaufman, 1994). I believe that the principles of this approach are valid, but it is doubtful whether this treatment, which has many supporters and many critics (Kaufman, 1976), is as effective as it claims.

Question for discussion

How easy do you think it is for parents of children with ASD to adhere to this treatment programme? Which challenges could they face?

Levy (1998) agrees that Son-Rise cannot guarantee positive results. It is based on learning through observation, prompting and supporting the development of the child with ASD in a tender and non-judgemental environment. The child with ASD leads the programme, while the parent copies his behaviour. When the parent attracts the child's attention by joining in an activity with him, she attempts to expand the activity in order to enhance his communication and social interaction skills (Kaufman, 1998; MacDonald and MacDonald, 1991). It does not teach any specific skills to the child, who is viewed as a rather passive recipient of the whole process. The programme does not place any demands on the child, accepting that his current functioning level is the best that he can achieve and that if he could do better he would (for example, if the child could follow orders, he would). If this viewpoint is endorsed, then some adults may abandon any efforts they make to train the child with ASD to overcome some of the difficulties that he faces. This treatment places emphasis on the unconditional acceptance of the child and encourages him to develop stronger motives to communicate and to actively participate in ongoing activities (Levy, 1998). There are no published scientifically valid studies that assess the efficacy of Son-Rise. The main testimony of its effectiveness comes from its founder, who claims that his son now has a high IQ and his behaviour does not resemble that of a person with ASD. However, this testimony cannot be regarded as proof for the efficacy of this treatment which lacks theoretical background (Jordan and Powell, 1993).

Further reading

Grandin, T. (1995) 'The learning style of people with autism: an autobiography', in K. Quill (ed.), *Teaching Children with Autism: Strategies to Enhance Communication and Socialization*. Arlington, TX: Future Horizons. pp. 33–52.

Jordan, R. and Powell, S.D. (1993) 'Reflections on the options method as a treatment for autism', *Journal of Autism and Developmental Disorders*, 23: 682–5.

Epilogue

When choosing the appropriate intervention for a child with ASD, professionals and parents have to answer the following questions (Jordan, 1999a):

1. Which intervention will be more effective for the particular child?
2. Was the particular intervention successful in the past?
3. Is intervention A better than intervention B for the specific child?
4. Is the intervention carried out the way it was planned?
5. Which child will benefit more from intervention A than from intervention B?

In order to answer these questions you can use the guidelines and the criteria that determine the extent to which a given therapy is supported empirically as being effective. Researchers usually draw a distinction between the efficiency and the effectiveness or the clinical use of a therapy (Lonigan et al., 1998). The studies that demonstrate a therapy's efficacy focus on whether it decreases the unwanted behaviours and it increases the functioning of the child with ASD, and they are conducted under extremely controlled conditions that include random assignment, control group and controls of the procedure's integrity. On the contrary, the therapy's effectiveness depends on how well it functions in certain contexts and situations where it is implemented (Gresham et al., 1999).

Another way to look at the distinction between efficacy and effectiveness is based on external and internal validity (Cook and Campbell, 1979). Internal validity refers to the extent to which changes in the dependent variable (for example, socialisation) are due to systematic changes in the independent variable (for example, in the use of the Circle of Friends) and not to other variables (for example, maturation, or the implementation of a play-based therapy). Therefore, internal validity is essential for determining a therapy's efficacy. External validity refers to the extent to which the findings of a study can be generalised to other settings, other children with ASD, other therapists and other parents/families. Therefore, external validity is essential for determining a therapy's effectiveness.

A report compiled by Bristol et al. (1996) noted several methodological and statistical issues that should be resolved in the future in order to estimate the effectiveness of a treatment of ASD:

1. Studies should use experimental designs that compare different therapeutic approaches. Is therapy A more effective than therapy B in a strictly controlled condition?

2. Children should be randomly assigned to each experimental condition and the therapy should not be applied only to children with high functioning ASD who are likely to do better.

3. Standardised therapeutic protocols will enable the assessment of a range of behaviours and skills both in the laboratory and in naturalistic settings.

4. It is recommended to use external assessors who are not informed about the research questions and the research hypotheses, a fact that hinders intentional or unintentional bias.

5. Therapies must be applied according to the predetermined guidelines. Even if a therapy is perfect in its conception and planning, if it is not applied properly and credibly then it may not be effective.

6. Longitudinal studies can assess the indirect, direct and long-term effects of a therapy and identify what makes it effective in the long term.

Freeman (1997) suggests a list to assess programmes or approaches for the treatment of ASD:

1. Be cautious about procedures or programmes claiming that they can 'cure' all or most children with ASD.

2. Look for scientific data that document the effectiveness of a programme and the way they were collected.

3. Pay attention to programmes that deny having any methodological weakness.

4. Check whether the school that the child attends will agree to implement some therapy.

5. Realise that any treatment is just one of many that exist for children with ASD.

6. Make sure that the intervention is based on the individual evaluation of information about the needs of each child.

7. Do not apply any new intervention before you determine which are the necessary evaluation processes that you need to design an appropriate treatment.

8. Remember that most new and promising therapies may not be scientifically sound, so try to be critical of what you hear and see.

It is difficult to evaluate the programmes and the therapeutic approaches that are used with children with ASD because: (1) there is variation in the behavioural characteristics of children with ASD, (2) it is difficult to control the variables that might affect every therapy, and (3) it is challenging to measure small, but possibly important, changes in behaviour. Even if a therapy is particularly effective for some children, it would be practically impossible to be equally effective for all children with ASD. It is equally plausible that a therapy that is ineffective for most children with ASD contributes to the progress of a few. The heterogeneity and the multiple possible causes of ASD make it difficult to prove the effectiveness of different therapeutic approaches (Lord, 1997). Perhaps a more sophisticated diagnosis of ASD in the future could include specific suggestions for therapy. Trainers, therapists and service providers should constantly evaluate the effectiveness of the therapy that they apply to every child with ASD and keep in mind that the most effective contemporary approach to ASD includes early intervention, low teacher/student ratio, family participation and individualised instruction.

Further reading

Sherer, M.R. and Schreibman, L. (2005) 'Individual behavioural profiles and predictors of treatment effectiveness for children with autism', *Journal of Consulting and Clinical Psychology*, 73: 525–38.

References

Accordino, R., Comer, R. and Heller, W.B. (2007) 'Searching for music's potential: a critical examination of research on music therapy with individuals in autism', *Research in Autism Spectrum Disorders*, 1, 101–15.

Adams, J.B., George, F. and Audhya, T. (2006) 'Abnormally high plasma levels of vitamin B6 in children with autism not taking supplements compared to controls not taking supplements', *The Journal of Alternative and Complementary Medicine*, 12, 59–63.

Adams, L. and Conn, S. (1997) 'Nutrition and its relationship to autism', *Focus on Autism and Other Developmental Disabilities*, 12, 53–8.

Adams, L., Gouvousis, A., VanLue, M. and Waldron, C. (2004) 'Social story intervention: improving communication skills in a child with an autism spectrum disorder', *Focus on Autism and Other Developmental Disorders*, 19, 87–94.

Agrotou, A. (1988) 'A case study: Lara', *Journal of British Music Therapy*, 2, 17–23.

Akhondzadeh, S., et al. (2008) 'A double-blind placebo controlled trial of piracetam added to risperidone in patients with autistic disorder', *Child Psychiatry and Human Development*, 39, 237–45.

Alberto, P. and Troutman, A.C. (1999) *Applied Behaviour Analysis for Teachers*, 5th edn. Saddle River, NJ: Merrill.

Aldridge, D. (1996) *Music Therapy Research and Practice in Medicine: From Out of the Silence*. London: Jessica Kingsley.

Aldridge, D., Gustorff, D. and Neugebauer, L. (1995) 'A preliminary study of creative music therapy in the treatment of children with developmental delay', *The Arts in Psychotherapy*, 21, 189–205.

Ali, S. and Frederickson, N. (2006) 'Investigating the evidence base of Social Stories', *Educational Psychology in Practice*, 22, 355–77.

Allgood, N. (2005) 'Parents' perceptions of family-based group music therapy for children with autism spectrum disorders', *Music Therapy Perspectives*, 23, 92–9.

Alvarez, A. (1992) *Live Company: Psychoanalytic Therapy with Autistic, Abused and Borderline Psychotic Children*. London: Routledge.

Alvin, J. (1975) *Music Therapy for the Autistic Child*. Oxford: Oxford University Press.

Alvin, J. and Warwick, A. (1997) *Music Therapy for the Autistic Child*, 3rd edn. Oxford: Oxford University Press.

Aman, M.G. and Langworthy, K.S. (2000) 'Pharmacotherapy for hyperactivity in children with autism and other pervasive developmental disorders', *Journal of Autism and Developmental Disorders*, 30, 451–9.

Aman, M.G., Lam, K.S.L. and Van Bourgondien, M.E. (2005) 'Medication patterns in patients with autism: temporal, regional, and demographic influences', *Journal of Child and Adolescent Psychopharmacology*, 15, 116–26.

American Academy of Child and Adolescent Psychiatry (AACAP) (1999) 'Practice parameters for the assessment and treatment of children, adolescents and adults with autism and other pervasive developmental disorders', *Journal of the American Academy of Child and Adolescent Psychiatry*, 38, 32–54.

American Psychiatric Association (APA) (2001) *Diagnostic and Statistical Manual – Revised*. 4th edn. Washington, DC: APA.

Anderson, A., Moore, D.W. and Bourne, T. (2007) 'Functional communication and other concomitant behaviour change following PECS training: a case study', *Behaviour Change*, 24, 173–81.

Anderson, A.E. (2002) 'Augmentative communication and autism. A comparison of sign language and the picture exchange communication system', *Dissertation Abstracts International: Section B: The Sciences and Engineering*, 62, 42–69.

Anderson, L.T., et al. (1984) 'Haloperidol in the treatment of infantile autism: effects on learning and behavioural symptoms', *American Journal of Psychiatry*, 141, 1195–202.

Anderson, S.R., Avery, D.L., DiPietro, E.K., Edwards, G.L. and Christian, W.P. (1987) 'Intensive home-based early intervention with autistic children', *Education and Treatment of Children*, 10, 352–66.

Angermeier, K., Schlosser, R.W., Luiselli, J.K., Harrington, C. and Carter, B. (2008) 'Effects of iconicity on requesting with the Picture Exchange Communication System in children with autism spectrum disorder', *Research in Autism Spectrum Disorders*, 2, 430–46.

Anyanwu, E.C. (2007) 'Autistic disorders: is the use of pharmacotherapy necessary in every case?', *International Journal on Disability and Human Development*, 7, 13–17.

Arendt, R.E., Maclean, W.E. and Baumeister, A.A. (1988) 'Critique of sensory integration therapy and its application in mental retardation', *American Journal of Mental Retardation*, 92, 401–11.

Attwood, T. (1998) *Asperger's Syndrome: A Guide for Parents and Professionals*. London: Jessica Kingsley.

Attwood, T. (2000) 'Strategies for improving the social integration of children with Asperger syndrome', *Autism*, 4, 85–100.

Attwood, T. (2004) 'Cognitive behaviour therapy for children and adults with Asperger's syndrome', *Behaviour Change*, 21, 147–61.

Ayres, A.J. (1979) *Sensory Integration and the Child*. Los Angeles, CA: Western Psychological Association.

Ayres, J. (1972) 'Improving academic scores through sensory integration', *Journal of Learning Disabilities*, 5, 338–43.

Ayres, J. and Tickle, L.S. (1980) 'Hyper-sensitivity to touch and vestibular stimuli as a predictor of positive response to sensory integration procedures by autistic children', *American Journal of Occupational Therapy*, 34, 375–81.

Baer, D., Wolf, M. and Risley, R. (1968) 'Some current dimensions of applied behaviour analysis', *Journal of Applied Behaviour Analysis*, 1, 91–7.

Baer, D., Wolf, M. and Risley, R. (1987) 'Some still-current dimensions of applied behaviour analysis', *Journal of Applied Behaviour Analysis*, 20, 313–27.

Baglio, C., Benavidiz, D., Compton, L., Matson, J. and Paclawskyj, T. (1996) 'Behavioural treatment of autistic persons: a review of research from 1980 to present', *Research in Developmental Disabilities*, 17, 433–65.

Baker, B. (1982) 'The use of music with autistic children', *Journal of Psychosocial Nursing and Mental Health Services*, 20, 31–4.

Baranek, G.T., Foster, L.G. and Berkson, G. (1997) 'Tactile defensiveness and stereotyped behaviours', *American Journal of Occupational Therapy*, 51, 91–5.

Barrett, W. and Randall, L. (2004) 'Investigating the Circle of Friends approach: adaptations and implications for practice', *Educational Psychology in Practice*, 20, 353–68.

Barry, L.M. and Burlew, S.B. (2004) 'Using Social Stories to teach choice and play skills to children with autism', *Focus on Autism and Other Developmental Disorders*, 19, 45–51.

Bartak, L. (1978) 'Educational approaches', in M. Rutter and E. Schopler (eds), *Autism: A Reappraisal of Concepts and Treatment*. New York: Plenum. pp. 423–38.

Bebko, J.M. (1990) 'Echolalia, mitigation, and autism: indicators from child characteristics for the use of sign language and other augmentative language systems', *Sign Language Studies*, 66, 61–78.

Beck V. and Rimland, B. (1998) *Unlocking the Potential of Secretin – Information and Questions for Parents and Physicians Who Want to Learn More about Secretin as Its Use Is Explored in Autism and Other Disorders*. San Diego, CA: Autism Research Institute.

Beckman, P. (1983) 'The relationship between behavioural characteristics of children and social interaction in an integrated setting', *Journal of the Division for Early Childhood*, 7, 69–77.

Bekoff, M. and Byers, J.A. (1981) *A Critical Reanalysis of the Ontogeny of Mammalian Social and Locomotion Play: An Ethological Hornet's Nest*. Cambridge: Cambridge University Press.

Bellini, S. and Peters, J.K. (2008) 'Social skills training for youth with autism spectrum disorders', *Child and Adolescent Psychiatric Clinics of North America*, 17, 857–73.

Benaroya, A.A., Wesley, S., Oglivie, H., Klein, L.S. and Clarke, E. (1979) 'Sign language and multisensory input training of children with communication and related developmental disorders: Phase II', *Journal of Autism and Developmental Disorders*, 9, 219–20.

Berard, G. (1993) *Hearing Equals Behaviour*. New Canaan: Keats.

Beratis, S. (1994) 'A psychodynamic model for understanding pervasive developmental disorders', *European Journal of Psychiatry*, 8, 209–14.

Berg, W., Wacker, D. and Steege, M. (1995) 'Best practices in assessment with persons who have severe or profound handicaps', in A. Thomas and J. Grimes (eds), *Best Practices in School Psychology III*. Bethesda, MD: National Association of School Psychologists. pp. 805–16.

Berger, D.S. (2002) *Music Therapy, Sensory Integration and the Autistic Child*. London: Jessica Kingsley.

Berkell, D.E., Malgeri, S.E. and Streit, M.K. (1996) 'Auditory integration training for individuals with autism', *Education and Training in Mental Retardation*, 31, 66–70.

Bettelheim, B. (1967) *The Empty Fortress*. New York: Free Press.

Bettison, S. (1996) 'The long-term effects of auditory training on children with autism', *Journal of Autism and Developmental Disorders*, 23, 361–74.

Beyer, J. and Gammeltoft, K.L. (2000) *Autism and Play*. London: Jessica Kingsley.

Biklen, D. (1992) 'Facilitated communication: Biklen responds', *American Journal of Speech and Language Pathology*, 1, 21–2.

Biklen, D. (1993) *Communication Unbound: How Facilitated Communication Is Challenging Traditional Views of Autism and Ability/Disability*. New York: Teachers College Press.

Biklen, D., Morton, M., Gold, D., Berrigan, C. and Swaminathan, S. (1992) 'Facilitated communication: implications for individuals with autism', *Topics in Language Disorders*, 12, 1–28.

Birnbauer, J.S. and Leach, D.J. (1993) 'The Murdoch early intervention programme after 2 years', *Behaviour Change*, 10, 63–74.

Boman, G. (1974) *What to Do about Your Brain-Injured Child*. New York: Square One.

Bondy, A. and Frost, L. (1994) 'The Picture Exchange Communication System', *Focus on Autistic Behaviour*, 9, 1–19.

Bondy, A., Tincani, M. and Frost, L. (2004) 'Multiple controlled verbal operants: an analysis and extension to the Picture Exchange Communication System', *The Behavior Analyst*, 27, 247–61.

Bonvillan, J.D. and Nelson, K.E. (1976) 'Sign language acquisition in a mute autistic boy', *Journal of Speech and Hearing Disorders*, 41, 339–47.

Bonvillan, J.D., Nelson, K.E. and Rhyne, J.M. (1981) 'Sign language and autism', *Journal of Autism and Developmental Disorders*, 11, 125–37.

Boso, M., Emanuele, E., Minazzi, V., Abbamonte, M. and Politi, P. (2007) 'Effect of long-term interactive music therapy on behavior profile and musical skills in young adults with severe autism', *The Journal of Alternative and Complementary Medicine*, 13, 709–12.

Boucher, J. (1999) 'Editorial: interventions with children with autism – methods based on play', *Child language Teaching and Therapy*, 15, 1–5.

Boucher, J. and Lewis, V. (1990) 'Guessing or creating? A reply to Baron-Cohen', *British Journal of Developmental Psychology*, 8, 205–6.

Brasic, J.R., et al. (1994) 'Clomipramine ameliorates adventitious movements and compulsions in prepubertal boys with autistic disorders and severe mental retardation', *Neurology*, 44, 1309–12.

Bristol, M., et al. (1996) 'State of the science in autism: report to the National Institutes of Health', *Journal of Autism and Developmental Disorders*, 26, 121–54.

Broadstock, M., Doughty, C. and Eggleston, M. (2007) 'Systematic review of the effectiveness of pharmacological treatments for adolescents and adults with autism spectrum disorder', *Autism*, 11, 335–48.

Brodkin, E.S., et al. (1997) 'Clomipramine in adults with pervasive developmental disorders: a prospective open-label investigation', *Journal of Child and Adolescent Psychopharmacology*, 7, 109–21.

Bromfield, R. (2000) 'It's the tortoise: long-term psychodynamic psychotherapy with a high-functioning autistic adolescent', *Psychoanalytic Inquiry*, 20, 732–45.

Brown, M.M. (1999) 'Auditory integration training and autism: two case studies', *British Journal of Occupational Therapy*, 62, 13–18.

Brown, S.M.K. (1994) 'Autism and music therapy: is change possible, and why music?', *British Journal of Music Therapy*, 8, 15–25.

Brownell, M.D. (2002) 'Musically adapted Social Stories to modify behaviours in students with autism: four case studies', *Journal of Music Therapy*, 39, 117–44.

Bruckner, C.T. and Yoder, P. (2007) 'Restricted object use in young children with autism: definition and construct validity', *Autism*, 11, 161–71.

Brunk, B.K. (1999) *Music Therapy: Another Path to Learning and Communication for Children in the Autistic Spectrum*. Arlington, TX: Future Horizons.

Bruscia, K. (1987) *Improvisational Models of Music Therapy*. Springfield: IL: Charles C. Thomas.

Bruscia, K.E. (1982) 'Music in the assessment of echolalia', *Music Therapy*, 2, 25–41.

Bryen, D.N. and Joyce, D.G. (1985) 'Language intervention with the severely handicapped: a decade of research', *Journal of Special Education*, 19, 7–39.

Bryson, S.E., Koegel, L.K., Koegel, R.L., Openden, D., Smith, I.M. and Nefdt, N. (2007) 'Large scale dissemination and community implementation of Pivotal Response Treatment: program description and preliminary data', *Research and Practice for Persons with Severe Disabilities*, 32, 142–53.

Buckman, S. (1995) 'Lovaas revisited: should we have ever left?', *Indiana Resource Center for Autism Newsletter*, 8, 1–7.

Buday, E.M. (1995) 'The effects of signed and spoken words taught with music on sign and speech imitation of children with autism', *Journal of Music Therapy*, 32, 189–202.

Bunge, M. (1994) 'What is pseudoscience?', *Skeptical Inquirer*, 9, 36–46.

Bunt, L. (1994) *Music Therapy: An Art Beyond Words*. London: Routledge.

Burke, R.V., Kuhn, B.R. and Peterson, J.L. (2004) 'Brief report: a "storybook" ending to children's bedtime problems – the use of a rewarding social story to reduce bedtime resistance and frequent night waking', *Journal of Pediatric Psychology*, 29, 389–96.

Burns, Y.R. (1988) 'Sensory integration or the role of sensation in movement', *American Journal on Mental Retardation*, 92, 412.

Buxbaum, J.D., et al. (2006) 'Mutation screening of the PTEN gene in patients with autism spectrum disorders and macrocephaly', *American Journal of Medical Genetics, Part B*, 144, 484–91.

Caban, M. (1994) 'A controlled evaluation of facilitated communication using open-ended and fill-in questions', *Journal of Autism and Developmental Disorders*, 24, 517–27.

Calabrese, R., Patterson, J., Liu, F., Goodvin, S., Hummel, C. and Nance, E. (2007) 'An appreciative inquiry into the Circle of Friends program: the benefits of social inclusion of students with disabilities', *International Journal of Whole Schooling*, 4, 20–49.

Campbell, M., et al. (1997) 'Neuroleptic-related dyskinesias in autistic children: a prospective, longitudinal study', *Journal of the American Academy of Child and Adolescent Psychiatry*, 36, 835–43.

Campbell, M., Schopler, E., Cueva, J.E. and Hallin, A. (1996) 'Treatment of autistic disorder', *Journal of the American Academy of Child and Adolescent Psychiatry*, 35, 134–43.

Carey, T., et al. (2002) 'Double-blind placebo-controlled trial of secretin: effects on aberrant behaviour in children with autism', *Journal of Autism and Developmental Disorders*, 33, 161–7.

Carlson, J.S., Brinkman, T. and Majewicz-Hefley, A. (2006) 'Medication treatment outcomes for school-aged children diagnosed with autism', *California School Psychologist*, 11, 21–30.

Carmody, D.P., Kaplan, M. and Gaydos, A.M. (2001) 'Spatial orientation adjustments in children with autism in Hong Kong', *Child Psychiatry and Human Development*, 31, 233–47.

Carr, D. and Felce, J. (2007a) 'Brief report: increase in production of spoken words in some children with autism after PECS teaching to Phase III', *Journal of Autism and Developmental Disorders*, 37, 780–7.

Carr, D. and Felce, J. (2007b) 'The effects of PECS teaching to Phase III on the communicative interactions between children with autism and their teachers', *Journal of Autism and Developmental Disorders*, 37, 724–37.

Carr, E.G. (1994) 'Emerging themes in the functional analysis of problem behaviour', *Journal of Applied Behaviour Analysis*, 27, 393–9.

Carr, E.G., Binkoff, J.A., Kologinsky, E. and Eddy, M. (1978) 'Acquisition of sign language by autistic children: expressive labelling', *Journal of Applied Behaviour Analysis*, 11, 489–501.

Carre, A.J., Le Grice, B., Blampied, N.M. and Walker, D. (2009) 'Picture exchange communication (PECS) training for young children: does training transfer at school and to home?', *Behaviour Change*, 26, 54–65.

Carter, C., Meckes, L., Pritchard, L., Swensen, S., Wittman, P.P. and Velde, B. (2004) 'The friendship club: an after-school program for children with Asperger Syndrome', *Family and Community Health*, 27, 143–50.

Cartwright, C. and Beskina, S. (2007) 'Review of engaging autism: using the Floortime approach to help children relate, communicate and think', *Journal of the American Academy of Child and Adolescent Psychiatry*, 46, 1498–9.

Case-Smith, J. and Arbesman, M. (2008) 'Evidence-based review of interventions for autism used in or of relevance to occupational therapy', *American Journal of Occupational Therapy*, 62, 412–29.

Case-Smith, J. and Bryan, T. (1999) 'The effects of occupational therapy with sensory integration emphasis on preschool-age children with autism', *American Journal of Occupational Therapy*, 53, 489–97.

Casey, L.O. (1978) 'Development of communicative behaviour in autistic children: a parent programme using manual signs', *Journal of Autism and Childhood Schizophrenia*, 8, 45–59.

Chaabane, D.B.B., Alber-Morgan, S.R. and DeBar, R.M. (2009) 'The effects of parent-implemented PECS training on improvisation of minds by children with autism', *Journal of Applied Behavior Analysis*, 42, 671–7.

Chalfant, A.M., Rapee, R. and Carroll, L. (2007) 'Treating anxiety disorders in children with high functioning autism spectrum disorders: a controlled trial', *Journal of Autism and Developmental Disorders*, 37, 1842–57.

Chan, J.M. and O'Reilly, M.F. (2008) 'A Social Stories intervention package for students with autism in inclusive classroom settings', *Journal of Applied Behaviour Analysis*, 41, 405–9.

Charlop, M.H. and Milstein, J.P. (1989) 'Teaching autistic children conversational speech using video modeling', *Journal of Applied Behaviour Analysis*, 22, 275–85.

Charlop-Christy, M.H., Carpenter, M.L.L., LeBlanc, L.A. and Kellet, K. (2002) 'Using the picture exchange communication system (PECS) with children with autism: assessment of PECS acquisition, speech, social-communicative behaviour, and problem behaviour', *Journal of Applied Behaviour Analysis*, 35, 213–31.

Charman, T. and Baron-Cohen, S. (1997) 'Brief report: prompted pretend play in autism', *Journal of Autism and Developmental Disorders*, 27, 325–32.

Cheung, P.P.P. and Siu, A.M.H. (2009) 'A comparison of patterns of sensory processing in children with and without developmental disabilities', *Research in Developmental Disabilities*, 30, 1468–80.

Chez, M.G., et al. (2000) 'Secretin and autism: a two-part clinical investigation', *Journal of Autism and Developmental Disorders*, 30, 87–94.

Christie, P. and Wimpory, D. (1986) 'Recent research into the development of communicative competence and its implications for the teaching of autistic children', *Communication*, 20, 4–7.

Clarkson, G. (1994) 'Creative music therapy and facilitated communication: new ways of reaching students with autism', *Preventing School Failure*, 38, 31–3.

Cogher, L. (1999) 'The use of non-directive play in speech and language therapy', *Child Language Teaching and Therapy*, 15, 7–15.

Collins, M. (2000) *Auditory Integration Therapy: Research Summaries*. London: Listen to Learn Centre.

Comoletti, D., et al. (2004) 'The Arg451Cys-Neuroligin-3 mutation associated with autism reveals a defect in protein processing', *The Journal of Neuroscience*, 24, 4889–93.

Coniglio, S.J., et al. (2001) 'A randomised, double-blind, placebo-controlled trial of single-dose intravenous secretin as treatment for children with autism', *Journal of Paediatrics*, 138, 649–55.

Cook, C.E. (1998) 'The Miller method: a case study illustrating use of the approach with children with autism in an interdisciplinary setting', *Journal of Developmental and Learning Disorders*, 2, 231–64.

Cook, D. (1991) 'A sensory approach to the treatment and management of children with autism', *Focus on Autistic Behaviour*, 5, 1–19.

Cook, E.H., Rowlett, R., Jaselskis, C. and Leventhal, B.L. (1992) 'Fluoxetine treatment of children and adults with autistic disorder and mental retardation', *Journal of the American Academy of Child and Adolescent Psychiatry*, 31, 739–45.

Cook, T. and Campbell, D. (1979) *Quasi-experimentation: Design and Analysis Issues for Field Settings*. Chicago, IL: Rand McNally.

Cooper, J.O., Heron, T. and Heward, W. (1989) *Applied Behaviour Analysis*. Columbus, OH: Merrill.

Cooper, L. and Harding, J. (1993) 'Extending functional analysis procedures to outpatient and classroom settings for children with mild disabilities', in J. Reichle and D. Wacker (eds), *Communicative Approaches to the Management of Challenging Behaviours: Integrating Functional Assessments and Intervention Strategies*. Baltimore, MD: Brookes. pp. 41–62.

Coucouvanis, J. (1997) 'Behavioural intervention for children with autism', *Journal of Child and Adolescent Psychiatric Nursing*, 10, 37–44.

Crossley, R. (1994) *Facilitated Communication Training*. New York: Teachers College Press.

Crossley, R. and McDonald, A. (1980) *Annie's Coming Out*. New York: Penguin Books.

Crozier, S. (2009) 'Social Stories', in A.E. Boutot and M. Tuscani (eds), *Autism Encyclopedia: The Complete Guide to Autism Spectrum Disorders*. Waco, TX: Prufrock Press. pp. 231–5.

Crozier, S. and Tincani, M.J. (2005) 'Using a modified social story to decrease disruptive behaviour of a child with autism', *Focus on Autistic Behaviour*, 20, 150–7.

Crozier, S. and Tincani, M.J. (2007) 'Effects of Social Stories on prosocial behaviour of preschool children with autism spectrum disorders', *Journal of Autism and Developmental Disorders*, 37, 1803–14.

Cullain, R.E. (2002) 'The effects of Social Stories on anxiety levels and excessive behavioural expressions of elementary school-aged children with autism', *Dissertation Abstracts International: Section A: Humanities and Social Sciences*, 62, 2383.

Cummings, A.R. and Williams, W.L. (2000) 'Visual identity matching and vocal imitation training with children with autism: a surprising finding', *Journal of Developmental Disabilities*, 7, 109–22.

Cummins, R.A. (1988) *The Neurologically-Impaired Child: Doman-Delacato Techniques Reappraised*. London: Croom Helm.

Dales, L., Hammer, S.J. and Smith, N.J. (2001) 'Time trends in autism and in MMR immunization coverage in California', *Journal of the American Medical Association*, 285, 1183–5.

Dallman, P.R. (1986) 'Biochemical basis for the manifestations of iron deficiency', *Annual Reviews of Nutrition*, 6, 13–40.

Daly, E., Witt, J., Martens, B. and Dool, E. (1997) 'A model for conducting a functional analysis of academic performance problems', *School Psychology Review*, 26, 554–74.

Darnley-Smith, R. and Patey, H.M. (2003) *Music Therapy*. London: Sage.

Daveson, B. and Edwards, J. (1998) 'A role for music therapy in special education', *International Journal of Disability, Development and Education*, 45, 449–57.

Dawson, G. and Adams, A. (1984) 'Imitation and social responsiveness in autistic children', *Journal of Abnormal Child Psychology*, 12, 209–26.

Dawson, G. and Osterling, J. (1997) 'Early intervention in autism', in M. Guralnick (ed.), *The Effectiveness of Early Intervention*. Baltimore, MD: Brookes. pp. 307–16.

Dawson, G. and Watling, R. (2000) 'Interventions to facilitate auditory, visual, and motor integration in autism: a review of the evidence', *Journal of Autism and Developmental Disorders*, 30, 415–21.

De Jaco, A., Miller, M., Comoletti, D., Dubi, N. and Taylor, P. (2008) 'Trafficking of neuroligin mutant proteins associated with autism', *The FASEB Journal*, 22, 1001–6.

Delacato, C. (1974) *The Ultimate Stranger: The Autistic Child*. Novato, CA: Arena.

Delano, M. and Snell, M.E. (2006) 'The effects of Social Stories on the social engagement of children with autism', *Journal of Positive Behaviour Interventions*, 8, 29–42.

DeLong, G.R., Teague, L.A. and Kamran, M.M. (1998) 'Effects of fluoxetine treatment in young children with idiopathic autism', *Developmental Medicine and Child Neurology*, 40, 551–62.

Dempsey, I.R. and Foreman, P. (2001) 'A review of educational approaches for individuals with autism', *International Journal of Disability, Development and Education*, 28, 103–16.

DeMyer, M.K., Hingtgen, J. and Jackson, R. (1981) 'Infantile autism reviewed: a decade of research', *Schizophrenia Bulletin*, 7, 388–451.

Deutsch, R.M. and Morrill, J.S. (1993) *Realities of Nutrition*. Palo Alto, CA: Bull.

Dodd, S., Hupp, S.D., Jewell, J.D. and Krohn, E. (2008) 'Using parents and siblings during a social story intervention for two children diagnosed with PPDD-NOS', *Journal of Developmental and Physical Disabilities*, 20, 217–29.

Dolske, M.C. (1993) 'A preliminary trial of ascorbic acid as a supplement therapy for autism', *Progress in Neuro-Psychopharmacology and Biological Psychiatry*, 17, 764–74.

Drew, G. (1996) 'The issue of directiveness in therapy', in *Caring to Communicate*. Royal College of Speech and Language Therapists proceedings. London: RCSLT.

Duchan, J.F. (1993) 'Issues raised by facilitated communication for theorising and research on autism', *Journal of Speech and Hearing Research*, 36, 1108–19.

Duffy, B. and Fuller, R. (2000) 'Role of music therapy in social skills development in children with moderate intellectual disability', *Journal of Applied Research in Intellectual Disabilities*, 13, 77–89.

Dunlap, G., Kern, L. and Worcester, J. (2001) 'ABA and academic instruction', *Focus on Autism and Other Developmental Disabilities*, 16, 129–36.

Dunlap, G., Kern-Dunlap, L., Clarke, S. and Robbins, F.R. (1991) 'Functional assessment, curricular revision, and severe behaviour problems', *Journal of Applied Behaviour Analysis*, 24, 387–97.

Dunn-Geier, J., et al. (2000) 'Effect of secretin on children with autism: a randomised control trial', *Developmental Medicine and Child Neurology*, 42, 796–802.

Durand, V., Crimmins, D., Caulfield, M. and Taylor, J. (1989) 'Reinforcer assessment I: using problem behaviours to select reinforcers', *Journal of the Association for Persons with Severe Handicaps*, 14, 113–26.

Eccles, C. and Pitchford, M. (1997) 'Understanding and helping a boy with problems: a functional approach to behaviour problems', *Educational Psychology in Practice*, 13, 115–22.

Edelson, S.M., Arin, D., Bauman, M., Lukas, S.E., Rudy, J.H., Sholar, M. and Rimland, B. (1999) 'Auditory integration training: a double-blind study of behavioural and electrophysiological effects in people with autism', *Focus on Autism and Other Developmental Disabilities*, 14, 73–81.

Edgerton, C.L. (1994) 'The effect of music therapy on the communicative behaviours of autistic children', *Journal of Music Therapy*, 31, 31–62.

Edwards, D. (1995) 'The efficacy of Daily Life therapy at the Boston Higashi School', in *Therapeutic Approaches to Autism: Research and Practice*. Collected conference papers. Sunderland: Autism Research Unit. pp. 115–27.

Elgar, S. (1989) 'Report of my visit to Dr Kiyo Kitahara's Boston Higashi, Boston, USA', *Communication*, 23, 5–6.

Elliot, S.N. and Busse, R.T. (1991) 'Social skills assessment with children and adolescents', *School Psychology International*, 12, 63–83.

Enderby, P. and Emerson, J. (1995) *Does Speech and Language Therapy Work?* Reading: Whurr.

Enwonwu, C.O. (1989) 'Functional significance of iron deficiency', in C.O. Enwonwu (ed.), *Annual Nutrition Workshop Series, Vol. III*. Nashville, TN: Meharry Medical College.

Epstein, L., Taubman, M.T. and Lovaas, O.I. (1985) 'Changes in self-stimulatory behaviour with treatment', *Journal of Applied Behaviour Analysis*, 18, 281–94.

Erickson, C.A., Posey, D.J., Stigler, K.A. and McDougle, C.J. (2007) 'Pharmacotherapy of autism and related disorders', *Psychiatric Annals*, 37, 490–500.

Esbensen, A.J., Greenberg, J.S., Seltzer, M.M. and Aman, M.G. (2009) 'A longitudinal investigation of psychotropic and non-psychotropic medication use among adolescents and adults with autism spectrum disorders', *Journal of Autism and Developmental Disorders*, 39, 1339–49.

Esch, B. and Carr, J.E. (2004) 'Secretin as a treatment for autism: a review of the evidence', *Journal of Autism and Developmental Disorders*, 34, 543–56.

Evangeliou, A., et al. (2003) 'Application of a ketogenic diet in children with autistic behaviour: pilot study', *Journal of Child Neurology*, 18, 113–18.

Fatemi, S.H., Realmuto, G.M., Khan, L. and Thuras, P. (1998) 'Fluoxetine in treatment of adolescent patients with autism: a longitudinal open trial', *Journal of Autism and Developmental Disorders*, 28, 303–7.

Fazlioglu, Y. and Baran, G. (2008) 'A sensory integration therapy on sensory problems for children with autism', *Perceptual and Motor Skills*, 106, 415–22.

Feinberg, M.J. (2002) 'Using Social Stories to teach specific social skills to individuals diagnosed with autism', *Dissertation Abstract International: Section B: The Sciences and Engineering*, 62, 3797.

Fenske, E.C., Zalenski, S., Krantz, P.J. and McClannahan, L.E. (1985) 'Age at intervention and treatment outcome for autistic children in a comprehensive intervention programme', *Analysis and Intervention in Intellectual Disabilities*, 5, 49–58.

Ferraro, F.R. (2001) 'Survey of treatments for childhood autism', *Psychology and Education: An Interdisciplinary Journal*, 38, 29–41.

Findling, R.L., Maxwell, K., Scotese-Wojtila, L. and Huang, J. (1997) 'High-dose pyridoxine and magnesium administration in children with autistic disorder: an absence of salutary effects in a double-blind placebo-controlled study', *Journal of Autism and Developmental Disorders*, 27, 467–78.

Fish, W.W. (2006) 'Perceptions of parents of students with autism towards the IEP meeting: a case study of one family support group chapter', *Education*, 127, 56–68.

Fisher, A.G. and Murray, E.A. (1991) 'Introduction to sensory integration theory', in A. G. Fisher, E.A. Murray and A.C. Bundy (eds), *Sensory Integration Theory and Practice*. Philadelphia, PA: F.A. Davis. pp. 15–17.

Fisher, A.G., Murray, E.A. and Bundy, A.C. (1991) *Sensory Integration Theory and Practice*. Philadelphia, PA: F.A. Davis.

Fombonne, E. (1998) 'Epidemiology of autism and related conditions', in R.F. Volkmar (ed.), *Autism and Pervasive Developmental Disorders*. New York: Cambridge University Press. pp. 32–63.

Fox, J.J. and McEvoy, M.A. (1993) 'Assessing and enhancing generalization and social validity of social-skills interventions with children and adolescents', *Behaviour Modification*, 17, 339–65.

Foxx, R.M. (2008) 'Applied behavior analysis treatment of autism: the state of the art', *Child and Adolescent Psychiatric Clinics of North America*, 17, 821–34.

Frankel, F., Myatt, R. and Feinberg, D. (2007) 'Parent-assisted friendship training for children with autism spectrum disorders: effects of psychotropic medication', *Child Psychiatry and Human Development*, 37, 337–46.

Frankel, F., Simon, J.Q. and Richey, V.E. (1987) 'Reward value of prosodic features of language for autistic, mentally retarded, and normal children', *Journal of Autism and Developmental Disorders*, 17, 103–13.

Frederickson, N. and Turner, J. (2003) 'Utilizing the classroom peer group to address children's social needs: an evaluation of the Circle of Friends intervention approach', *The Journal of Special Education*, 36, 234–45.

Frederickson, N., Warren, L. and Turner, J. (2005) '"Circle of Friends" – an exploration of impact over time', *Educational Psychology in Practice*, 21, 197–217.

Freeman, B.J. (1997) 'Guidelines for evaluating intervention programs for children with autism', *Journal of Autism and Developmental Disorders*, 27, 641–51.

Freundlich, B.M., Pike, L. and Schwartz, V. (1989) 'Dance and music for children with autism', *Journal of Physical Education, Recreation and Dance*, 60, 50–3.

Frost, L., Daly, M. and Brondy, A. (1997) 'Speech features with and without access to PECS for children with autism', paper presented at COSAC, New Jersey.

Fuggle, K., Fixter, A. and Brown, S.W. (1995) 'Music therapy in the treatment of a child with epilepsy and autism', *Epilepsia*, 36, 3–6.

Fullerton, A., Stratton, J., Coyne, P. and Gray, C. (1996) *Higher Functioning Adolescents and Young Adults with Autism*. Austin, TX: Pro-Ed.

Gamby, T.E. (2002) 'Remediating generalization deficits in children with autism: an empirical investigation', *Dissertation Abstracts International: Section B: The Sciences and Engineering*, 62, 5962.

Ganz, J.B. and Simpson, R.L. (2004) 'Effects of communicative requesting and speech development of the Picture Exchange Communication System in children with characteristics of autism', *Journal of Autism and Developmental Disorders*, 34, 395–410.

Ganz, J.B., Simpson, R.L. and Corbin-Newsome, J. (2008) 'The impact of the Picture Exchange Communication System on requesting and speech development in preschoolers with autism spectrum disorders and similar characteristics', *Research in Autism Spectrum Disorders*, 2, 157–69.

Gerlach, E.K. (1993) *Autism Treatment Guide*. Eugene, OR: Four Leaf Press.

Gibson, J.A., Grey, I.M. and Hastings, R.P. (2009) 'Supervisor support as a predictor of burnout and therapeutic self-efficacy in therapists working in ABA schools', *Journal of Autism and Developmental Disorders*, 39, 1024–30.

Gillberg, C. (1996) 'The psychopharmacology of autism and related disorders', *Journal of Psychopharmacology*, 10, 5463.

Gillberg, C., et al. (1997) 'Auditory integration training in children with autism: a brief report of an open pilot study', *Autism*, 1, 97–100.

Gillberg, C., et al. (1998) 'Auditory integration training in children with autism: reply to Rimland and Edelson', *Autism*, 2, 93–4.

Goldstein, H. (2000) 'Commentary: interventions to facilitate auditory, visual, and motor integration: "Show me the data"', *Journal of Autism and Developmental Disorders*, 30, 423–5.

Goldstein, H. (2002) 'Communication intervention for children with autism: a review of treatment efficacy', *Journal of Autism and Developmental Disorders*, 32, 373–95.

Golnik, A.E. and Ireland, M. (2009) 'Complimentary alternative medicine for children with autism: a physician survey', *Journal of Autism and Developmental Disorders*, 39, 996–1005.

Gordon, C.T., et al. (1992) 'Differential response of seven subjects with autistic disorder to clomipramine and desipramine', *American Journal of Psychiatry*, 149, 363–6.

Gordon, C.T., State, R.C., Nelson, J.E., Hamburger, S.D. and Rapport J.L. (1993) 'A double-blind comparison of clomipramine, desipramine, and placebo in the treatment of autistic disorder', *Archives of General Psychiatry*, 50, 441–7.

Gorman, B.J. (1999) 'Facilitated communication: rejected in science, accepted in court – a case study and analysis of the use of FC evidence under Frye and Daubert', *Behavioural Sciences and the Law*, 17, 517–41.

Goulet, M., et al. (2001) 'Neural transmission of Fos protein in the central amygdala after intravenous injection of secretin', paper presented at the International Meeting of Autism Research, San Diego, CA.

Grandin, T. (1995) 'The learning style of people with autism: an autobiography', in K. Quill (ed.), *Teaching Children with Autism: Strategies to Enhance Communication and Socialization*. Arlington, TX: Future Horizons. pp. 33–52.

Grandin, T. (1996) 'Brief report: response to National Institutes of Health Report', *Journal of Autism and Developmental Disorders*, 26, 185–7.

Gravel, J.S. (1994) 'Auditory integrative training: placing the burden of proof', *American Journal of Speech and Language Pathology*, 3, 25–9.

Gray, C. (1994) *The New Social Story Book*. Arlington, TX: Future Horizons.

Gray, C. (1995) 'Teaching children with autism to read social situations', in K.A. Quill (ed.), *Teaching Children with Autism*. New York: Delmar. pp. 219–41.

Gray, C. (2000) *New Social Stories*, 2nd edn. Arlington, TX: Future Horizons.

Gray, C. (2004) *Writing Social Stories with Carol Gray*. Arlington, TX: Future Horizons.

Gray, C.A. and Garand, J.D. (1993) 'Social Stories: improving responses of students with autism with accurate social information', *Focus on Autistic Behaviour*, 8, 1–10.

Green, D. (2001) 'Autism and "voodoo science" treatments', *Priorities for Health*, 13, 27–32.

Green, G. (1994) 'The quality of the evidence', in H.C. Shane (ed.), *Facilitated Communication: The Clinical and Social Phenomenon*. San Diego, CA: Singular Press. pp. 157–226.

Green, G. (1996a) 'Evaluating claims about treatments for autism', in C. Maurice, G. Green and S.C. Luce (eds), *Behavioral Intervention for Young Children with Autism: A Manual for Parents and Professionals*. Austin, TX: Pro-Ed. pp.15–28.

Green, G. (1996b) 'Early behavioural intervention for autism: what does research tell us?', in C. Maurice, G. Green and S.C. Luce (eds), *Behavioural Intervention for Young Children with Autism: A Manual for Parents and Professionals.* Austin, TX: Pro-Ed. pp. 29–44.

Green, V.A. (2007) 'Parental experience with treatments for autism', *Journal of Developmental and Physical Disabilities*, 19, 91–101.

Green, V.A., et al. (2006) 'Internet survey of treatments used by parents of children with autism', *Research in Developmental Disabilities*, 27, 70–84.

Greenspan, S.I. (1992) 'Reconsidering the diagnosis and treatment of very young children with autistic spectrum or pervasive developmental disorder', *Zero to Zhree, National Center for Clinical Infant Programmes*, 13, 1–9.

Greenspan, S.I. (1998) 'A developmental approach to problems in relating and communicating in autistic spectrum disorders and related syndromes', *SPOTLIGHT on Topics in Developmental Disabilities*, 1, 1–6.

Greenspan, S.I. and Wieder, S. (2000) 'Developmentally appropriate interactions and practices', in S.I. Greenspan (ed.), *The Interdisciplinary Council on Developmental and Learning Disorders Clinical Practice Guidelines.* Bethesda, MD: Interdisciplinary Council on Developmental and Learning Disorders. Ch. 12.

Greenspan, S.I. and Wieder, S. (2006) *Engaging Autism: Using the Floortime Approach to Help Children Relate, Communicate, and Think.* Cambridge, ME: Da Capo Press.

Gresham, F.M. and MacMillan, D.L. (1998) 'Early intervention project: can its claims be substantiated and its effects replicated?', *Journal of Autism and Developmental Disorders*, 28, 5–13.

Gresham, F.M., Beebe-Frankenberger, M.E. and MacMillan, D.L. (1999) 'A selective review of treatments for children with autism: description and methodological considerations', *School Psychology Review*, 28, 559–76.

Grossman, R.B., Scneps, M.H. and Tager-Flusberg, H. (2009) 'Slipped lips: onset asynchrony detection of auditory-visual language in autism', *Journal of Child Psychology and Psychiatry*, 50, 491–7.

Guralnick, M.J. (1990) 'Major accomplishments and future directions in early childhood mainstreaming', *Topics in Early Childhood Special Education*, 10, 1–17.

Gus, L. (2000) 'Autism: promoting peer understanding', *Educational Psychology in Practice*, 16, 461–8.

Gutierrez, A., Hale, M.N., Gossens-Archuleta, K. and Sobrino-Sanchez, V. (2007) 'Evaluating the social behaviour of preschool children with autism in an inclusive playground setting', *International Journal of Special Education*, 22, 25–9.

Gutstein, S.E. and Sheely, R.K. (2002) *Relationship Development Intervention with Children, Adolescents and Adults: Social and Emotional Development Activities for Asperger Syndrome, Autism, PDD and NLD.* New York: Jessica Kingsley.

Hagiwara, T. and Myles, B.S. (1999) 'A multimedia social story intervention: teaching skills to children with autism', *Focus on Autism and Other Developmental Disabilities*, 14, 82–95.

Hagopian, L., Fisher, W., Sullivan, M., Acquisto, J. and LeBlanc, L. (1998) 'Effectiveness of functional communication training with and without extinction and punishment: a summary of 21 inpatient cases', *Journal of Applied Behaviour Analysis*, 31, 211–35.

Hairston, M.P. (1990) 'Analyses of responses of mentally retarded autistic and mentally retarded nonautistic children to art therapy and music therapy', *Journal of Music Therapy*, 27, 137–50.

Hall, L.J. (1997) 'Effective behavioural strategies for the defining characteristics of autism', *Behaviour Change*, 14, 139–54.

Hall, L.J. (2009) *Autism Spectrum Disorders: From Theory to Practice*. New York: Merrill.

Hall, L.J., McClannahan, L.E. and Krantz, P.J. (1995) 'Promoting independence in integrate', *Education and Training in Mental Retardation and Developmental Disabilities*, 30, 208–17.

Handen, B.L. and Hofkosh, D. (2005) 'Secretin in children with autistic disorder: a double-blind, placebo-controlled trial', *Journal of Developmental and Physical Disabilities*, 17, 95–106.

Handen, B.L. and Lubetsky, M. (2005) 'Pharmacotherapy in autism and related disorders', *School Psychology Quarterly*, 20, 155–71.

Hare, D.J. (1997) 'The use of cognitive behavioural therapy with people with Asperger syndrome: a case study', *Autism*, 1, 215–25.

Harris, M. (1992) *Language Experience and Early Language Development: From Input to Intake*. Hove: Lawrence Erlbaum.

Harris, S.L., Handleman, J.S., Gordon, R., Kristoff, B. and Fuentes, F. (1991) 'Changes in cognitive and language functioning of preschool children with autism', *Journal of Autism and Developmental Disorders*, 21, 281–90.

Harrison, E.J., et al. (2006) 'The gluten-free, casein-free diet in autism: results of a preliminary double blind clinical trial', *Journal of Autism and Developmental Disorders*, 36, 413–20.

Hastings, R.P. (2003) 'Behavioural adjustment of siblings of children with autism engaged in applied behaviour analysis early intervention programmes: the moderating role of social support', *Journal of Autism and Developmental Disorders*, 33, 141–50.

Hatch-Rasmussen, C. (1995) *Sensory Integration*. Salem, OR: Center for the Study of Autism.

Hayes, R. and Gordon, A. (1977) 'Auditory abnormalities in autistic children', *Lancet*, 2, 767.

Hayes, S.C. (2001) 'The greatest dangers facing behaviour analysis today', *The Behaviour Analyst Today*, 2, 61–3.

Hazell, P. (2007) 'Drug therapy for attention-deficit/hyperactivity disorder-like symptoms in autistic disorder', *Journal of Paediatrics and Child Health*, 43, 19–24.

Heflin, L.J. and Alberto, P.A. (2001) 'ABA and instruction of students with autism spectrum disorders: introduction to the special series', *Focus on Autism and Other Developmental Disabilities*, 16, 66–7.

Hendrickson, J.M., Shokoohi-Yekta, M., Hamre-Nietupski, S. and Gable, R.A. (1996) 'Middle and high school students' perceptions of being friends with peers with severe disabilities', *Exceptional Children*, 63, 19–28.

Herbert, J.D. and Brandsma, L.L. (2002) 'Applied behaviour analysis for childhood autism: does the emperor have clothes?', *The Behaviour Analyst Today*, 3, 45–56.

Herbert, J.D. and Sharp, I.R. (2001) 'Pseudoscientific treatments for autism', *Priorities for Health*, 13, 23–6, 59.

Herbert, J.D., Lilienfeld, S.O., Lohr, J.M., et al. (2000) 'Science and pseudoscience in the development of eye movement desensitization and reprocessing: implications for clinical psychology', *Clinical Psychology Review*, 20, 945–71.

Hilton, J.C. and Seal, B.C. (2007) 'Brief report: comparative ABA and DIR trials in twin brothers with autism', *Journal of Autism and Developmental Disorders*, 37, 1197–201.

Hingtgen, J.N. and Bryson, C.Q. (1972) 'Recent developments in the study of early childhood psychoses: infantile autism, childhood schizophrenia, and related disorders', *Schizophrenia Bulletin*, 5, 8–54.

Hoehn, T.P. and Baumeister, A.A. (1994) 'A critique of the application of sensory integration therapy to children with learning disabilities', *Journal of Learning Disabilities*, 27, 338–51.

Hollander, E., et al. (2006) 'Liquid fluoxetine versus placebo for repetitive behaviours in childhood autism', in J.L. Cummings (ed.), *Progress in Neurotherapeutics and Neuropsychopharmacology*. New York: Cambridge University Press. pp. 105–13.

Holmes, E. and Willoughby, T. (2005) 'Play behaviour of children with autism spectrum disorders', *Journal of Intellectual and Developmental Disability*, 30, 156–64.

Honey, E., Leekam, S., Turner, M. and McConahie, H. (2007) 'Repetitive behaviour and play in typically developing children and children with autism spectrum disorders', *Journal of Autism and Developmental Disorders*, 37, 1107–15.

Horner, R., O'Neill, R. and Flannery, K. (1993) 'Building effective behaviour support plans from functional assessment information', in M. Snell (ed.), *Instruction of Persons with Severe Handicaps*, 4th edn. Columbus, OH: Merrill. pp. 184–214.

Horner, R., Vaughn, B., Day, H. and Ard, F. (1996) 'The relationship between setting events and problem behaviour', in L.K. Koegel, R. Koegel and G. Dunlap (eds), *Positive Behavioural Support: Including People with Difficult Behaviour in the Community*. Baltimore, MD: Brookes. pp. 381–402.

Horvath, K., et al. (1998) 'Autistic behaviour and secretin', *Journal of the Association for Academic Minority Physicians*, 9, 9–15.

Howes, C. (1988) 'Same- and cross-sex friends: implications for interaction and social skills', *Early Childhood Research Quarterly*, 3, 21–7.

Howlin, P. (1996) *A Visit to the Light and Sound Therapy Centre*. London: National Autistic Society.

Howlin, P. (1997) *Autism: Preparing for Adulthood*. London: Routledge.

Howlin, P., Gordon, R.K., Pasco, G., Wade, A. and Charman, T. (2007) 'The effectiveness of a Picture Exchange Communication System (PECS) training for teachers of children with autism: a pragmatic, group randomised controlled trial', *Journal of Child Psychology and Psychiatry*, 48, 473–81.

Hoyson, M., Jamieson, B. and Strain, P.S. (1984) 'Individualised group instruction of normally developing and autistic-like children: the LEAP curriculum model', *Journal of the Division of Early Childhood*, 8, 157–72.

Hutchins, T.L. and Prelock, P.A. (2005) 'Using Social Stories and comic strip conversations to promote socially valid outcomes for children with autism',

Seminars in Speech and Language, 27, 47–59.

Hutchins, T.L. and Prelock, P.A. (2008) 'Supporting theory of mind development: considerations and recommendations for professionals providing services to individuals with autism spectrum disorder', *Topics in Language Disorders*, 28, 340–64.

Idjradinata, P. and Pollit, E. (1993) 'Reversal of developmental delay in iron deficient infants treated with iron', *Lancet*, 341, 1–4.

Iobst, E.A., Nabors, L.A. and McGrady, M.E. (2008) 'Social Stories as a social skills intervention for children with autism', in J.A. Patterson and I.N. Lipschitz (eds), *Psychological Counseling Research Focus*. Hauppage, NY: Nova Science. pp. 71–82.

Irvin, D. (2006) 'Using analog assessment procedures for determining the effects of a gluten-free and casein-free diet on rate of problem behaviours for an adolescent with autism', *Behavioural Interventions*, 21, 281–6.

Ivey, M.L., Heflin, L.J. and Alberto, P. (2004) 'The use of Social Stories to promote independent behaviours in novel events for children with PDD-NOS', *Focus on Autism and Other Developmental Disorders*, 19, 164–76.

Jacobson, J.W., Mulick, J.A. and Schwartz, A.A. (1995) 'A history of facilitated communication: science, ps', *American Psychologist*, 50, 750–65.

James, A. and Leyden, G. (2008) 'A grounded theory study of circles of friends groups: the power of the set-up meeting as a tool for the opening of the social field of isolated children in schools', *Educational and Child Psychology*, 25, 48–58.

Janzen, J. (1996) *Understand the Nature Of Autism: A Practical Guide*. San Antonio, TX: Therapy Skill Builders.

Jarrold, C., Boucher, J. and Smith, P. (1996) 'Generativity deficits in pretend play in autism', *British Journal of Developmental Psychology*, 14, 275–300.

Jones, E.A., Carr, E.D. and Feeley, K.M. (2006) 'Multiple effects of joint attention intervention for children with autism', *Behavioural Modification*, 30, 782–834.

Jordan, R. (1999a) *Autistic Spectrum Disorders: An Introductory Handbook for Practitioners*. London: David Fulton.

Jordan, R. (1999b) 'Evaluating practice: problems and possibilities', *Autism*, 3, 411–34.

Jordan, R. and Libby, S. (1997) 'Developing and using play in curriculum', in S. Powell and R. Jordan (eds), *Autism and Learning: A Guide to Good Practice*. London: David Fulton.

Jordan, R. and Powell, S. (1995) *Understanding and Teaching Children with Autism. London: Wiley.*

Jordan, R., Jones, G. and Murray, D. (1998) *Educational Interventions for Children with Autism: A Literature Review of Recent and Current Research*. London: Department of Education and Employment.

Jung, K.-E., Lee, H.-J., Lee, Y.-S, and Lee, J.-H. (2006) 'Efficacy of sensory integration treatment based on virtual reality – tangible interaction for children with autism', *Annual Review of CyberTherapy and Telemedicine*, 4, 45–4.

Jurgens, A., Anderson, A. and Moore, D.W. (2009) 'The effect of teaching PECS to a child with autism on verbal behaviour, play and social functioning', *Behaviour Change*, 26, 66–81.

Kalyva, E. (2009) 'Comparison of eating attitudes between adolescent girls with and without Asperger syndrome: daughters' and mothers' reports', *Journal of Autism and Developmental Disorders*, 39, 480–6.

Kalyva, E. (2010) 'Teachers' perspectives of the sexuality of children with autism spectrum disorders', *Research in Autism Spectrum Disorders*, 4, 433–7.

Kalyva, E. and Agaliotis, I. (2009) 'Can Social Stories enhance the interpersonal conflict resolution skills of children with LD?', *Research in Developmental Disabilities*, 30, 192–202.

Kalyva, E. and Avramidis, E. (2005) 'Improving communication between children with autism and their peers through the "Circle of Friends": a small scale intervention study', *Journal of Applied Research in Intellectual Disabilities*, 18, 253–61.

Kamps, D.M., Barbetta, P.M., Leonard, B.R. and Delquadri, J. (1994) 'Classwide peer tutoring: an integration strategy to improve reading skills and promote peer interactions among students with autism and general education peers', *Journal of Applied Behaviour Analysis*, 27, 49–61.

Kaplan, B.J., Polatajko, H.J., Wilson, B.N. and Faris. P.D. (1993) 'Reexamination of sensory integration treatment: a combination of two efficacy studies', *Journal of Learning Disabilities*, 26, 342–7.

Kaplan, M., Edelson, S.M. and Seip, J.L. (1998) 'Behavioural changes in autistic individuals as a result of wearing ambient transitional prism lenses', *Child Psychiatry and Human Development*, 29, 65–76.

Kaplan, R.M., Carmody, D.P. and Gaydos, A. (1996) 'Postural orientation modifications in autism in response to ambient lenses', *Child Psychiatry and Human Development*, 27, 87–91.

Kaplan, R.S. and Steele, A.L. (2005) 'An analysis of music therapy goals and outcomes for clients with diagnoses on the autism spectrum', *Journal of Music Therapy*, 42, 2–19.

Katagiri, J. (2009) 'The effect of background music and song texts on the emotional understanding of children with autism', *Journal of Music Therapy*, 46, 15–31.

Kaufman, B.N. (1976) *Son-Rise*. New York: Harper and Row.

Kaufman, B.N. (1994) *Son-Rise: The Miracle Continues*. Tiburon, CA: H.J. Kramer.

Kaufman, S. (1998) 'The Son-Rise programme at the Option Institute', *Communication*, 32, 19–23.

Kaye, J.A., Melero-Montes, M. and Jick, H. (2001) 'Mumps, measles, and rubella vaccine', *British Medical Journal*, 322, 460–3.

Keel, J.H., Mesibov, G.B. and Woods, A.V. (1997) 'TEACCH supported employment programme', *Journal of Autism and Developmental Disorders*, 27, 3–9.

Kelly, B. (1999) 'Circle time: a systems approach to emotional and behavioural difficulties', *Educational Psychology in Practice*, 15, 40–4.

Kenny, M.C. and Winick, C.B. (2000) 'An integrative approach to play therapy with an autistic girl', *International Journal of Play Therapy*, 9, 11–33.

Kern, J.K., et al. (2002) 'Efficacy of porcine secretin in children with autism and pervasive developmental disorder', *Journal of Autism and Developmental Disorders*, 32, 153–60.

Kern, P. and Aldridge, D. (2006) 'Using embedded music therapy interventions to support outdoor play of young children with autism in an inclusive community-based child care program', *Journal of Music Therapy*, 43, 270–94.

Kern, P., Wakeford, L. and Aldridge, D. (2007) 'Improving the performance of a young child with autism during self-care tasks using embedded song intervention: a case study', *Music Therapy Perspectives*, 25, 43–51.

Kerrin, R.G., Murdock, J.Y., Sharpton, W.R. and Jones, N. (1998) 'Who's doing the pointing? Investigating facilitated communication in a classroom setting with students with autism', *Focus on Autism and Other Developmental Disabilities*, 13, 73–9.

Kezuka, E. (2002) 'A history of the facilitated communication controversy' (in Japanese), *Japanese Journal of Child and Adolescent Psychiatry*, 43, 312–27.

Kiernan, C. (1983) 'The use of nonvocal communication techniques with autistic individuals', *Journal of Child Psychology and Psychiatry*, 24, 339–75.

Kiernan, C. and Reid, B. (1984) 'The use of augmentative communication systems in schools and units for autistic and aphasic in the United Kingdom', *British Journal of Disorders of Communication*, 19, 47–61.

Kim, J., Wigram, T. and Gold, C. (2008) 'The effects of improvisational music therapy on joint attention behaviors in autistic children: a randomized controlled study', *Journal of Autism and Developmental Disorders*, 38, 1758–66.

Kim, J., Wigram, T. and Gold, C. (2009) 'Emotional, motivational and interpersonal responsiveness of children with autism in improvisational music therapy', *Autism*, 13, 389–409.

King, B.H. (2000) 'Pharmacological treatment of mood disturbances, aggression, and self-injury in persons with pervasive developmental disorders', *Journal of Autism and Developmental Disorders*, 30, 439–45.

King, L.J. (1987) 'A sensory-integrative approach to the education of the autistic children', *Occupational Therapy in Health Care*, 4, 77–85.

Kitahara, K. (1984a) *Daily Life Therapy: A Method of Educating Autistic Children*. Record of actual education at Musashino Higashi Gakuen School, Japan. Vol. 1. Boston, MA: Nimrod Press.

Kitahara, K. (1984b) *Daily Life Therapy: A Method of Educating Autistic Children*. Record of actual education at Musashino Higashi Gakuen School, Japan. Vol. 2. Boston, MA: Nimrod Press.

Kitahara, K. (1984c) *Daily Life Therapy: A Method of Educating Autistic Children*. Record of actual education at Musashino Higashi Gakuen School, Japan. Vol. 3. Boston, MA: Nimrod Press.

Klin, A., Volkmar, F.R. and Sparrow, S.S. (1992) 'Autistic social dysfunction: some limitations of the theory of mind hypothesis', *Journal of Child Psychology and Psychiatry*, 33, 861–86.

Klinger, L.G. and Williams, A. (2009) 'Cognitive-behavioral interventions for students with autism spectrum disorders', in M.J. Mayer, J.E. Lochman and R. Van Acker (eds), *Cognitive-Behavioral Interventions for Emotional and Behavioral Disorders: School-Based Practice*. New York: Guilford Press. pp. 328–62.

Koegel, L., Koegel, R. and Dunlap, G. (1996) *Positive Behavioural Support*. Baltimore, MD: Paul Brookes.

Koegel, L.K., Koegel, R.L., Hurley, C. and Frea, W.D. (1992) 'Improving social skills and disruptive behaviour in children with autism through self-management', *Journal of Applied Behaviour Analysis*, 25, 341–53.

Koegel, R.L. and Koegel, L.K. (2006) *Pivotal Response Treatments for Autism: Communication, Social, and Academic Development.* Baltimore, MD: Paul H. Brookes.

Koegel, R.L., Koegel, L.K. and Carter, C.M. (1999) 'Pivotal teaching interactions for children with autism', *School Psychology Review*, 28, 576–94.

Koegel, R.L., O'Dell, M. and Dunlap, G. (1988) 'Producing speech use in nonverbal autistic children by reinforcing attempts', *Journal of Autism and Developmental Disorders*, 18, 525–38.

Koegel, R.L., Rincover, A. and Egel, A.L. (1982a) *Educating and Understanding Autistic Children.* San Diego, CA: College-Hill Press.

Koegel, R.L., Russo, D.C., Rincover, A. and Schreibman, L. (1982b) 'Assessing and training teachers', in R.L. Koegel, A. Rincover and A.L. Egel (eds), *Educating and Understanding Autistic Children.* San Diego, CA: College-Hill Press. pp. 178–202.

Kohler, F.W., Strain, P.S. and Goldstein, H. (2005) 'Learning experiences – an alternative program for preschoolers and parents: peer-mediated interventions for young children with autism', in E.D. Hibbs and P.S. Jensen (eds), *Psychosocial Treatments for Child and Adolescent Disorders: Empirically Based Strategies for Clinical Practice*, 2nd edn. Washington, DC: American Psychological Association. pp. 659–87.

Kohler, F.W., Strain, P.S. and Shearer, D.D. (1996) 'Examining levels of social inclusion within an integrated preschool for children with autism', in L. Koegel, R.L. Koegel and G. Dunlap (eds), *Positive Behavioural Support: Including People with Difficult Behaviour in the Community.* Baltimore, MD: Brookes. pp. 305–32.

Kohler, F.W., Strain, P.S., Hoyson, M. and Jamieson, B. (1997) 'Merging naturalistic teaching and peer-based strategies to address the IEP objectives of preschoolers with autism: an examination of structural and child behaviour outcomes', *Focus on Autism and Other Developmental Disabilities*, 12, 196–206.

Kolevzon, A. (2009) 'The pharmacologic treatment of attention deficit and hyperactivity in autism', *Primary Psychiatry*, 16, 55–60.

Konstantareas, M. (2006) 'Social skills training in high functioning autism and Asperger's disorder', *Hellenic Journal of Psychology*, 3, 39–56.

Konstantareas, M.M. and Gravelle, G. (1998) 'Facilitated communication: the contribution of physical, emotional and mental support', *Autism*, 2, 389–414.

Konstantareas, M.M., Webster, C.D. and Oxman, J. (1979) 'Manual language acquisition and its influence on other areas of functioning in four autistic and autistic-like children', *Journal of Child Psychology and Psychiatry*, 20, 337–50.

Konstantareas, M.M., Webster, C.D. and Oxman, J. (1980) 'An alternative to speech training: simultaneous communication', in C.D. Webster, M.M. Konstantareas, J. Oxman and J.E. Mack (eds), *Autism: New Direction in Research and Education.* Oxford: Pergamon Press. pp. 187–201.

Kossoff, E.H., Zupec-Kania, B.A. and Rho, J.M. (2009) 'Ketogenic diets: an update for child neurologists', *Journal of Child Neurology*, 24, 979–88.

Kostka, M.J. (1993) 'A comparison of selected behaviours of a student with autism in special education and regular music classes', *Music Therapy Perspectives*, 11, 57–60.

Kravits, T.R., Kamps, D.M., Kemmerer, K. and Potucek, J. (2002) 'Brief report: increasing communication skills for an elementary-aged student with autism using the picture exchange communication system', *Journal of Autism and Developmental Disorders*, 32, 225–30.

Kunce, L. and Mesibov, G.B. (1998) 'Educational approaches to high-functioning autism and Asperger syndrome', in E. Schopler and G.B. Mesibov (eds), *Asperger Syndrome or High-Functioning Autism? Current Issues in* Autism. New York: Plenum Press. pp. 227–61.

Kuttler, S. and Myles, B.S. (1998) 'The use of Social Stories to reduce precursors to tantrum behaviour in a student with autism', *Focus on Autism and Other Developmental Disabilities*, 13, 176–82.

Kvinsberg, A.M., Reichelt, K.L., Nodland, M. and Hoien, T. (1996) 'Autistic syndromes and diet: a follow-up study', *Scandinavian Journal of Educational Research*, 39, 223–36.

Langworthy-Lam, K.S.M., Aman, M.G. and Van Bourgondien, M.E. (2002) 'Prevalence and patterns of use of psychoactive medicines in individuals with autism in the Autism Society of North Carolina', *Journal of Child and Adolescent Psychopharmacology*, 12, 311–21.

Lantz, J.F., Nelson, J.M. and Lofin, R.L. (2004) 'Guiding children with autism in play: applying the integrated play group model in school settings', *Teaching Exceptional Children*, 37, 8–14.

Larkin, A.S. and Gurry, S. (1998) 'Brief report: progress reported in three children with autism using Daily Life therapy', *Journal of Autism and Developmental Disorders*, 28, 339–42.

Larrington, G.G. (1987) 'A sensory integration based programme with a severely retarded/autistic teenager: an occupational therapy case report', in Z. Mailloux (ed.), *Sensory Integration Approaches*. New York: Hawthorn Press. pp. 101–17.

Latif, A., Heinz, P. and Cook, R. (2002) 'Iron deficiency in autism and Asperger syndrom', *Autism*, 6, 103–14.

Lawson, D.W. (2001) 'Transdermal secretin for autism: a case report', *Alternative Medicine Review*, 6, 311–13.

Layton, T.L. (1988) 'Language training with autistic children using four different modes of presentation', *Journal of Communication Disorders*, 21, 333–50.

Lehmkuhl, H.D., Storch, E.A., Bodfish, J.W. and Geffken, G.R. (2008) 'Brief report: exposure and response prevention for obsessive compulsive disorder in a 12-year-old with autism', *Journal of Autism and Developmental Disorders*, 38, 977–81.

Levy, J. (1998) 'The autism treatment center of America: the Son-Rise Programme for families with special children', available at: http://www.option.org.

Levy, S.E. and Hyman, S.L. (2008) 'Complementary and alternative medicine treatments for children with autism spectrum disorders', *Child and Adolescent Psychiatric Clinics of North America*, 17, 803–20.

Levy, S.E., et al. (2007) 'Relationship of dietary intake to gastrointestinal symptoms in children with autistic spectrum disorders', *Biological Psychiatry*, 61, 492–7.

Lewis, V. (1987) *Development and Handicap*. London: Blackwell.

Lewy, A.L. and Dawson, G. (1992) 'Social stimulation and joint attention in young autistic children', *Journal of Abnormal Psychology*, 20, 555–66.

Liddle, K. (2001) 'Implementing the Picture Exchange Communication System (PECS)', *International Journal of Language and Communication Disorders*, 36, 391–5.

Lilienfield, S.O. (1998) 'Pseudoscience in contemporary clinical psychology: what it is and what we can do about it', *The Clinical Psychologist*, 51, 3–9.

Lim, S.M., Kattapuram, A. and Lian, W.B. (2007) 'Evaluation of a pilot clinic-based social skills group', *British Journal of Occupational Therapy*, 70, 35–9.

Link, H.M. (1997) 'Auditory Integration Training (AIT): sound therapy? Case studies of three boys with autism who received AIT', *British Journal of Learning Disabilities*, 25, 106–10.

Livanis, A., Solomon, E.R. and Ingram, D.H. (2007) 'Guided Social Stories: group treatment of adolescents with Asperger's disorder in the schools', in R.W. Christner, J.L. Stewart and A. Freeman (eds), *Handbook of Cognitive-Behaviour Group Therapy with Children and Adolescents: Specific Settings and Behaviour Problems*. New York: Routledge/Taylor and Francis Group. pp. 389–407.

Locascio, J.J., et al. (1991) 'Factors related to haloperidol response and dyskinesias in autistic children', *Psychopharmacology Bulletin*, 27, 119–26.

Lonigan, C., Elbert, J. and Johnson, S. (1998) 'Empirically supported psychosocial interventions for children: an overview', *Journal of Clinical Child Psychology*, 27, 138–45.

Lonsdale, D. and Shamberger, R.J. (2000) 'A clinical study of secretin in autism and pervasive developmental delay', *Journal of Nutritional and Environmental Medicine*, 10, 271–80.

Lord, C. (1997) 'Ask the editor', *Journal of Autism and Developmental Disorders*, 27, 349.

Lord, C. and Schopler, E. (1989) 'The role of the age at assessment, developmental level, and test in the stability of intelligence scores in young autistic from preschool years through early school age', *Journal of Autism and Developmental Disorders*, 18, 234–53.

Lord, C. and Schopler, E. (1994) 'TEACCH services for preschool children', in S.L. Harris and J.S. Handleman (eds), *Preschool Education Programmes for Children with Autism*. Austin, TX: Pro-Ed. pp. 87–106.

Lorimer, P.A., Simpson, R.L., Myles, B.S. and Granz, J.B. (2002) 'The use of Social Stories as a preventive behavioural intervention in a home setting with a child with autism', *Journal of Positive Behaviour Interventions*, 4, 53–60.

Lovaas, O.I. (1977) *The Autistic Child: Language Development Through Behaviour Modification*. New York: Irvington.

Lovaas, O.I. (1987) 'Behavioural treatment and normal educational and intellectual functioning in young autistic children', *Journal of Consulting and Clinical Psychology*, 5, 3–9.

Lovaas, O.I. (1993) *Treating Developmentally Disabled Children: The Me Book*. Austin, TX: Pro-Ed.

Lovaas, O.I. and Smith, T. (1988) 'Intensive behavioural treatment for young autistic children', in B.B. Lahey and A.E. Kazdin (eds), *Advances in Clinical Child Psychology*, Vol. 11. New York: Plenum. pp. 285–324.

Lovaas, O.I., Koegel, R.L., Simmons, J.Q. and Long, J.S. (1973) 'Some generalization and follow-up measures on autistic children in behaviour therapy', *Journal of Applied Behaviour Analysis*, 6, 131–66.

Lovaas, O.I., Newsom, C. and Hickman, C. (1987) 'Self-stimulatory behaviour and perceptual reinforcement', *Journal of Applied Behaviour Analysis*, 20, 45–68.

Lovaas, O.I., Smith, T. and McEachin, J. (1989) 'Clarifying comments on the young autism study: reply to Schopler, Short, and Mesibov', *Journal of Consulting and Clinical Psychology*, 57, 165–7.

Lozoff, B. (1988) 'Behavioural alteration in iron deficiency', *Advances in Paediatrics*, 35, 331–60.

Lund, S.K. and Troha, J.M. (2008) 'Teaching young people who are blind and have autism to make requests using a variation on the picture exchange communication system with tactile symbols: a preliminary investigation', *Journal of Autism and Developmental Disorders*, 38, 719–30.

Lynch, S. (1998) 'Case study: intensive behavioural intervention with a 7-year-old girl with autism', *Autism*, 2, 181–97.

MacDonald, H. and MacDonald, A. (1991) 'Option method – Part two', *Communication*, 25, 5–6.

MacDuff, G.S., Krantz, P.J. and McClannahan, L.E. (1993) 'Teaching children with autism to use photographic activity sheets: maintenance and generalization of complex response chains', *Journal of Applied Behaviour Analysis*, 26, 89–97.

Mace, F.C. and Lalli, J.S. (1991) 'Linking descriptive and experimental analyses in the treatment of bizarre speech', *Journal of Applied Behaviour Analysis*, 24, 553–62.

MacNeil, J.S. (2001) 'Is autism's answer in the gut?', Repligen Corporation, available at: www.vaccinationnews.com.

Magiati, I. and Howlin, P. (2003) 'A pilot evaluation study of the Picture Exchange Communication System (PECS) for children with autistic spectrum disorders', *Autism*, 7, 297–320.

Mahlberg, M. (1973) 'Music therapy in the treatment of an autistic child', *Journal of Music Therapy*, 10, 189–93.

Mahler, M. (1968) *On Human Symbiosis and the Vicissitudes of Individuation*. New York: International Universities Press.

Manning, A. (1999) 'Vaccine–autism link feared', *USA Today*, 16 August.

Marcus, L. (2004) 'Structured teaching', available at: www.teacch.com.

Margolin, K.N. (1994) 'How shall facilitated communication be judged? Facilitated communication and the legal system', in H.C. Shane (ed.), *Facilitated Communication: The Clinical and Social Phenomenon*. San Diego, CA: Singular Press. pp. 227–58.

Marrosu, F., Marrosu, G., Rachel, M.G. and Biggio, G. (1987) 'Paradoxical reactions elicited by diazepam in children with classic autism', *Functional Neurology*, 3, 335–61.

Martell, R. (1996) 'Vision need not be a miracle', *Therapy Weekly*, 22, 4.

Martens, B.K., Witt, J.C., Dally, E.J. and Vollmer, T.R. (1999) 'Behaviour analysis: theory and practice in educational settings', in C. Reynolds and T.B. Gutkin (eds), *The Handbook of School Psychology*, 3rd edn. New York: Wiley.

Mason, S.A. and Iwata, B.A. (1990) 'Artifactual effects of sensory-integrative therapy on self-injurious behaviour', *Journal of Applied Behavioural Analysis*, 23, 361–70.

Mastrangelo, S. (2009) 'Play and the child with autism spectrum disorder: from possibilities to practice', *International Journal of Play Therapy*, 18, 13–30.

Matson, J. L. and Dempsey, T. (2008) 'Autism spectrum disorders: pharmacotherapy for challenging behaviours', *Journal of Developmental and Physical Disabilities*, 20, 175–91.

Matson, J.L., Benavidez, D.A., Compton, L.S., Paclawksyj, T. and Baglio, C. (1996) 'Behaviour treatment of autistic persons: a review of research from 1980 to the present', *Research in Developmental Disabilities*, 17, 433–65.

Matson, J.L., Taras, M E, Sevin, J.A., Love, S.R. and Fridley, D. (1990) 'Teaching self-help skills to autistic and mentally retarded children', *Research in Developmental Disabilities*, 11, 361–78.

Maurice, C. (1993) *Let Me Hear Your Voice*. London: Robert Hale.

Maurice, C., Green, G. and Luce, S. (1996) *Behavioural Intervention for Young Children with Autism*. Austin, TX: Pro-Ed.

McAbee, G.N., et al. (2009) 'Permanent visual loss due to dietary vitamin A deficiency in an autistic adolescent', *Journal of Child Neurology*, 24, 1288–9.

McCormick, L.H. (1997) 'Treatment with buspirone in a patient with autism', *Archives of Family Medicine*, 6, 368–70.

McDonald, M.E. and Hemmes, N.S. (2003) 'Increases in social initiation toward an adolescent with autism: reciprocity effects', *Research in Developmental Disabilities*, 24, 453–65.

McDougle, C.J., Kresch, L.E. and Posey, D.J. (2000) 'Repetitive thoughts and behaviour in pervasive developmental disorders: treatment with serotonin reuptake inhibitors', *Journal of Autism and Developmental Disorders*, 30, 427–35.

McEachin, J.J., Smith, T. and Lovaas, O.I. (1993) 'Long term outcome for children with autism who received early intensive behavioural treatment', *American Journal on Mental Retardation*, 4, 359–72.

McGee, G.G., Krantz, P.J. and McClannahan, L.E. (1985) 'The facilitative effects of incidental teaching on preposition use by autistic children', *Journal of Applied Behaviour Analysis*, 18, 17–31.

Mesibov, G. (1997) 'Formal and informal measures on the effectiveness of the TEACCH programme', *Autism*, 1, 25–35.

Mesibov, G. and Howley, M. (2003) *Accessing the Curriculum for Pupils with Autistic Spectrum Disorders: Using the TEACCH Programme to Help Inclusion*. London: David Fulton.

Mesibov, G.B. (1993) 'Commentaries on McEachin, Smith and Lovaas: treatment outcome is encouraging', *American Journal on Mental Retardation*, 97, 379–80.

Mesibov, G.B. and Schopler, E. (1983) 'The development of community-based programmes for autistic adolescents', *Children's Health Care*, 12, 20–4.

Mesibov, G.B., Schopler, E., Schaffer, B. and Landrus, R. (1988) *Adolescent and Adult Psychoeducational Profile*. Austin, TX: Pro-Ed.

Meyen, E.L. (1978) *Exceptional Children and Youth*. Denver, CO: Love.

Miller, A. and Chretien, K. (2007) *The Miller MethodReg.: Developing the Capacities of Children on the Autism Spectrum*. London: Jessica Kingsley.

Miller, A. and Eller-Miller, E. (2000) *The Miller Method: A Cognitive-Developmental*

Systems Approach for Children with Body Organization, Social, and Communication Issues. Boston, MA: Language and Cognitive Development Centre.

Moffatt, M.E.K., Langestaffe, S., Besant, J. and Dureski, C. (1994) 'Prevention of iron deficiency and psychomotor decline in high-risk infants through use of iron-fortified infant formula: a randomised clinical trial', *Journal of Paediatrics*, 125, 527–33.

Molloy, C.A., et al. (2002) 'Lack of benefit of intravenous synthetic human secretin in the treatment of autism', *Journal of Autism and Developmental Disorders*, 32, 545–51.

Monti, R. (1985) 'Music therapy in a therapeutic nursery', *Music Therapy*, 5, 22–7.

Moore, M. and Russ, S. (2006) 'Pretend play', *Journal of Developmental and Behavioural Pediatrics*, 27, 237–48.

Moore, P.S. (2004) 'The use of Social Stories in a psychology service for children with learning disabilities: a case study of a sleep problem', *British Journal of Learning Disabilities*, 32, 133–8.

Moreno, J. and O'Neal, M. (2004) 'Help for parents with Aspergers children', available at: http://www.myaspergerschild.com/2009/11/aspergers-students-iep-and-ard.html.

Mostert, M.P. (2001) 'Facilitated communication since 1995: a review of published studies', *Journal of Autism and Developmental Disorders*, 31, 287–313.

Mudford, O.C., Cross, B.A., Bren, S., Cullen, C., Reeves, D., Gould, J. and Douglas, J. (2000) 'Auditory integration training for children with autism: no behavioural benefits detected', *American Journal on Mental Retardation*, 105, 118–29.

Mulick, J.A., Jacobson, J.W. and Kobe, F. (1993) 'Anguished silence and helping hands: autism and facilitated communication', *Sceptical Inquirer*, 17, 270–80.

Mundy, P. (1993) 'Normal versus high-functioning status in children with autism', *American Journal of Mental Retardation*, 97, 381–4.

Mundy, P. and Stella, J. (2001) 'Joint attention, orienting, and nonverbal communication in autism', in A.M. Wetherby and B.M. Prizant (eds), *Autism Spectrum Disorders: A Transactional Developmental Perspective.* Baltimore, MD: Brookes. pp. 55–77.

Murray, E.A. and Anzalone, M.E. (1991) 'Integrating sensory integration theory and practice with other intervention approaches', in A.G. Fisher, E.A. Murray and A.C. Bundy (eds), *Sensory Integration Theory and Practice.* Philadelphia: F.A. Davis. p. 378.

Myers, E.G. (1979) 'The effect of music therapy in a paired-association task with EMR children', *Journal of Music Therapy*, 16, 190–8.

Myles, B.S. and Simpson, R.L. (1996) 'Collateral behavioural and social effects of using facilitated communication with individuals with autism', *Focus on Autism and Other Developmental Disorders*, 11, 163–9.

Myles, B.S., Simpson, R.L. and Smith, S.M. (1996) 'Impact of facilitated communication combined with direct instruction on academic performance of individuals with autism', *Focus on Autism and Other Developmental Disabilities*, 11, 37–44.

Nelson, D., Anderson, V. and Gonzales, A. (1984) 'Music activities as therapy for children with autism and other pervasive developmental disorders', *Journal of Music Therapy*, 21, 100–16.

Newsom, C. and Rincover, A. (1989) 'Autism', in J. Marsh and R.A. Barkley (eds), *Treatment of Childhood Disorders*. New York: Guilford Press. pp. 286–346.

Newton, C., Taylor, G. and Wilson, D. (1996) 'Circles of friends: an inclusive approach to meeting emotional and behavioural need', *Educational Psychology in Practice*, 11, 41–8.

Nickels, K.C., et al. (2008) 'Stimulant medication treatment of target behaviours in children with autism: a population-based study', *Journal of Developmental and Behavioural Paediatrics*, 29, 75–81.

Nolan, A. (1989) 'Music therapy with autistic children', *Communication*, 23, 30–1.

Nordoff, P. and Robbins, C. (1985) *Therapy in Music for Handicapped Children*. London: Gollancz.

Norgate, R. (1998) 'Reducing self-injurious behaviour in a child with severe learning difficulties: enhancing predictability and structure', *Educational Psychology in Practice*, 14, 176–82.

Norris, V. and Dattilo, J. (1999) 'Evaluating effects of a social story intervention on a young girl with autism', *Focus on Autism and Other Developmental Disabilities*, 14, 180–6.

O'Neill, M. and Jones, R.S.P. (1997) 'Sensory-perceptual abnormalities in autism: a case for more research?', *Journal of Autism and Developmental Disorders*, 27, 283–93.

O'Neill, R., Horner, R., Albin, R., Sprague, J., Storey, R. and Newton, J. (1997) *Functional Assessment and Programme Development for Problem Behaviour: A Practical Handbook*. Pacific Grove, CA: Brooks/Cole.

Oberman, L.M. and Ramachandran, V.S. (2008) 'Preliminary evidence for deficits in multisensory integration in autism spectrum disorders: the mirror neuron hypothesis', *Social Neuroscience*, 3, 348–55.

Odom, S.L. and Strain, P.S. (1984) 'Peer mediated approaches to promoting children's social interaction: a review', *Journal of Orthopsychiatry*, 54, 544–57.

Oke, J.N. and Schreibman, L. (1990) 'Training social initiations to a high-functioning autistic child: assessment of collateral behaviour change and generalization in a case study', *Journal of Autism and Developmental Disorders*, 20, 479–97.

Olley, J.G. and Gutentag, S.S. (1999) 'Autism: historical overview, definitions, and characteristics', in D.B. Zager (ed.), *Autism: Identification, Education and* Treatment. Mahwah, NJ: Erlbaum. pp. 3–22.

Oski, F.A. (1993) 'Iron deficiency in infancy and childhood', *New England Journal of Medicine*, 329, 190–3.

Oswald, D.P. and Sonenklar, N.A. (2007) 'Medication use among children with autism-spectrum disorders', *Journal of Child and Adolescent Psychopharmacology*, 17, 348–55.

Ottenbacher, K. (1982) 'Sensory integration therapy: affect or effect', *American Journal of Occupational Therapy*, 36, 571–8.

Owley, T., et al. (1999) 'A double-blind placebo-controlled trial of secretin for the treatment of autistic disorder', *Medscape General Medicine*, 1. Available at: http://www.medscape.com/medscape/ GeneralMedicine/journal/1999/v01.n10/mgm1006.owle/mgm1006.owle-01.html (accessed 6 December 2002).

Oxman, J. and Konstantareas, M.M. (1981) 'On the nature and variability of linguistic impairment in autism', *Clinical Psychology Review*, 1, 337–52.

Ozdemir, S. (2008) 'The effectiveness of Social Stories on decreasing disruptive behaviours of children with autism: three case studies', *Journal of Autism and Developmental Disorders*, 38, 1689–96.

Ozonoff, S. and Cathcart, K. (1998) 'Effectiveness of a home programme intervention for young children with autism', *Journal of Autism and Developmental Disorders*, 28, 25–32.

Panerai, S., Ferrante, L. and Caputo, V. (1997) 'The TEACCH strategy in mentally retarded children with autism: a multidimensional assessment: pilot study', *Journal of Autism and Developmental Disorders*, 27, 345–7.

Panerai, S., Ferrante, L. and Zingale, M. (2002) 'Benefits of the Treatment and Education of Autistic and Communication Handicapped Children (TEACCH) programme as compared with a non-specific approach', *Journal of Intellectual Disability Research*, 46, 318–27.

Panerai, S., Zingale, M., Trubia, G., Finocchiaro, M., Zuccarello, R., Ferri, R., et al. (2009) 'Special education versus inclusive education: the role of the TEACCH program', *Journal of Autism and Developmental Disorders*, 39, 874–82.

Pasiali, V. (2004) 'The use of prescriptive therapeutic songs in a home-based environment to promote social skills acquisition by children with autism: three case studies', *Music Therapy Perspectives*, 22, 11–20.

Pavlicevic, M. (1997) *Music Therapy in Context: Music, Meaning and Relationship*. London: Jessica Kingsley.

Peacock, G. (1994) *Higashi: Implementing Daily Life Therapy in Japan: A Visit to the Musashino Higashi Gakuen School in Tokyo*. London: National Autistic Society.

Perry, R., Cohen, I. and DeCarlo, R. (1995) 'Case study: deterioration, autism and recovery in two siblings', *Journal of the American Academy of Child and Adolescent Psychiatry*, 34, 232–7.

Persson, B. (2000) 'Brief report: a longitudinal study of quality of life and independence among adult men with autism', *Journal of Autism and Developmental Disorders*, 30, 61–6.

Piaget, J. (1948) *Language and Thought of the Child*. London: Routledge and Kegan Paul.

Pierce, K. and Schreibman, L. (1995) 'Multiple peer use of pivotal response training social behaviours of classmates with autism: results from trained and untrained peers', *Journal of Applied Behaviour Analysis*, 30, 157–60.

Pierce, K. and Schreibman, L. (1997) 'Using peer trainers to promote social behaviour in autism: are they effective at enhancing multiple social modalities?', *Focus on Autism and Other Developmental Disabilities*, 12, 207–18.

Pierce, K.C. and Schreibman, L. (1994) 'Teaching daily living skills to children with autism in unsupervised settings through pictorial self-management', *Journal of Applied Behaviour Analysis*, 27, 471–81.

Posey, D.J., Erickson, C.A. and McDougle, C.J. (2008) 'Developing drugs for core social and communication impairment in autism', *Child and Adolescent Psychiatric Clinics of North America*, 17, 787–801.

Powers, M.D. (1992) 'Early intervention for children with autism', in D.E. Berkell (ed.), *Autism: Identification, Education and Treatment*. Hillsdale, NJ: Lawrence Erlbaum Associates. pp. 225–52.

Prendeville, J.-A., Prelock, P. and Urwin, G. (2006) 'Peer play interventions to support the social competence of children with autism spectrum disorders', *Seminars in Speech and Language: Language, Social, and Cognitive Communication in Children with Autism Spectrum Disorders*, 27, 32–46.

Prevezer, W. (1990) 'Strategies for tuning into autism', *Therapy Weekly*, 18, 4–7.

Prizant, B.M. and Wetherby, A.M. (1987) 'Communicative intent: a framework for understanding social-communicative behaviour in autism', *Journal of the American Academy of Child and Adolescent Psychiatry*, 26, 472–9.

Probst, P. (2005) '"Communication unbound or unfound"? An integrative review on the effectiveness of facilitated communication (FC) in nonverbal persons with autism and mental retardation' (in German), *Zeitschrift fur Klinische Psychologie, Psychiatrie und Psychotherapie*, 53, 93–128.

Quill, K. (1989) 'Daily Life therapy: a Japanese model of educating children with autism', *Journal of Autism and Developmental Disorders*, 19, 625–35.

Quilty, K.M. (2007) 'Teaching paraprofessionals how to write and implement Social Stories for students with autism spectrum disorders', *Remedial and Special Education*, 28, 182–9.

Quirmbach, L.M., Linclon, A.J., Feinberg-Gizzo, M.J., Ingersoll, B.R. and Andrews, S.M. (2009) 'Social Stories: mechanisms of effectiveness in increasing game play skills in children diagnosed with autism spectrum disorders using a pretest posttest repeated measures control group design', *Journal of Autism and Developmental Disorders*, 39, 299–321.

Randall, T. (1999) 'Harvey's auditory integration training: a parent's view', *The Autism File*, 1, 7–9.

Rapin, I. (1997) 'Current concepts: autism', *New England Journal of Medicine*, 337, 97–104.

Ratey, J.J., Mikkelsen, E. and Chmielinski, H.E (1989) 'Buspirone therapy for maladaptive behaviours and anxiety in developmentally disabled persons', *Journal of Clinical Psychiatry*, 50, 382–4.

Ray, T., King, L. and Grandin, T. (1988) 'The effectiveness of self-initiated vestibular stimulation in producing speech sounds in an autistic child', *The Occupational Therapy Journal of Research*, 8, 186–90.

Realmuto, G.M., August, G.J. and Garfinkel, B.D. (1989) 'Clinical effects of buspirone in autistic children', *Clinical Psychopharmacology*, 9, 122–5.

Reaven, J. and Hepburn, S. (2003) 'Cognitive-behavioural treatment of obsessive-compulsive disorder in a child with Asperger syndrome: a case study', *Autism*, 7, 145–64.

Reaven, J.A. (2009) 'Children with high-functioning autism spectrum disorders and co-occuring anxiety symptoms: implications for assessment and treatment', *Journal for Specialists in Pediatric Nursing*, 14, 192–9.

Reaven, J.A., Blakeley-Smith, A., Nichols, S., Dasari, M., Flanigan, E. and Hepburn, S. (2009) 'Cognitive-behavioral group treatment for anxiety symptoms in children with high-functioning autism spectrum disorders: a pilot study', *Focus on Autism and Other Developmental Disabilities*, 24, 27–37.

Regehr, K. and Feldman, M. (2009) 'Parent-selected interventions for infants at-risk for autism spectrum disorders and their affected sibling', *Behavioural Interventions*, 24, 237–48.

Reichelt, K. (1981) 'Biologically active peptide: containing fractions in schizophrenia and childhood autism', *Advanced Biochemical Psychopharmacology*, 28, 627–43.

Reichelt, K. (1998) 'A top doctor's deep concern', *Looking Up*, 1, 17.

Reid, D.H., Hill, B.K., Rawers, R.J. and Montegar, C.A. (1975) 'The use of contingent music in teaching social skills to a nonverbal hyperactive boy', *Journal of Music Therapy*, 12, 2–18.

Repp, A., Felce, D. and Banton, L. (1988) 'Basing the treatment of stereotypic and self-injurious behaviours on hypotheses of their causes', *Journal of Applied Behaviour Analysis*, 21, 281–9.

Restall, C. and Magill-Evans, J. (1994) 'Play and preschool children with autism', *The American Journal of Occupational Therapy*, 48, 113–20.

Reynhout, G. and Carter, M. (2006) 'Social Stories for children with disabilities', *Journal of Autism and Developmental Disorders*, 36, 445–69.

Reynhout, G. and Carter, M. (2007) 'Social story efficacy with a child with autism spectrum disorder and moderate intellectual disability', *Focus on Autism and Other Developmental Disabilities*, 22, 173–82.

Richer, J. (1991) 'Changing autistic behaviour: the place of holding', *Communication*, 23, 35–9.

Richer, J. (1992) *Holding: A Brief Guide for Parents*. New York: Simon and Schuster.

Ricks, D.M. and Wing, L. (1976) 'Language, communication and the use of symbols', in L. Wing (ed.), *Early Childhood Autism*. Oxford: Pergamon Press. pp. 93–134.

Rimland, B. (1987) *Evaluation of the Tokyo Higashi Programme for Autistic Children by Parents of the International Division Students*. CA: Autism Research Institute.

Rimland, B. (1996) 'Dimethylglycine (DMG), a non-toxic metabolite, and autism', *Autism Research Review International*, 14, 3.

Rimland, B. (1997) 'What is the right "dosage" for Vitamin B6, DMG and other nutrients useful in autism?', *Autism Research Review International*, 11, 3.

Rimland, B. (1998) 'The autism–secretin connection', *Autism Research Review International*, 12, 3.

Rimland, B. and Edelson, S. M. (1992) *Auditory Integration Training in Autism: A Pilot Study*. San Diego, CA: Autism Research Institute.

Rimland, B. and Edelson, S.M. (1994) 'The effects of auditory integration training on autism', *American Journal of Speech and Language Pathology*, 3, 16–24.

Rimland, B. and Edelson, S.M. (1995) 'A pilot study of auditory integration training in autism', *Journal of Autism and Developmental Disorders*, 25, 61–70.

Rimland, B. and Edelson, S.M. (1998) 'Response to Howlin on the value of auditory integration training', *Journal of Autism and Developmental Disorders*, 28, 169–70.

Rimland, B. and Edelson, S.M. (1999) 'Letter about auditory integration training', *Autism*, 2, 91–2.

Robinson, T.W. (2001) 'Homeopathic secretin in autism: a clinical pilot study', *British Homeopathic Journal*, 90, 86–91.

Roeyers, H. (1995) 'A peer-mediated proximity intervention to facilitate the social interactions of children with a pervasive developmental disorder', *British Journal of Special Education*, 22, 161–4.

Roeyers, H. (1996) 'The influence of non-handicapped peers on the social interaction of children with a pervasive developmental disorder', *Journal of Autism and Developmental Disorders*, 26, 307–20.

Rogers, S.J. (1998) 'Empirically supported comprehensive treatments for young children with autism', *Journal of Clinical Child Psychology*, 27, 168–79.

Rogers, S.J. and DiLalla, D. (1991) 'A comparative study of a developmentally based preschool curriculum on young children with autism and young children with autism and young children with other disorders of behaviour and development', *Topics in Early Childhood Special Education*, 11, 29–48.

Rogers, S.J. and Lewis, H. (1989) 'An effective day treatment model for young children with pervasive developmental disorders', *Journal of the American Academy of Child and Adolescent Psychiatry*, 28, 207–14.

Rogers, S.J., Hayden, D., Hepburn, S., Charlifue-Smith, R., Hall, T. and Hayes, A. (2006) 'Teaching young nonverbal children with autism useful speech: a pilot study of the Denver model and PROMPT interventions', *Journal of Autism and Developmental Disorders*, 36, 1007–24.

Rogers, S.J., Herbison, J., Lewis, H., Pantone, J. and Reis, K. (1986) 'An approach for enhancing the symbolic, communicative, and interpersonal functioning of young children with autism and severe emotional handicaps', *Journal of the Division of Early Childhood*, 10, 135–48.

Rogers, S.J., Lewis H.C. and Reis, K. (1987) 'An effective procedure for training early special education teams to implement a model programme', *Journal of the Division of Early Childhood*, 11, 180–8.

Rogoff, B. (1990) *Apprenticeship in Thinking*. Oxford: Oxford University Press.

Ross, R.K. (2007) 'Beyond autism treatment: the application of applied behaviour analysis in the treatment of emotional and psychological disorders', *International Journal of Behavioral Consultation and Therapy*, 3, 528–35.

Rowe, C. (1999) 'Do Social Stories benefit children with autism in mainstream primary schools?', *British Journal of Special Education*, 26, 12–14.

Rust, J. and Smith, A. (2006) 'How should the effectiveness of Social Stories to modify the behaviour of children on the autistic spectrum be tested? Lessons from the literature', *Autism*, 10, 125–38.

Rutherford, M., Young, G., Hepburn, S. and Rogers, S. (2007) 'Longitudinal study of pretend play in autism', *Journal of Autism and Developmental Disorders*, 37, 1024–39.

Rutter, M. (1965) 'Speech disorders in a series of autistic children', in A.W. Franklin (ed.), *Children with Communication Problems*. London: Pittman.

Sallows, G. (2000) 'Educational interventions for children with autism in the UK', *Early Child Development Health and Care*, 163, 25–47.

Sanchez, L.E., et al. (1996) 'A pilot study of clomipramine in young autistic children', *Journal of the American Academy of Child and Adolescent Psychiatry*, 35, 537–44.

Sansosti, F.J. and Powell-Smith, K.A. (2006) 'Using Social Stories to improve the social behaviour of children with Asperger syndrome', *Journal of Positive Behaviour Interventions*, 8, 43–57.

Sansosti, F.J. and Powell-Smith, K.A. (2008) 'Using computer-presented Social Stories and video models to increase the social communication skills of children with high-functioning autism spectrum disorders', *Journal of Positive Behaviour Interventions*, 10, 162–78.

Sansosti, F.J., Powell-Smith, K.A. and Kincaid, D. (2004) 'A research synthesis of social story interventions for children with autism spectrum disorders', *Focus on Autism and Other Developmental Disorders*, 19, 194–204.

Sapon-Shevin, M., Dobbelaere, A., Corrigan, C.R., Goodman, K. and Mastin, M.C. (1998) 'Promoting inclusive behaviour in inclusive classrooms: 'You can't say you can't play'', in L.M. Meyer, H.-S. Park, I.S. Schwartz and B. Harry (eds), *Making Friends: The Influence of Culture on Development*. Baltimore, MD: Brookes. pp. 105–32.

Sasso, G., Reimers, J., Cooper, L., Wacker, D., Berg, W., Steege, M., Kelly, L. and Allaire, A. (1992) 'Use of descriptive and experimental analyses to identify functional properties of aberrant behaviour in school settings', *Journal of Applied Behaviour Analysis*, 25, 809–21.

Sato, M., Nishimura, B., Watamaki, T. and Wakabayashi, S. (1987) 'Sign language acquisition in a totally mute autistic child', *Japanese Journal of Child and Adolescent Psychiatry*, 28, 149–68.

Scahill, L. (2008) 'How do I decide whether or not to use medication for my child with autism? Should I try behaviour therapy first?', *Journal of Autism and Developmental Disorders*, 38, 1197–8.

Scahill, L., Koenig, K., Carroll, D.H. and Pachler, M. (2007) 'Risperidone approved for the treatment of serious behavioural problems in children with autism', *Journal of Child and Adolescent Psychiatric Nursing*, 20, 188–90.

Scarlett, W.G. (2004) *Children's Play*. Thousand Oaks, CA: Sage.

Scattone, D. (2008) 'Enhancing the conversation skills of a boy with Asperger's disorder through Social Stories and video modeling', *Journal of Autism and Developmental Disorders*, 38, 395–400.

Scattone, D., Tingstrom, D.H. and Wilczynski, S. (2006) 'Increasing appropriate social interactions of children with autism spectrum disorders using Social Stories', *Focus on Autism and Other Developmental Disabilities*, 21, 211–22.

Scattone, D., Wilczynski, S.M. and Edwards, R.P. (2002) 'Decreasing disruptive behaviours of children with autism using Social Stories', *Journal of Autism and Developmental Disorders*, 32, 535–43.

Schaaf, R.C. and Miller, L.J. (2005) 'Occupational therapy using a sensory integrative approach for children with developmental disabilities', *Mental Retardation and Developmental Disabilities Research Reviews*, 11, 143–8.

Schiavo, P., Tressoldi, P. and Martinez, E.M. (2005) 'Autism and facilitated communication: the results of an authorship test' (in Italian), *Giornale Italiano delle Disabilita*, 5, 3–17.

Schmidt, D.C., Franklin, R. and Edwards, J.S. (1976) 'Reinforcement of autistic children's responses to music', *Psychological Reports*, 39, 571–7.

Schneider, N. and Goldstein, H. (2009) 'Social Stories improve the on-task behaviour for children with language impairment', *Journal of Early Intervention*, 31, 250–64.

Schopler, E. (1991) *Current and Past Research on Autistic Children and their Families*. Chapel Hill, NC: Division TEACCH.

Schopler, E. (1992) 'Editorial commentary', *Journal of Autism and Developmental Disorders*, 22, 337–8.

Schopler, E. and Mesibov, G. (1984) *The Effects of Autism on the Family*. New York: Plenum.

Schopler, E. and Mesibov, G. (1995) 'Structured teaching in the TEACCH system', in *Learning and Cognition in Autism*. New York and London: Plenum Press.

Schopler, E. and Mesibov G.B. (2000) 'Cross-cultural priorities in developing autism services', *International Journal of Mental Health*, 29, 3–21.

Schopler, E. and Olley, J.G. (1980) 'Public school programming for autistic children', *Exceptional Children*, 46, 461–3.

Schopler, E. and Reichler, R.J. (1971) 'Parents as cotherapists in the treatment of psychotic children', *Journal of Autism and Childhood Schizophrenia*, 1, 87–102.

Schopler, E., Mesibov, G.B. and Baker, A. (1982) 'Evaluation of treatment for autistic children and their parents', *Journal of the American Academy of Child Psychiatry*, 21, 262–7.

Schopler, E., Reichler, R.J. and Renner, B. (1988) *The Childhood Autism Rating Scale (CARS)*. Baltimore, MD: University Park Press.

Schopler, E., Reichler, R.J., Bashford, A., Lansing, M.D. and Marcus, L.M. (1990) *Individual Assessment and Treatment for Autistic and Developmentally Disabled Children. Vol. 1: Psychoeducatonal Profile Revised*. Austin, TX: Pro-Ed.

Schopler, E., Short, A. and Mesibov, G. (1989) 'Relation of behavioural treatment to "normal functioning": comments on Lovaas', *Journal of Consulting and Clinical Psychology*, 57, 162–4.

Schreck, K. (2000) 'It can be done: an example of a behavioral Individualized Education Program (IEP) for a child with autism', *Behavioral Interventions*, 15, 279–300.

Schreck, K.A. and Mazur, A. (2008) 'Behavior analyst use of and beliefs in treatments for people with autism', *Behavioral Intervention*, 23, 201–12.

Schreibman, L. (2000) 'Intensive behavioral/psychoeducational treatments for autism: research needs and future directions', *Journal of Autism and Developmental Disorders*, 30, 373–8.

Schreibman, L., Kaneko, W.M. and Koegel, R.L. (1991) 'Positive', *Behaviour Therapy*, 22, 479–90.

Schultheis, S.F., Boswell, B.B. and Decker, J. (2000) *Focus on Autism and Other Developmental Disabilities*, 15, 159–62.

Schwartz, I.S., Garfinkle, A.N. and Bauer, J. (1998) 'The Picture Exchange Communication System: communicative outcomes for young children with disabilities', *Topics in Early Childhood Special Education*, 18, 144–59.

Seung, H., Rogalski, Y., Shankar, M. and Elder, J. (2007) 'The gluten- and casein-free diet and autism: communication outcomes from a preliminary double-blind clinical trial', *Journal of Medical Speech-Language Pathology*, 15, 337–45.

Shane, H.C. (1994) *Facilitated Communication: The Clinical and Social Phenomenon.* San Diego, CA: Singular.

Sheehan, C.M. and Matuozzi, R.T. (1996) 'Investigation of the validity of facilitated communication through the disclosure of unknown information', *Mental Retardation,* 34, 94–107.

Sheinkopf, S.J. and Siegel, B. (1998) 'Home-based behavioural treatment of young children with autism', *Journal of Autism and Developmental Disorders,* 28, 15–23.

Sherratt, D. (2002) 'Developing pretend play in children with autism: a case study', *Autism,* 6, 169–79.

Sherrill, C. (1998) *Adapted Physical Activity, Recreation, and Sport: Cross Disciplinary and Lifespan,* 5th edn. Dubuque, IA: McGraw Hill.

Shimizu, N. (1988) 'Sign language training for children with developmental retardation in speech', *RIEEC Report,* 37, 73–8.

Shore, B.A. (1994) 'Sensory-integrative therapy', *Self-injury Abstracts and Reviews,* 3, 1–7.

Shotton, G. (1998) 'A Circle of Friends approach with socially neglected children', *Educational Psychology in Practice,* 13, 22–5.

Siaperas, P. and Beadle-Brown, J. (2006) 'A case study of the use of a structured teaching approach in adults with autism in a residential home in Greece', *Autism,* 10, 330–43.

Siaperas, P., Higgins, S. and Proios, P. (2007) 'Challenging behaviours on people with autism: a case study on the effect of a residential training programme based on structured teaching and TEACCH method', *Psychiatriki,* 18, 343–52.

Siegel, B. (1996) *The World of the Autistic Child: Understanding and Treating Autistic Spectrum Disorders.* New York: Oxford University Press.

Sigafoos, J. and Saggers, E. (1995) 'A discrete-trial approach to the functional analysis of aggressive behaviour in two boys with autism', *Australia and New Zealand Journal of Developmental Disabilities,* 20, 287–97.

Silverman, F. (1995) *Communication for the Speechless,* 3rd edn. Boston, MA: Allyn and Bacon.

Simeonnson, R.J., Olley, J.G. and Rosenthal, S.L. (1987) 'Early intervention for children with autism', in M. Guralnick and F.C. Bennett (eds), *The Effectiveness of Early Intervention for At-Risk and Handicapped Children.* New York: Plenum. pp. 275–96.

Simpson, R. (1993) 'Tips for practitioners', *Focus on Autistic Behaviour,* 8, 15–16.

Simpson, R.L. (1995) 'Individualised Education Programmes for students with autism: including parents in the process', *Focus on Autistic Behaviour,* 10, 11–15.

Simpson, R.L. (2001) 'ABA and students with autism spectrum disorders: issues and considerations for effective practice', *Focus on Autism and Other Developmental Disabilities,* 16, 68–71.

Simpson, R.L. and Fiedler, C.R. (1989) 'Parent participation in Individualised Educational Programme (IEP) conferences: a case for individualisation', in M.J. Fine (ed.), *The Second Handbook on Parent Education.* San Diego, CA: Academic Press. pp. 145–71.

Simpson, R.L. and Myles, B.S. (1995) 'Effectiveness of facilitated communication with children and youth with autism', *Journal of Special Education*, 28, 424–39.

Simpson, R.L. and Regan, M. (1998) *Management of Autistic Behaviour*. Austin, TX: Pro-Ed.

Smith, C. (2001) 'Using Social Stories to enhance behaviour in children with autistic spectrum difficulties', *Educational Psychology in Practice*, 17, 337–45.

Smith, C. and Cooke, T. (2000) 'Collaboratively managing the behaviour of a reception class pupil', *Educational Psychology in Practice*, 16, 235–42.

Smith, E.G. and Bennetto, L. (2007) 'Audiovisual speech integration and lipreading in autism', *Journal of Child Psychology and Psychiatry*, 48, 813–21.

Smith, T. (1993) 'Autism', in T.R. Giles (ed.), *Handbook of Effective Psychotherapy*. New York: Plenum Press. pp. 107–33.

Smith, T. (1996) 'Are other treatments effective?', in C. Maurice, G. Green and S.C. Luce (eds), *Behavioural Intervention for Young Children with Autism: A Manual for Parents and Professionals*. Austin, TX: Pro-Ed. pp. 45–49.

Solomon, R., Necheles, J., Ferch, C. and Bruckman, D. (2007) 'Pilot study of a parent training program for young children with autism: the P.L.A.Y. Project Home Consultation Program', *Autism*, 11, 205–24.

Soraci, S., Deckner, C.W., McDaniel, C. and Blanton, R.L. (1982) 'The relationship between rate of rhythmicity and the stereotypic behaviours of abnormal children', *Journal of Music Therapy*, 19, 46–54.

Spencer, V.G., Simpson, C.G. and Lynch, S.A. (2008) 'Using Social Stories to increase positive behaviours for children with autism spectrum disorders', *Intervention in School and Clinic*, 44, 58–61.

Stahmer, A.C. (1995) 'Teaching symbolic play skills to children with autism using pivotal response training', *Journal of Autism and Developmental Disorders*, 25, 123–41.

Stahmer, A.C. (1999) 'Using pivotal response training to facilitate appropriate play in children with autistic spectrum disorders', *Child Language Teaching and Therapy*, 15, 29–40.

Staley, M.J. (2002) 'An investigation of social story effectiveness using reversal and multiple baseline designs', *Dissertation Abstracts International Section B: The Sciences and Engineering*, 62, 4770.

Stanley, G. and Konstantareas, M. (2007) 'Symbolic play in children with autism spectrum disorder', *Journal of Autism and Developmental Disorders*, 37, 1215–23.

Stehli, A. (1991) *The Sound of a Miracle: A Child's Triumph Over Autism*. New York: Doubleday.

Strain, P.S. (1983) 'Generalization of autistic children's social behaviour change: effects of developmentally integrated and segregated settings', *Analysis and Intervention in Developmental Disabilities*, 3, 23–34.

Strain, P.S. and Cordisco, L. (1994) 'LEAP preschool', in S. Harris and J. Handleman (eds), *Preschool Education Programmes for Children with Autism*. Austin, TX: Pro-Ed. pp. 225–52.

Strain, P.S. and Fox, J. (1981) 'Peers as behaviour change agents for withdrawn classmates', in B. Lahey and A. Kazdin (eds), *Advances in Clinical Child Psychology*. New York: Plenum. pp. 167–98.

Strain, P.S., Shores, R.E. and Timm, M. (1977) 'Effects of peer social initiations on the behaviour of withdrawn preschool children', *Journal of Applied Behaviour Analysis*, 10, 289–98.

Stull, S., Edkins, E.C., Krause, M., McGavin, G., Brand, L.H. and Webster, C.D. (1980) 'Individual differences in the acquisition of sign language by severely communicatively-impaired children', in C.D. Webster, M.M. Konstantareas, J. Oxman and J.E. Mack (eds), *Autism: New Direction in Research and Education*. Oxford: Pergamon Press. pp. 202–11.

Sturmey, P. (2005) 'Secretin is an ineffective treatment for pervasive developmental disabilities: a review of 15 double-blind randomized controlled trials', *Research in Developmental Disabilities*, 26, 87–97.

Sulzer-Azaroff, B. and Mayer, R. (1991) *Behaviour Analysis for Lasting Change*. Fort Worth, TX: Holt, Reinhart and Winston.

Sulzer-Azaroff, B., Hoffman, A.O., Horton, C.B., Bondy, A. and Frost, L. (2009) 'The Picture Exchange Communication System (PECS): what do the data say?', *Focus on Autism and Other Developmental Disabilities*, 24, 89–103.

Swaggart, B.L., Brenda, L. and Gragnon, E.C. (1995) 'Using Social Stories to teach social and behavioural skills to children with autism', *Focus on Autism Behaviour*, 10, 1–16.

Sze, K.M. and Wood, J.J. (2007) 'Cognitive behavioral treatment of comorbid anxiety disorders and social difficulties in children with high-functioning autism: a case report', *Journal of Contemporary Psychotherapy*, 37, 133–43.

Tarnai, B. and Wolfe, P.S. (2008) 'Social Stories for sexuality education for persons with autism/pervasive developmental disorders', *Sexuality and Disability*, 26, 29–36.

Taylor, G. (1997) 'Community building in schools: developing a "Circle of Friends"', *Educational and Child Psychology*, 14, 3.

Terpstra, J.E., Higgins, K. and Pierce, T. (2002) 'Can I play? Classroom-based interventions for teaching play skills to children with autism', *Focus on Autism and Other Developmental Disabilities*, 17, 119–28.

Tews, L. (2007) 'Early intervention for children with autism: methodologies critique', *Developmental Disabilities Bulletin*, 35, 148–68.

Tharpe, A.M. (1999) 'Auditory Integration Training: the magical mystery cure', *Language, Speech, and Hearing Services in Schools*, 30, 378–82.

Thaut, M.H. (1984) 'A music therapy treatment model for autistic children', *Music Therapy Perspectives*, 1, 7–13.

The Option Institute and Fellowship (1997) *The Option Institute: The Worldwide Teaching Center for the Option Process*. Programme catalogues.

Thiemann, K.S. and Goldstein, H. (2001) 'Social Stories written text cues and video feedback: effects on social communication of children with autism', *Journal of Applied Behaviour Analysis*, 34, 425–46.

Thorp, D.M., Stahmer, A.C. and Schreibman, L. (1995) 'Effects of sociodramatic play training on children with autism', *Journal of Autism and Developmental Disorders*, 25, 265–81.

Tiegeman, E. and Primavera, L. (1987) 'Object manipulation: an interactional strategy with autistic children', *Journal of Autism and Developmental Disorders*, 11, 427–38.

Timbergen, N. and Timbergen, E.A. (1983) *Autistic Children: New Hope for a Cure.* London: Allen and Unwin.

Toda, Y., et al. (2006) 'Administration of secretin for autism alters dopamine metabolism in the central nervous system', *Brain and Development*, 28, 99–103.

Toigo, D. (1992) 'Autism: integrating a personal perspective with music therapy practice', *Music Therapy Perspectives*, 10, 13–20.

Tolbert, L.C., Haigler, T., Waits, M.M. and Dennis, T. (1993) 'Brief report: lack of response in an autistic population to a low dose clinical trial of pyrodoxine plus magnesium', *Journal of Autism and Developmental Disorders*, 23, 193–9.

Tomatis, A. (1978) *Education and Dyslexia.* Fribourg: AIAPP.

Tomatis, A. (1991) *The Conscious Ear.* Barrytown, NY: Station Hill Press.

Tomatis, A. (1996) *The Ear and Language.* Norval: Moulin.

Tomchek, S.D. and Dunn, W. (2007) 'Sensory processing in children with and without autism: a comparative study using the Short Sensory Profile', *American Journal of Occupational Therapy*, 61, 190–200.

Toolan, P.G. and Coleman, S.Y. (1994) 'Music therapy, a description of progress: engagement and avoidance in five people with learning disabilities', *Journal of Intellectual Disability Research*, 38, 433–44.

Toplis, R. and Hadwin, J.A. (2006) 'Using Social Stories to change problematic lunchtime behaviour in school', *Educational Psychology in Practice*, 22, 53–67.

Trehin, P. (1998) *Some Basic Information about TEACCH.* Chapel Hill, NC: Division TEACCH.

Trevarthen, C. (2002) 'Autism, sympathy of motives, and music therapy', *Enfance*, 54, 86–99.

Trevisanello, G. and Gremigni, P. (2008) 'Privotal response treatment to treat autism: a review' (in Italian), *Psicoterapia Cognitiva e Comportamentale*, 14, 65–79.

Tsakanikos, E., et al. (2007) 'Behaviour management problems as predictors of psychotropic medication and use of psychiatric services in adults with autism', *Journal of Autism and Developmental Disorders*, 37, 1080–5.

Tsang, S.K.M., Shek, D.T.L., Lam, L.L., Tang, F.L.Y. and Cheung, P.M.P. (2007) 'Brief report: application of the TEACCH program on Chinese pre-school children with autism. Does culture make a difference?', *Journal of Autism and Developmental Disorders*, 37, 390–6.

Tuchman, R. (2004) 'AEDs and psychotropic drugs in children with autism and epilepsy', *Mental Retardation and Developmental Disabilities Research Reviews*, 10, 135–8.

Tustin, F. (1981) *Autistic States in Children.* Boston, MA: Routledge.

Unis, A.S., et al. (2002) 'A randomised, double-blind, placebo-controlled trial of porcine versus synthetic secretin for reducing symptoms of autism', *Journal of the American Academy of Child and Adolescent Psychiatry*, 4, 1322–3.

Upton, G. (1992) 'Two hours in the Musashino Higashi Gakuen', *Communication*, 26, 9–12.

Van Bourgondien, M.E. and Schopler, E. (1996) 'Intervention for adults with autism', *Journal of Rehabilitation*, 62, 65–71.

Van Bourgondien, M.E., Reichle, N.C. and Schopler, E. (2003) 'Effects of a model treatment approach on adults with autism', *Journal of Autism and Developmental Disorders*, 33, 131–40.

Vismara, L.A. and Rogers, S. J. (2008) 'The Early Start Denver Model: a case study of an innovative practice', *Journal of Early Intervention*, 31, 91–108.

Vismara, L.A., Colombi, C. and Rogers, S.J. (2009) 'Can one hour per week of therapy lead to lasting changes in young children with autism?', *Autism*, 13, 93–115.

Volkmar, F.R., Lord, C., Bailey, A., Schultz, R.T. and Klin, A. (2004) 'Autism and pervasive developmental disorders', *Journal of Child Psychology and Psychiatry*, 45, 135–70.

Von Bertallanfy, L. (1968) *Organismic Psychology and Systems Theory*. Worcester: Clark University Press with Barre Publishers.

Von Tetzchner, S. (1984) 'Use of signs with psychotic/autistic children: theory, method and a case study', *Tidsskrift for Norsk Psykologforening*, 21, 3–15.

Vygotsky, L.S. (1962) *Thought and Language*. Cambridge, MA: MIT Press.

Walter, T., DeAmdraca, I., Chadud, P. and Perales, C.G. (1989) 'Iron deficiency anaemia: adverse effects on infant psychomotor development', *Paediatrics*, 84, 7–17.

Waterhouse, L., Morris, R., Allen, D., Dunn, M., Fein, D., Feinstein, C., Rapin, I. and Wing, L. (1996) 'Diagnosis and classification in autism', *Journal of Autism and Developmental Disorders*, 26, 59–86.

Watling, R., Deitz, J., Kanny, E.M. and McLaughlin, J.F. (1999) 'Current practice of occupational therapy for children with autism', *American Journal of Occupational Therapy*, 53, 498–505.

Weber, R.C. and Thorpe, J. (1992) 'Teaching children with autism through task variation in physical education, *Exceptional Children*, 59, 77–86.

Webster, C.D., McPherson, H., Sloman, L., Evans, M.A., Kuchar, E. and Fuchter, D. (1980) 'Gestures as a mean of communication with an autistic boy: a case study', in C.D. Webster, M.M. Konstantareas, J. Oxman and J.E. Mack (eds), *Autism: New Direction in Research and Education*. Oxford: Pergamon Press. pp. 179–85.

Wehrenfenning, A. and Surian, L. (2008) 'Autism and facilitated communication: a review of the experimental studies' (in Italian), *Psicologia Clinica dello Sviluppo*, 12, 437–64.

Welch, M.G. (1989) *Holding Time*. London: Century Hutchinson.

Welch, M.G. (1998) *Holding Time: How to Eliminate Conflict, Temper Tantrums, and Sibling Rivalry and Raise Happy, Loving Successful Children*. New York: Simon and Schuster.

Werner, H. and Kaplan, B. (1963) *Symbol Formation: An Organismic Developmental Approach to Language and the Expression of Thought*. New York: Wiley and Sons.

West, L., Waldrop, J. and Brunssen, S. (2009) 'Pharmacologic treatment for the core deficits and associated symptoms of autism in children', *Journal of Paediatric Health Care*, 23, 75–89.

Wheeler, B. (1995) *Music Therapy Research: Qualitative and Quantitative Perspectives*. Phoenixville, PA: Barcelona.

Wheeler, D.L., Jacobson, J.W., Paglieri, R.A. and Schwartz, A.A. (1993) 'An experimental assessment of facilitated communication', *Mental Retardation*, 31, 49–59.

Whipple, J. (2004) 'Music in intervention for children and adolescents with autism: a meta-analysis', *Journal of Music Therapy*, 41, 90–106.

Whitaker, P., Barratt, P., Joy, H., Potter, M. and Thomas, G. (1998) 'Children with autism and peer group support: using "Circle of Friends"', *British Journal of Special Education*, 25, 60–4.

White, C. (2002) 'The social play record: the development and evaluation of a new instrument for assessing and guiding the social interaction of children with autistic spectrum disorders', *Good Autism Practice*, 3, 63–78.

Whitley, P., Rodgers, J., Savery, D. and Shattock, P. (1999) 'A gluten-free diet as an intervention for autism and associated spectrum disorders: preliminary findings', *Autism*, 3, 45–65.

Wigram, T. (2000) 'A method of music therapy assessment for the diagnosis of autism and communication disorders in children', *Music Therapy Perspectives*, 18, 13–22.

Wigram, T. and DeBacker, J. (1999) *Clinical Applications of Music Therapy in Developmental Disabilities, Paediatrics and Neurology*. London: Jessica Kingsley.

Wigram, T. and Gold, C. (2006) 'Music therapy in the assessment and treatment of autistic spectrum disorder: clinical application and research evidence', *Child: Care, Health and Development*, 32, 535–42.

Williams, K. (1995) 'Understanding the student with Asperger syndrome: guidelines for teacher', *Focus on Autistic Behaviour*, 10, 10–17.

Williams, K.R. and Wishart, J.G. (2003) 'The Son-Rise programme intervention for autism: an investigation into family experiences', *Journal of Intellectual Disability Research*, 47, 291–9.

Wilson, S.L. (1995) 'Single case experimental designs', in G.M. Breakwell, S. Hammond and C. Fife-Shaw (eds), *Research Methods in* Psychology. London: Sage. pp. 69–84.

Wimpory, D. (1995) 'Brief report: musical interaction therapy for children with autism: an evaluative case study with two-year follow-up', *Journal of Autism and Other Developmental Disorders*, 25, 541–52.

Wisniewski, T., Brimacombe, M.B. and Ming, X. (2007) 'Pharmaceutical studies in autism and ADHD: a design based review of study quality', *Journal of Paediatric Neurology*, 5, 189–97.

Wolfberg, P.J. (2005) 'Definitions for imagination, Integrated Play Groups (IPG) model, spontaneous play, social play and symbolic play', in J. Neisworth and P.S. Wolfe (eds), *The Autism Encyclopedia*. Baltimore, MD: Brookes.

Wolfberg, P.J. (2006a) 'Foreword', in H. McCracken, *That's What's Different about Me: Friend 2 Friend Social Learning Model*. Shawnee Mission, KS: Autism Asperger Publishing Company.

Wolfberg, P.J. (2006b) 'Regular and continuous support: Integrated Play Groups (IPG) Model', in H. McCracken, *That's What's Different about Me: Friend 2 Friend Social Learning Model*. Shawnee Mission, KS: Autism Asperger Publishing Company. pp. 32–6.

Wolfberg, P.J. (2007) 'Essays on play oriented therapies, Integrated Play Groups model, social play, symbolic play, spontaneous play, and imagination', in B. Myles, T. Cooper Swanson and J. Holverstott (eds), *Autism Spectrum Disorders: A Handbook for Parents and Professionals*. Westport, CT: Greenwood.

Wolfberg, P.J. and Schuler, A.L. (1999) 'Fostering peer interaction, imaginative play and spontaneous language in children with autism', *Child Language Teaching and Therapy*, 15, 41–52.

Wolfberg, P.J. and Schuler, A.L. (2006) 'Promoting social reciprocity and symbolic representation in children with ASD: designing quality peer play interventions', in T. Charman and W. Stone (eds), *Early Social Communication in Autism Spectrum Disorders*. New York: Guilford Publications. pp. 180–219.

Wolfberg, P.J., McCracken, H. and Tuchel, T. (2008) 'Fostering peer play and friendships: creating a culture of inclusion', in K. Buron and P.J. Wolfberg (eds), *Learners on the Autism Spectrum: Preparing Highly Qualified Educators*. Shawnee Mission, KS: Autism Asperger Publishing Company. pp. 182–207.

Wood, J.J., Drahota, A., Sze, K., Har, K., Chiu, A. and Langer, D.A. (2009a) 'Cognitive behavioral therapy for anxiety in children with autism spectrum disorders: a randomized, controlled trial', *Journal of Child Psychology and Psychiatry*, 50, 224–34.

Wood, J.J., Drahota, A., Sze, K., Van Dyke, M., Decker, K., Fujii, C., et al. (2009b) 'Brief report: effects of cognitive behavioral therapy on parent-reported autism symptoms in school-age children with high- functioning autism', *Journal of Autism and Developmental Disorders*, 39, 1608–12.

Yencer, K.A. (1998) 'The effects of auditory integration training for children with Central Auditory Processing Disorder (CAPD)', *American Journal of Audiology*, 7, 32–44.

Yokoyama, K., Naoi, N. and Yamamoto, J. (2006) 'Teaching verbal behaviour using the Picture Exchange Communication System (PECS) with children with autistic spectrum disorders', *Japanese Journal of Special Education*, 43, 89–103.

Zanobini, M., Camba, R. and Scopesi, A. (2008) 'Psychological lexicon in facilitated communication of autistic boys' (in Italian), *Eta Evolutiva*, 91, 72–81.

Zimbelman, M., Paschal, A., Hawley, S.R., Molgraard, C.A. and St. Romain, T. (2007) 'Addressing physical inactivity among developmentally disabled students through visual schedules and Social Stories', *Research in Developmental Disabilities*, 28, 386–96.

Zollweg, W., Palm, D. and Vance, V. (1997) 'The efficacy of auditory integration training: a double-blind study', *American Journal of Audiology*, 6, 39–47

Index

I CAN'T DO THAT!

My Social Stories to Help with Communication, Self-Care and Personal Skills

Second Edition

John Ling

'This continues to be a very helpful resource for parents and professionals working with children with a range of social communication difficulties. Particularly useful, besides the examples of social stories provided, are the additional features, including how to use them, how to write your own and the further reading lists' - *Sarah Worth, Specialist Speech and Language Therapist, Cheshire Autism Support and Development Team*

Are you teaching or supporting students with special educational needs (SEN) who are struggling with social rules and conventions?

This book introduces you to the concept of social stories which are a positive and practical way to help children with these difficulties. The new edition of this book has over 90 examples of social stories, including over 30 new stories and also contains a new sections on:

- why social stories are important
- how to use them in your setting
- how to write your own social stories.

Suitable for use with children of any age, the book includes examples for those children with language delays, communication difficulties, difficult behaviour, antisocial behaviour as well as those with autism.

Broken down into eight sections, it is easy to find an example suitable for the situation you are facing so you can work together with the child to create their personal story.

LUCKY DUCK BOOKS

September 2010 • 120 pages
Paper (978-0-85702-044-4) • £21.99

ALSO FROM SAGE

MARTIAN IN THE PLAYGROUND

Understanding the Schoolchild with Asperger's Syndrome

Second Edition

Clare Sainsbury

'This deceptively little book contains more truth and provides more insight into what it is like to have Asperger's Syndrome than many a weighty tome on the subject. It offers a view from the inside, but it is not yet another autobiography. Admirably and refreshingly, the author has refrained from giving an account solely based on her own experiences. Instead she sets out observations from 25 different suffers, giving often astonishing and sometimes harrowing glimpses of what actually happens to a child with Asperger's Syndrome in the classroom, in the playground, in the lunch queue and at home' - *The Journal of Child Psychology and Psychiatry*

This award-winning book illuminates what it means to be a person who has Aspergers Syndrome by providing a window into a unique and particular world. Drawing on her own experience of schooling, and that of a network of friends and correspondents who share her way of thinking and responding, Clare Sainsbury reminds us of the potential for harm which education holds for those who do not fit.This book holds insights that take us beyond the standard guidance on how to manage autistic spectrum disorder. It challenges the way we might handle obsessional behaviour.It invites us to celebrate the pure passion of the intellect, which such obsessions can represent, and to recognise the delight which can be experienced by children who love to collect. This revised edition includes an additional introduction and extensive summary of research in the field of Asperger's Syndrome, both by Tony Attwood.

LUCKY DUCK BOOKS
2009 • 144 pages
Paper (978-1-84920-000-4) • £17.99

ALSO FROM SAGE

EDUCATION AND CARE FOR ADOLESCENTS AND ADULTS WITH AUTISM

A Guide for Professionals and Carers

Kate Wall *University of Chichester*

Kate Wall shows a depth of knowledge in the subject area of autism and her experience as a practitioner shines through...For anyone working with or planning services for adolescents and adults with autism this is definitely a useful book to have on the shelf' *- Support for Learning*

'[This] is the first book I have read which covers both education and care. There is some very useful information, some of which is very thought provoking....The book promotes the importance of everyone working together to achieve a better understanding' *- National Autistic Society*

By providing case studies and examples that show the reader how to put theory into practice in multi-disciplinary settings, this book clearly explains how changes in policy and provision have affected the ways in which young people and adults with autism are cared for and educated. This book offers up-to-date, accessible information on:

- the nature and effects of Autistic Spectrum Disorders (ASDs)
- family issues surrounding caring for and educating those with ASDs
- possible intervention programmes
- how to support the family

Based on years of experience gained in education and care settings, this book offers strategies for all those working with adolescents and adults who are on the autistic spectrum.

2007 • 168 pages
Cloth (978-1-4129-2381-1) • £69.00
Paper (978-1-4129-2382-8) • £21.99
Electronic (978-1-84860-754-5) • £69.00

ALSO FROM SAGE